BEYOND THE LATINO WORLD WAR II HERO

Beyond the Latino
WORLD WAR II HERO
THE SOCIAL AND POLITICAL LEGACY OF A GENERATION

EDITED BY

Maggie Rivas-Rodríguez and Emilio Zamora

WITH A FOREWORD BY JOSÉ LIMÓN

UNIVERSITY OF TEXAS PRESS ☖ AUSTIN

Requests for permission to reproduce material
from this work should be sent to:
   Permissions
   University of Texas Press
   P.O. Box 7819
   Austin, TX 78713-7819
   www.utexas.edu/utpress/about/bpermission.html

∞ The paper used in this book meets the minimum
requirements of ANSI/NISO Z39.48-1992 (R1997)
(Permanence of Paper).

Library of Congress Cataloging-in-Publication Data

Beyond the Latino World War II hero : the social and political
legacy of a generation / edited by Maggie Rivas-Rodríguez and
Emilio Zamora ; with a foreword by José Limón. — 1st ed.
   p. cm.
   Includes bibliographical references and index.
   ISBN 978-0-292-72580-5
   1. World War, 1939–1945—Participation, Hispanic American. 2. World
War, 1939–1945—Personal narratives, American. 3. Hispanic Americans—
Social conditions—20th century. 4. Hispanic American women—Social
conditions—20th century. 5. United States—Armed Forces—Hispanic
Americans. I. Rivas-Rodríguez, Maggie. II. Zamora, Emilio.
   D769.8.H58B496 2009
   940.53089'68073—dc22   2009026123

To everyone involved in recovering, preserving, and interpreting the Latino historical record, particularly the thousands who joined the Defend the Honor campaign in 2007 to promote the fair and just representation of Mexican American World War II veterans in U.S. history and who continue their efforts even today.

CONTENTS

CONTENTS

FOREWORD

The dominant narratives of World War II seem determined to exclude the representation of Latinos and Latinas, as, for example, the 2007 documentary by Ken Burns. In the controversy surrounding that documentary, one of the editors of this volume—Maggie Rivas-Rodríguez—provided stalwart critical leadership for this community against such exclusion. Hers is a leadership richly informed by the successful and distinguished U.S. Latino & Latina World War II Oral History Project at the University of Texas at Austin, which she founded and directs. But such exclusion begins in ignorance, ignorance of the pervasive and persistent participation of Latinos and Latinas in all services, at all levels, and in all theaters of the war, including the vital home front. We Latinos and Latinas, especially we older ones, have long known of such participation, mostly anecdotally, from those who actually participated, such as my three uncles from Laredo, Texas—Pedro, in the Aleutians; Beto, at the Coral Sea on the *Lexington*; and Ruperto, crossing the beach at Normandy and dying in the hedgerow country. The Oral History Project has done a magnificent job of collecting the narratives of those veterans and other participants who survived, and such oral evidence is now providing part of the firm evidentiary basis for published accounts and analysis of both this participation and its consequences after 1945. Rivas-Rodríguez and the fine UT Austin historian Emilio Zamora are bringing such published research into being, as is evident in the essays collected in this volume. Future dominant narratives about the war will no longer have the excuse of ignorance unless it be willful. We at the Center for Mexican American Studies are very proud of the support we have given to the Oral History Project in the past, and we are equally proud to endorse this wonderful volume.

JOSÉ E. LIMÓN

Mody C. Boatright Regents Professor of
American and English Literature

Director, Center for Mexican American Studies
The University of Texas at Austin

ACKNOWLEDGMENTS

Numerous persons have assumed varied roles and responsibilities in the production of this book. The Latinos/as who left a legacy of service and sacrifice under the difficult circumstances of the World War II period deserve recognition. Their singular experiences provide the basis for our interpretation of the larger Latino historical record, as well as that of World War II and its impact on U.S. society. The Latino men and women who have shared their memories, as well as the researchers who have interviewed them and created valuable oral narratives, have been especially important in recovering and preserving this historical record. Research programs like the U.S. Latino & Latina World War II Oral History Project at the University of Texas at Austin have served as focal points in recalling this memory and recovering the record.

The book would not have been possible without the considerable support of members of the College of Communication's Tech Team, who dub tapes for us and help with equipment needs, as well as troubleshoot in myriad ways. The School of Journalism staff at the University of Texas at Austin, particularly Janice Brandon and Sonia Reyes-Krempin, has always been supportive. We are especially indebted to the dedicated work of bibliographers, researchers, and archivists associated with the U.S. Latino & Latina World War II Oral History Project. Marc Hamel, the project's photographer, was instrumental in adding the special touches to the photographs to prepare them for publication. Raquel Garza, project manager, helped in various aspects of the processing of the manuscript. We are also grateful to the blind reviewer who offered helpful suggestions to an early draft of the manuscript. Rosemary Wetherold, a freelance copy editor, also gave our manuscript the meticulous attention that it needed.

We especially wish to thank the contributors to the anthology. They invested time and energy that exceeded the usual demands that editors place on such authors. The scholars were especially helpful in agreeing to participate in the planning of the publication. The scholarly meetings that brought them together involved discussions on the theory and practice of oral history, the conceptualization of Latino history during the war years, and the importance and use of oral narratives generated by the U.S. Latino & Latina World War II Oral History Project. The shared research findings and views provided the authors a valuable frame of reference as they prepared the final drafts of their essays. Their decision to make generous use of oral narratives enriched their work with firsthand accounts and interpretations that one does not often see in the writing of history.

We would be remiss if we did not thank the sponsors of the 12 September 2004 symposium in Washington, D.C., that served as a foundation for this book. They included the University of Texas at Austin's College of Communication; American Airlines; Univision Communications Inc.; Pew Hispanic Center; the Ernesto Galarza Applied Research Center, University of California, Riverside; Coors Brewing Company; the University of Texas at Austin's Center for Mexican American Studies; and the University of New Mexico's Center for Regional Studies. We are also mindful that the University of Texas at Brownsville's College of Liberal Arts provided equipment and time to videographer Juan Aguilar of UTB's Media Services. Mr. Aguilar videotaped our 2004 symposium at the U.S. Navy Memorial Foundation, Naval Heritage Center Theatre.

The success of the symposium was largely due to the staff of the Latino & Latina World War II Oral History Project, including Yazmín Lazcano (then project manager), Valentino Mauricio (photographer), Rajesh Reddy (technical assistance), Laura Querubin (administrative help), Kristian D. Stewart (then database manager and administrative assistance), and Brenda Sendejo (indexing and transcribing supervisor). Kelly Tarleton also deserves recognition for the graphic design that appeared on the cover of the symposium's program. Melissa DiPiero-D'Sa, the project graphic designer, was instrumental in producing the program for the symposium.

Lastly, but most importantly, we thank our respective spouses, Gil Rodríguez and Angela Valenzuela, and our children, Ramón and Agustín Rodríguez and Clara and Luz Zamora. We are fortunate that they believe in the importance of our work, not only for our families and Latinos/as, but for the country's understanding of itself.

BEYOND THE LATINO WORLD WAR II HERO

INTRODUCTION

▬

MAGGIE RIVAS-RODRÍGUEZ & EMILIO ZAMORA

The war in Europe and the subsequent entry of the United States into the world conflagration set the country on a path to build what President Franklin D. Roosevelt called "the arsenal of democracy." The United States managed to assemble the required arsenal for the war, although it was not as successful in guaranteeing egalitarian values at home. War production nevertheless made possible the dramatic growth and expansion of the economy. It also allowed the United States to make a decisive contribution to the outcome of the war and to emerge from the hostilities as a major world power with imposing imperial designs. The martial spirit was no less significant at the home front. At least sixteen million men and women of varied social backgrounds gave expression to the heightened sense of national duty that overtook the country by agreeing to serve in the military.[1]

While the expansion of U.S. industrial capacity exceeded early wartime aims, the lofty wartime rhetoric of justice and equality for workers, women, and national minorities consistently fell short of declared expectations. The unprecedented and growing opportunities in employment, the single most important democratizing effect of the war, suggested a more equal and just society, but the change resulted more from an expanded wartime economy than from a more democratic and just society, as asserted in official pronouncements. Moreover, Latinos/as may have benefited from employment opportunities to a lesser extent than other groups in U.S. society. Despite the unequal access to jobs, wartime opportunities pulled the country out of the hard times of the Depression and allowed hundreds of thousands of workers to improve their lives with higher-skilled and better-paying jobs. The public language of democracy and justice, coupled with continuing discrimination and inequality, also encouraged protests and claims of entitlement among marginalized groups, including the Mexican, Puerto Rican, and Cuban men and women who are at the center of this anthology.[2]

The focus on Latinos/as, or U.S. communities that trace their ancestry to the Spanish-speaking peoples in the Caribbean, Mexico, Central America, and South America, requires some conceptual explanation. An obvious point of departure is the assertion that Latinos/as are too diverse to be considered a single group of persons with markedly shared experiences. Obvious differences in nationality, class, race, culture, places of origin, and length of residence in the United States suggest different historical trajectories and contemporary sociocultural formations. Compelling similarities, however, are also evident.

U.S. military, trade, and immigration policies, although varying in their intent and consequences in the history of relations with countries in the Americas, have produced generally similar results in the lives of Latinos/as. The history of U.S. expansionism during the last half of the nineteenth century, for instance, explains the absorption of one-half of Mexico's northern territory, the establishment of a dependent commonwealth in Puerto Rico, and the tumultuous relationship that the United States continues to share with Cuba. In all these instances, the United States mediated its expanded economic influence with trade and immigration policies that regulated the movement of capital, manufacturing, goods, and technology abroad and Latino/a labor for low-wage work in the United States.

Once in the United States, as well as in Puerto Rico, Latinos/as have been subjected to a process of racialization that set them socially and culturally apart from the rest of society as territorial minorities, working-class groups, racially distinct populations, and immigrant communities. The preponderant experience of immigration in the history of Latinos/as and their largely working-class status has also blurred intergroup differences and reinforced a view of sameness in the public imagination. Latinos/as have acted on this process by self-identifying as a distinct group and promoting pan-Latino/a views and interests.

Recent works by Juan Gonzalez, Marcelo Suárez-Orozco, Mariela Páez, and José Alamillo remind us that scholars generally consider Latinos/as a distinct U.S. community and an appropriate category of analysis, although they do not always explain the pan-Latino/a identity that they use or consistently acknowledge the obvious conceptual challenge.[3] Gonzalez, for instance, uses a quick-witted journalistic style to offer a broad and integrated historical treatment of Latinos/as that recognizes diverse experiences but mostly assumes common binding threads. Suárez-Orozco and Páez, on the other hand, provide a more explicit interpretative framework in their anthology's introductory essay. They underscore the importance of U.S. foreign policy in the history of migration of Latinos/as and the process of racially incorporating them into society to argue for a common Latino/a experience. Juan Flores offers nuance to the discourse on Latino/a identity by underscoring the unique Puerto Rican identity, its place within the wider Latino/a community, and the ongoing influence of consumerist marketing forces in shaping this process. Alamillo notes the growing scholarly literature, its general assumption of sameness in the face of intergroup difference, and the consequent pan-Latino/a perspective that characterizes it.[4]

Although this anthology assumes that Latinos/as possess a common set of experiences that warrants our undivided attention, it also seeks to test the validity of this view during the years of the Second World War. The wartime language of justice and democracy, the sense of common national purpose, the widespread employment opportunities, and the democratizing foxhole conditions at the front suggest the social and cultural incorporation of Latinos/as, along with a diminished Latino/a identity. Society, however, continued to marginalize them and to underscore their distinctiveness during the war years. Carlos Castañeda, the eminent historian from the University of Texas at Austin in the 1940s, sardonically described this experience in the Mexican community as second-class citizenship, made all the more obvious by the recovery from the hard times of the Depression and heightened democratic sensibilities.[5]

The secondary literature on Latinos/as has recognized the trends of discrimination, inequality, and improved employment opportunities as well as their important contributions to both home and war fronts. With some exceptions, however, the scholarship has failed to explain the common experiences, preferring instead to make the familiar general observations of Latino/a wartime history. Outside the field of Latino/a studies, researchers have been generally inattentive, preferring instead to assume that the Latino/a experience has not been sufficiently different from the general social and political trends and, consequently, cannot possibly render worthwhile empirical or theoretical returns to their efforts. As a result, U.S. military and home front studies typically give scant attention to Latinos/as while the scholarship devoted to them provides little empirical corroboration to their otherwise accurate but broad depictions.[6]

In the study of Mexicans, the largest of the Latino/a groups, general histories by Mario García, David Montejano, George J. Sánchez, Guadalupe San Miguel, and Juan Gómez-Quiñones have noted that Mexicans made significant contributions as low-wage workers and activists who promoted the wartime values of democracy and justice.[7] The general outline of the story also notes impressive contributions in the battlefields and posits that Latino/a soldiers returned with a new Americanized identity and a determined desire to fashion a rejuvenated civic culture and social movement for equal rights. Although scholars have expanded this narrative with new information and important nuance, they mostly use the general framework established soon after the end of the war by writers like Pauline Kibbe, Carey McWilliams, Alonso Perales, and Raul Morín.[8]

Kibbe's *Latin Americans in Texas* provided an original regional study on the living and working conditions of Mexicans, with a focus on discriminatory practices. Her primary concern was for government agencies to encourage racial understanding in order to achieve wartime unity in the Americas. Discrimination and inequality, she noted, remained relatively unchecked during the war despite its obvious deleterious effect on U.S. relations with Latin American nations. In seeking to justify improved attitudes, particularly in the Anglo population, she also underscored the important contributions that Mexicans made at the war front and the home front. This observation no doubt encouraged the refurbished Americanized identity that historians attribute to the returning veterans and the renewed civil rights cause of the postwar period.[9]

McWilliams' impressive survey of the history of "the Spanish-speaking" focused on Mexicans in the Southwest, particularly their development as an ethnic group and a bottom segment of the working class. He was especially critical of discrimination as an obstacle to equality and an impediment to the wartime goals of democracy and justice. Mexicans, he argued, were prevented from making full use of the wartime experience of recovery. McWilliams pointed out the slow movement of workers out of agriculture and into the urban-based skilled ranks, plus the expansion of the immigrant population and the growth of the migratory workforce. He was especially adept at using cases of discrimination, at times involving Mexican servicemen in uniform, to underscore its significance during the war years. He also acknowledged Mexico's efforts to make discrimination an issue in its diplomatic relations with the United States.

Perales, a cofounder of the League of United Latin American Citizens (LULAC) and one of the most active civil rights leaders of the 1940s, used the voice of the aggrieved Mexicans and the claims for equal rights by his contemporaries in the civil rights movement to bring added attention to discrimination and the cause for equal rights. His book *Are We Good Neighbors?* gave ample justification to the critique of discrimination and inequality with numerous personal accounts of discrimination and reprinted speeches, articles, and testimonies by civil rights leaders of the interwar period. Contributing authors like Carlos Castañeda, Robert Lucey, and José de la Luz Saenz, speaking from experience in the cause for equal rights, acknowledged significant social improvements but gave emphasis to the enduring practice of discrimination and the persistence of inequality.[10]

Discrimination and inequality, made especially obvious by the wartime promise of recovery, also moved Morín to put pen to paper. Although he published his account in 1963, Morín began his work during his "training days" when he reflected on the meaning of military service. Subsequent interviews and conversations with former servicemen whom he located in hospitals and veterans' organizations imbued his book with compassion. Morín was especially moved by the "glaring omissions of the Spanish-named soldiers" in the emerging literature and a realization that they "were being treated with second-class citizenship."[11] Morín also echoed the veterans' lament that they had made sacrifices at the battlefield but were denied equality at home. He underscored this point by contrasting accounts of refusal of service in businesses and government offices with the impressive record of citations, including Medals of Honor, Silver Stars, and other commendations for heroic sacrifices in the major theaters of war.

The issue of changing cultural sensibilities among veterans as well as immigrants, youth, and other members of Mexican communities also drew increasing attention from sociologists and anthropologists. Beginning with Emory S. Bogardus' study, which preceded World War II, U.S. scholars have expressed an interest in how Mexicans were adjusting to American life. Works by Ruth D. Tuck, Ozzie G. Simmons, Arthur J. Rubel, William Madsen, and John H. Burma, for example, used the war years as a point of departure in studying changing social conditions and acculturation in Latino/a communities. In some cases, they made explicit reference to World War II as a benchmark in the development of the civil rights movement and to the emergence of veterans in community leadership roles.[12]

Other writers helped maintain a focus on discrimination and inequality, often as evidence of maladjustments in society. Authors like Walter Fogel, a labor economist, and Tomás López, a creative writer, are cases in point.

Fogel used census data to confirm the view that occupational inequality continued throughout the war years and the postwar period. López drew on the experiences of Alfonso A. Rodríguez, a veteran and a successful construction company executive, to craft a biographical novel that recounted a rags-to-riches story. The story emphasized Rodríguez' military service and the unfriendly reception he received to underscore the larger contribution that Latinos/as made to the war effort and to justify their energized social movement.[13]

The contemporary literature on Latinos/as may not have added significant detail to the scholarly narrative of the war years and the postwar period, but recent oral history and archival collection initiatives promise a new generation of scholarship that will expand our knowledge of Latinos/as in World War II. At least two successful oral history and archival collections provide an empirical basis for such a possibility. The Recovering the U.S. Hispanic Literary Heritage Project, at the University of Houston, has been collecting and preserving historical and literary material written by and about Latinos/as for almost twenty years. The more focused U.S. Latino & Latina World War II Oral History Project, in its tenth year of operation at the University of Texas at Austin, has amassed more than six hundred oral narratives and much archival material. The recovery project has found common themes in its collection of personal papers, books, and newspapers, including the establishment of alternative institutions to offset the indifference of the dominant society, a concern for maintaining and promoting the Spanish language, a nostalgic view of the Latino/a past, and a preoccupation with discrimination as an obstacle to social advancement and self-realization. The U.S. Latino & Latina Oral History Project is more relevant to our purposes because of its emphases and the role that it has played in the production of this anthology.[14]

The Latino & Latina Project has affirmed the value of casting a wide unifying net in the study of Latino/a groups. The project's staff and associated researchers have also encouraged scholars to integrate the oral narratives into their work by sponsoring scholarly meetings that have produced two publications, including this anthology. A conference in the spring of 2000, which resulted in the first publication—an anthology edited by Maggie Rivas-Rodríguez—demonstrated that Mexicans, Puerto Ricans, and Cubans faced discrimination even as they benefited from occupational opportunities, albeit to a lesser extent than other groups. Latinos/as also served in the U.S. military in proportionally large numbers, participated in the major theaters of the war primarily as foot soldiers, outdid other identifiable groups in recognized cases of valor and sacrifice, waged a social movement that helped elevate discrimination to a level of hemispheric importance, and contributed significantly to production demands at the home front.[15]

Two more meetings held at Austin and Washington, D.C., in 2002 and 2004 were especially important in the production of this anthology. Invited scholars discussed their work on Latinos/as during the war years and examined the oral narratives.[16] The consensus was that Latinos/as shared important experiences and that the project's oral narratives could be used to expand the enterprise.

This volume addresses some of the same themes that appeared in the first anthology and introduces new ones. It examines the general experience of Latinos/as, including their contributions as workers in agriculture and nonagricultural industries and discrimination as an obstacle to mobility and a cause of continuing inequality. The authors acknowledge the unprecedented opportunities that made it possible for Latinos/as, and especially Latinas, to improve their lives and, in that way, establish the basis for generational change as well. Military service was given its due consideration, including the ubiquitous problem of discrimination and the participation of Mexican nationals in the U.S. military, the camaraderie and faith expressions that resulted in the dire circumstances of combat, the righteous sense of fairness and equality that veterans and their family members translated into individual claims and popular causes for equal rights, and psychological disorders and maladjustments that often haunted the servicemen upon their return home.

The authors use different terms to identify Latinos/as. In all cases, they have taken into account the popular usage of self-referents during the war years, including names like Mexican, Mexican American, and Puerto Rican. Sometimes they use terms interchangeably, but they always take care to denote nativity, citizenship, and gender when the discussion warrants it. The editors also agreed to use gender-neutral terms like "Latino/a" and "Latinos/as" to signify inclusion and fairness in representation. Moreover, we decided to honor the wishes of most of the women interviewees by using their married surnames. We also included maiden names when it was necessary to acknowledge familial associations and provide full bibliographic entries.

Richard Griswold del Castillo opens the anthology with a general interpretative essay, "The Paradox of War: Mexican American Patriotism, Racism, and Memory," that underscores the dilemma of embracing an Americanized identity on patriotic terms while facing racial discrimination. Latinos/as remember their youthful experiences in molding an American identity, one that incorporated patriotism and an abiding belief in the American dream, all the while fashioning a sense of self that was uniquely Latino/a.

Maggie Rivas-Rodríguez looks at how Latino men often listened to Spanish-language radio—in some cases broadcast from thousands of miles away—in an effort to maintain their mother tongue and give free expression to feelings of nostalgia. Rivas-Rodríguez observes that the practice is particularly noteworthy because of the widespread contempt for the Spanish language in mainstream America. It was common practice for schoolchildren to be punished harshly for speaking Spanish on school grounds. The radio listening practice as well as other uses of the Spanish language were mostly individual expressions of cultural solidarity. The social context of hostility, dismissal, and acts of defiance, however, provide for an appreciation of the importance of language in maintaining a sense of cultural identity and collective purpose.

Dionicio Valdés looks at another way that Latinos/as were transformed by the war experience. Many were migrant farmworkers, and although they advanced their situation with better-paying jobs, wartime agriculture continued to exploit them and to deny them the full measure of recovery that wartime production promised its workers. Valdés demonstrates the value of using oral narratives to place the human side of the experience of exploitation and assertiveness at center stage in agricultural development. Recollections of families living under trees because no other shelter was available provide added perspective to the history of Latinos/as during the war years. The individual claims for equal consideration also tell us that agency was the everyday expression of will, self-realization, and survival.

For Latinas in civilian life, World War II provided a new vantage point to life and work—away from the protective gaze of family and the obliging influence of tradition. Joanne Rao Sánchez measures the extent to which the larger story of women during World War II applies to Latinas. She concludes that Latinas joined in the unprecedented movement out of homes and into industrial employment as well as military service. They too registered improvements in their lives and contributed to generational advancements in their communities. These gains were all the more significant because they traveled a long distance from their working-class and Mexican cultural origins. Latinas, however, faced both gender and racial discrimination in their quest for a better life.

Emilio Zamora reminds us that 15,000 Mexican nationals served in the U.S. military and that the Mexican government included them when its officials advocated for equal Mexican rights in the United States. Not content with only recovering this history of continental unity and service, Zamora uses it to comment on broader issues such as scholarly neglect, discriminatory recruitment practices, the "citizenship draft," a "1.5 generation" that straddled the cultural line separating the Mexico- and the U.S.-born,, and the uneven influence of the war on Mexican socioeconomic mobility.

Silvia Alvarez Curbelo addresses the case of Puerto Ricans serving in the U.S. military, in units segregated by race and language. She examines the contradiction between declared principles of equality abroad and racial discrimination at home as a backdrop to two important themes in the history of Puerto Ricans during World War II. The first concerns the incorporation of Puerto Ricans into a racial-minded military. The second involves Puerto Rican officials who did not press for the end to discrimination and segregation in the military for fear of jeopardizing their improved wartime standing with the United States and the prospects of negotiating reforms for the island. The U.S. military was caught in its own contradiction when it sought to apply the longtime tradition of racial segregation to Puerto Rican soldiers. The U.S. Bureau of the Census declared that Puerto Ricans were White. The military, however, pointed to popular racial expressions against Puerto Ricans and used the presence of Afro–Puerto Rican soldiers to adopt its version of a "one-drop rule" to establish separate military units for them.

Rea Ann Trotter's essay emphasizes the importance of faith and spirituality among Latino soldiers. These two values often came to mean the difference between life and death for many of them. Men who had been casual churchgoers before the war now found solace and even redemption in prayer and in their Christian faith. Some confronted the profound remorse about killing another human being, while others wondered why they had been spared from death but their friends had not. They made sense of these and other issues by turning to the hope that their faith provided them.

Ricardo Ainslie and Daphny Domínguez tell of other men who were not able to banish the demons that haunted them. The stress of war has always represented an intense source of disorienting and disquieting change on battlefields and on the return home. World War II was no different, nor was the effect less injurious on Latinos. As with other veterans, society had a difficult time recognizing the war-related problems associated with "shell shock" and "nerves." Society was also ill-prepared to devise the necessary treatment for these ailments. The problem may have been more serious in the Latino/a community. In some cases, Latino veterans were advised to get married, presumably because the warmth and intimacy of one's own home along with traditional care of dutiful wives would cure their problems.

Finally, Brenda Sendejo addresses how Latina mothers of World War II used their new experiences to translate the inherited roles of their own mothers into the new generation of daughters who became adults in the postwar period. Sendejo notes that although women largely returned to the role of homemakers after the war, they urged their daughters to be self-sufficient and assume leadership roles in their families and communities. Sendejo's generational, case study approach provides a reliably close method by which to better understand change over time and the influence of the war years in this process.

The authors have made obvious individual contributions that are important to the study of Latinos/as. Taken together, those contributions achieve greater importance. The authors consistently observe that Latinos/as were integral to the war effort and that they often made extraordinary contributions despite their position as a racialized community of low-wage workers. They also suggest subterranean wells of resentment that mirror and no doubt contributed to emergent critiques and aspirations associated with the cause for equal rights that extends into our times.

The use of oral narratives and the role that memory played in the preparation of the essays represent another less obvious underlying theme in the anthology. This was made possible by the scholarly meetings in which the contributing authors discussed their work in light of the value of oral narratives and the need to use them responsibly. Oral narratives assumed an important role during the early development of Latino/a history as a way to supplement a record of neglect in the literature. They are no less important now that so many interviews have been conducted, including the ones at the Latino & Latina World War II Oral History Project.

The oral interviews demonstrate that our narrators—former migratory workers, soldiers, Latinas who entered the industrial workforce in the 1940s, and radio listeners of the times—have long-range and clear memories and that these recollections repeatedly point to suffering, defiance, fulfilling experiences, and collective identities. Moreover, the memories are filtered through a concern in the present for remembering an important past in the formation of our communities. It is as if the past reclaims and reshapes the present while the present reinterprets the past. Nowhere is this more evident than in the idea of "shared authorship," whereby the narrator and the interpreter of the oral narrative share somewhat equally in the interpretation of the past. And so our contributing authors as well as the narrators who shared their stories must be credited with recalling their strong conviction to making this volume what it is.[17]

THE PARADOX OF WAR

Mexican American Patriotism, Racism, and Memory

RICHARD GRISWOLD DEL CASTILLO

One of the themes running through the more than six hundred interviews gathered by the U.S. Latino & Latina World War II Oral History Project at the University of Texas at Austin is that of struggle against poverty, discrimination, and the perception of Mexican Americans as foreigners and outsiders during the Great Depression and World War II. Largely because of this experience, many Mexican Americans developed a life philosophy that enabled them to cope with harsh realities. World War II also afforded them the opportunity to put that philosophy to the test: they were called upon to sacrifice for their country, a nation that increasingly came to represent freedom, tolerance, and human dignity for them. This conflicted consciousness of being a patriotic American while experiencing second-class citizenship led to the formation of a tough and resilient worldview, one that would make Mexican Americans a backbone of what came to be called middle America.

This chapter explores the ways in which Mexican American men and women remembered their youthful experience with racism and discrimination while molding an American identity, one that incorporated patriotism and an abiding belief in the American dream. It also suggests that the U.S. Latino & Latina World War II Oral History Project archive deserves closer examination by scholars who seek to explain what has been termed "the Mexican American generation."[1]

When the United States entered World War II, about three and a half million people of Mexican descent lived in the United States. They represented a diversity of backgrounds, ranging from families who had lived within the present-day United States for centuries to those who had recently crossed the border to find new and promising jobs in the factories and fields of their adopted country. According to the 1940 count of the U.S. Bureau of the Census, a majority of them were U.S.-born for the first time in their history. Most were sons and daughters of the immigrants who crossed the border during the period between 1910 and 1930, the years of the great migration from Mexico.[2]

Despite their status as citizens and the internal differences that they exhibited in appearance, status, and regional affiliation, most were classified as "Mexican" by the U.S. Census and by public opinion. Moreover, their Spanish language, skin color (typically brown) and working-class status—resulting from a century of economic and political submersion—made them visible and subject to continued discrimination and segregation. Suspected of being disloyal to the United States, in part because they were perceived as foreigners, most Mexican Americans lived in the shadows of their barrios, or segregated communities, and in forgotten rural enclaves, hardly noticed except when needed for low-wage work or subject to the prejudiced watch of law enforcement officials. During the 1920s and 1930s they grew up expecting hard work, poverty, hunger, and rejection, but they learned to survive.[3]

The life stories that follow, taken from the U.S. Latino & Latina World War II Oral History Project, illustrate how Mexican American youth emerged from the hard times of the Great Depression and used their sense of patriotic sacrifice, born out of the war emergency of the 1940s, to redefine themselves as men and women who expected fair treatment and impartial justice.

Antonio Campos is a case in point. He was raised in Houston, Texas, during the 1930s. Campos vividly recalled the discrimination that Mexican Americans faced in restaurants: "If you wanted to get fed you had to go in the back. Mexicans and dogs were in the back. You had to get a sandwich and go home."[4]

As a child, he joined a segregated Boy Scouts troop with secondhand uniforms, and he joined a Mexican high school band after being rejected by the all-Anglo band. Campos volunteered for the U.S. Army and served as a paratrooper in France. After the war, he received his undergraduate education with the help of the GI Bill of Rights and later attended Baylor Law School. When he finished law school, Campos organized an English-teaching campaign for U.S.- and foreign-born Mexican youth. He also ran for mayor and for a position on the city council but was defeated after a bitter contest. He remembered that a local government official taunted him: "If you don't like it why don't you go back to Mexico?"[5] The remark triggered a response that defined Campos' new sense of self: "I was born here in Texas. I went overseas and put my life on the line so you people can make decisions."[6]

Campos believed that he was a patriot who had earned the right to expect and demand respect, and he found himself demonstrating that belief often. Even after he had served his country willingly and honorably, he did not feel that he was valued or that he could give up his fight for recognition and respect. Later, Campos, using his wartime confidence and personal resolve, led a coalition of activists to end discrimination in the public establishments of Baytown, Texas.[7]

Mexican veterans like Moisés Flores often expressed a patriotism that mixed with a Mexican identity in complicated ways. Flores was born in the Colonia Dublán of Chihuahua, Mexico. He crossed the border to join the U.S. Army and served in the Pacific theater, where he was wounded in action. After the war, he settled in El Paso, where he expressed the new identity that he had adopted: "I am very proud to be American. Sometimes I even call myself 'gringo,' which I'm not. I'm still Mexican, but I'm an American first."[8] Flores' *mestizaje*, or mixture of ideas, reflects the impact of a war that recast Mexicans as Americans and led some of them to occasionally blur the difference between "gringos" and Mexicans, if only to claim a changed identity.

For some, including Andrew Tamayo, the war experience accentuated resentments and even anger over the persistent social inequality at home. Tamayo was raised in San Antonio by a single mother. He recalled that the discrimination continued after he completed military service. "I remember how they used to treat us over here," he said.[9]

Tamayo served with distinction in the Thirty-ninth Field Artillery Battalion, Third Infantry Division of the U.S. Army. He earned a Bronze Star, a Purple Heart, and eight bronze campaign stars. When he finished his military service, Tamayo returned to San Antonio to find that conditions were relatively the same. He became bitter over the years, to the point of becoming angry about "helping the gringos" in their war. Tamayo, unlike some of his fellow Mexican veterans, used this anger to explicitly define his new defiant sense of self. His new identity, however, was also born out of military service.

Mexican veterans like Luis Leyva also experienced betrayals that contributed to a conditional form of American identity. Leyva was born in Mexico and grew up in Laredo as an adopted orphan. Since he had grown up in an

Andrew Tamayo, 1943. Courtesy of the U.S. Latino & Latina World War II Oral History Project.

all-Mexican neighborhood and attended all-Mexican schools, he never felt that he had experienced discrimination. An undocumented resident, Leyva was not drafted into the military; he volunteered soon after the Pearl Harbor attack. He explained, "I know no other country. . . . This is my country; this is where I live."[10] Leyva, however, witnessed discrimination when he asked some African American cooks to come into his barracks to see a photograph of his girlfriend and they told him that they were not allowed to enter the segregated building.

"I couldn't understand it," he recalled. "I was in the U.S. Army fighting for the freedom of people in Europe, and we were having the same problem here in the United States."[11] His more immediate concern involved a promise of citizenship that was never kept. Leyva had been assured citizenship if he served in the U.S. military. For some unexplained reason, he did not receive his citizenship papers. The bitter disappointment that he has carried all his life limited and impaired his Americanized identity.

For soldiers like Raymond J. Flores, the war experience strengthened a politicized identity previously shaped by his family's involvement in struggles against discrimination that stretched back over generations. He was born in the mining town of Miami, Arizona, one of seventeen brothers and sisters. His mother encouraged him to fight for his beliefs, including equality for his community. Not one to simply "do as I say," she modeled behavior for him.[12] Raymond joined his mother as well as his brothers and sisters to fight for the integration of an all-White class in the local elementary school. In high school, Flores also led a walkout of Mexican students to protest the school's decision to schedule the taking of the class picture according to the students' national origin. Flores described his resolve in no uncertain terms: "It was a period of racism to the extreme when I was growing up. If you get accustomed to it, it doesn't hurt as much. But we didn't want to be accustomed to that. It was just not our way."[13]

While in the military, Flores also encountered racial discrimination. He noted, "I hate to discredit different parts of the military, but racism was rampant."[14] Even in the military, Flores used his ability to teach by helping non-English-speaking Latino soldiers from Texas to learn "Army English." For two hours every morning, he taught the grateful soldiers the words they needed to understand in order to follow basic commands and avoid punishment. After the war, Flores continued with his activism against discrimination, including boycotts in college. He used the educational benefits of the GI Bill to become a teacher and took the opportunity while working in schools to challenge inequality and injustice everywhere.

María Elisa Rodríguez represented yet another case of a newfound identity. She was born into a Mexican immigrant family of nine children in Waco, Texas. Her father was a day laborer who encouraged his children to secure an education because he believed that this would protect them from prejudice and discrimination. Rodríguez remembered Waco had "lots of prejudice and that's the reason my dad always emphasized education."[15] She felt discrimination as a little girl, recalling, "We couldn't even belong to the Girl Scouts or anything like that. There was a lot of discrimination. So we couldn't even get into the public swimming pools."[16] As a teenager, she decided to become a secretary even though she knew that Mexican girls did not usually secure those kinds of jobs; they were expected to be maids and cooks. When she applied for the job, the interviewers questioned her citizenship and made her feel like a foreigner. She was forced to identify herself as an American of Mexican descent:

> There were very few secretaries at that time. . . . In fact I was the first secretary to come here and be hired . . . and they would see my name and the patient would say, "What nationality are you?" I'd say, "I'm Mexican and I am an American of Mexican descent." And they'd say, "Well, I've never seen a Mexican in an office." And I'd say, "Well, you're seeing one now." Because most of them [Hispanic women] were working in clothing stores because that was as high as you could get. There weren't too many opportunities offered to Mexican American women.[17]

Rodríguez worked as a civilian clerk for the army during the war. She felt the contradiction of the double identity as Mexican Americans were being called upon to be loyal Americans and sacrifice for their country while they were facing discrimination at home. She also observed the disparity in the lives of the young men who were serving in the military:

> And that's why I couldn't ever understand that they'd see these boys go and fight for this country and they'd come back and they couldn't get good jobs. That's the only thing I felt bad about. That they didn't give us the opportunity. Because our boys went out and died on the battlefront, and I thought we were entitled to everything. But as it was, we weren't. Discrimination still existed.[18]

Rodríguez married a World War II veteran and raised a family. She also continued working for the army as a monitor for fair employment practices in the military. She became active in several Mexican American rights organizations, including the League of United Latin American Citizens (LULAC), the Incorporated Mexican American Government Employees, and the American GI Forum. She also volunteered to teach citizenship classes in Waco. During the war years, she changed from a timid girl who accepted segregation and discrimination as a fact of life to an adult who considered herself an American and expected respect and equal treatment.

About the time that Rodríguez was attending school in Waco, Andrew Aguirre was growing up in Otay Mesa on the U.S.-Mexican border, south of San Diego. Aguirre's earliest memories spoke of poverty, hunger, and work. The entire family—eight children and their Mexican immigrant parents—

María Elisa Rodríguez, 1943. Courtesy of the U.S. Latino & Latina World War II Oral History Project.

worked as laborers in the agricultural fields or in town. Aguirre reached only the eighth grade and then dropped out to work for the family. In school, he remembered fights and punishments because he spoke only Spanish and because he was Mexican. When he was asked if the troubles in school were "a racial thing," his response was one of stoic acceptance but also of self-criticism:

> Yeah, there was racial stuff involved, let's face it. Because, let's face it, we've been racially picked on since we crossed the border. That's why as you get older you learn to assimilate more. . . . But I think that part of the problem

was that the Chicanos were their own worse enemies... because everybody was in a barrio.... You feel comfortable in your own language and your own culture. So when a person tries to escape the barrio and assimilate into the Anglos, he was picked on.... We were our own worst enemies.[19]

Aguirre no doubt learned this self-criticism after seeing the benefits of fitting in and because he bore the criticism of his barrio friends for speaking English and working with Anglos. The cultural pressure to stay with the group and not become *agabachado*, or Anglicized, represented a reaction to the favored treatment that the more accommodationist Mexicans received. The terms *vendido, vende patria,* or *malinchista* were often used as insults against persons who acculturated. Hence, persons like Aguirre had to contend with American racism, which excluded and segregated Mexicans, as well as with cultural values that singled out those who sought to advance on Anglo-American terms. This is why Aguirre noted that "we were our own worst enemies."[20] Barrio life, as a restrictive environment, added a complicating psychological layer to a developing double consciousness.

In 1944, as Aguirre was about to be drafted, his uncle persuaded him to join the Marine Corps. In the marines, he found the sense of belonging and the pride that he had been seeking. After serving in Okinawa, Aguirre decided to become a career marine. He subsequently fought in Korea, where he was captured and held in a North Korean prison camp. Reflecting on his experience in the marines, he commented:

I joined the Marine Corps and I really loved it. At first I hated it. I hated those robots you know—hep, hup, hey. They wore their hats down here [he pointed to below his eyebrows].... They brought their face right up, practically spitting on you. But gradually you start to develop a sense of unity, a sense of importance because you're part of something big, you know....
At first you really hate it; then you start to take pride in yourself, your buddies, and your platoon. You get gung ho! In fact when I got released [from a North Korean prison], they asked me if the Chinese had brainwashed me, and I said no, the Marine Corps had beaten them to it.[21]

For Aguirre, the Marine Corps became a way of making it in American society, despite his poverty, his lack of education, and the reactions to his Mexican heritage. He became a proponent of assimilation, but not at the expense of his identity as a Chicano—a self-referent of more recent origin than "Mexican American," which he still uses today. Quiet perseverance and a tough self-confidence defined Aguirre's identity. He underscored a deter-mined outlook in a message to youth: "To succeed, you need self-discipline and goals."²² Aguirre recognized that Anglos continue to discriminate against Mexican Americans. He believed, however, that some of the bad treatment was due to the refusal of Mexicans to accommodate to U.S. society. Aguirre's experience validates his philosophy. He was able to escape poverty and the criticism of his Mexican peers by joining the marines during World War II.

Hector De Peña Jr. offers the last example of how racism and discrimi-nation have shaped a Mexican American identity. The son of a small mer-chant from South Texas, De Peña excelled academically and graduated from high school in three years. His family life was not typical of most Mexican Americans living in Texas during the 1930s. His father provided so well for the family that De Peña was able to attend college. He entered a prelaw pro-gram at Texas A&I University in Kingsville and graduated with a teaching certificate.²³ De Peña, however, was not able to get a job as a teacher, largely because Mexicans typically were not allowed to teach Anglos. Undeterred and believing in the power of education, a value he had learned from his fam-ily, he went to San Antonio in 1937 and attended law school in the evenings. He received his law degree in three years and opened a small private practice in Corpus Christi. De Peña remembered the discrimination he encountered there: "They would not serve us in any downtown restaurant. If we wanted to go to the movie we went upstairs with the Blacks. My brother was the first secretary of the organization [the League of United Latin American Citi-zens]. Later, I joined LULAC."²⁴

De Peña remembered that LULAC fought against discrimination before the war. He knew some of the important Mexican American civil rights lead-ers who were active in civil rights lawsuits. They included Hector P. García, a local LULAC officer and later a cofounder of the American GI Forum. As a member and future leader of LULAC at the time, De Peña participated in two civil rights battles that took place during the postwar period. One of them in-volved an ordinance that prohibited Mexicans from using a swimming pool in a city-owned park: "I recall two major projects I was involved in, and one of them was the city council would not permit any Hispanics to swim at Cole Park.... So we went and appeared before them to do something about it. We were trying to improve their [Hispanics'] standing, to get them their rights. And they did open it up."²⁵

The other LULAC project spearheaded opposition against a segregated Black-only school in the barrio. It was common practice throughout Texas to have segregated Mexican schools as well as separate schools for African Americans.[26] In this case, the (all-White) school board had decided to build a school for African American students in the Mexican barrio because the land was cheap and a suitable parcel in the African American ghetto could not be found. The effort to build a new school in the barrio exposed a racial divide between Mexican Americans and Blacks as each community struggled to maintain a sense of self-respect within the bounds of segregation. Mexicans were classified as a separate race in the 1930 U.S. census, and throughout the 1930s LULAC and other middle-class Mexican American organizations had fought to have the government classify Mexicans as "White," hoping that this designation would improve their status. The school board's plan was defeated.

De Peña did not serve in the military during the war, because of a medical condition. Instead he worked as a civilian censor for the government. Clearly, his civil rights consciousness was developing before the war, and his activism reflected a growing popular consciousness throughout the country among Mexican American professionals. His formation as a civil rights advocate was also due to his association with other Mexican American professionals and his South Texas roots, which told him not to ignore discrimination even though he was relatively well-off.

The life stories from the Latino & Latina World War II Oral History Project underscore the diversity of ways that Mexican American men and women developed their awareness of civil rights during and prior to the Second World War. The common denominator in their experiences is that they became especially aware of the contradiction of being treated as outcasts while being told that they were expected to be patriotic Americans. The contradiction was stronger among this generation than in previous ones, because of the harsh experiences of the 1930s and the economic recovery that occurred during World War II, as well as the celebration of their status as citizens of the United States. This double consciousness of discrimination and being "American" would continue to be a force in shaping the actions of later generations as they struggled to achieve social and political justice.

2

EMBRACING THE ETHER

The Use of Radio by the Latino World War II Generation

MAGGIE RIVAS-RODRÍGUEZ

During World War II, my father, Ramón Rivas, a young army private, eagerly volunteered for overnight guard duty when he was stationed in Dutch Harbor, in the Aleutian Island chain off the coast of Alaska. It wasn't that he preferred solitude or that he relished the cold and darkness. Rather, it was that now and then, when the AM radio waves bounced just right, he could tune in a radio station, on the Mexican border, that carried the music and the language of his people, five thousand miles away. In 1999 he recalled his desperate homesickness and fear of losing Spanish, the only language spoken by his family and friends in South Texas. Finding the Spanish-language radio stations from Del Rio, Texas, was one of the ploys he used to hold fast to his native language. "Since I was the only Mexican American in my outfit," he recalled, "I used to have to practice speaking Spanish. I used to keep myself speaking Spanish so I could speak to people when I came home."[1]

Back in Texas, one of his contemporaries, Joe Bernal, grew up listening intently to the diction of the announcers on San Antonio's English-language radio stations. He sought to perfect his adopted language, believing that mastering English was his ticket to a better future. His parents, who spoke only limited English, encouraged their children to learn the language. They told young Bernal: "We don't want you to be like us, we couldn't get good jobs. So you need to speak English and graduate from high school and get good jobs."[2]

Ramón Rivas, 1945. Courtesy of the U.S. Latino &
Latina World War II Oral History Project.

But along with English-language radio, Bernal and his family also tuned
in to Spanish-language radio to hear the language of their people. Years
later, after a long career as a bilingual teacher, school administrator, and
then Texas state representative and senator, Bernal said that both English
and Spanish were vital to him. English was necessary to communicate with
the outside world. "But the Spanish part, it's something that you grew up
with, it's part of you," he said. "It was part of you—you couldn't take it out of
you. It was part of you."[3]

Bernal and my father were among the Latinos and Latinas of the World War II generation who navigated two cultures and two languages—and who used radio to live within that reality. While it was a common practice for them to seek out Spanish-language broadcasts before, during, and after the war, they similarly appreciated the offerings of mainstream English-language stations of the day—the music of Glenn Miller, Artie Shaw, Tommy Dorsey, the Andrews Sisters.

In the 1930s and the 1940s, the years in which a new generation of Mexican Americans reached adulthood, radio played a major role in U.S. society: it was the mass medium that could be heard by people in the country as well as in cities; it was accessible to illiterate people or those with limited ability to read; and it was free (except for the price of the receiver).[4] Americans gravitated to radio. In 1922 fewer than 1 percent of American households had a radio—but 40 percent of American homes did by 1930. A decade later, a whopping 80 percent of American households owned radios.[5]

There has been substantial research on radio, which will be discussed later in this chapter, in particular, its early years, its development, how it shaped communications theory, law and policy, how it was the proving ground for broadcast journalism, what it represented to the country. What has received little attention is how World War II–generation Americans used radio and in particular how Latinos/as used radio. This essay explores the importance of radio to Latinos/as of the World War II generation and uses interviews to illustrate how and why they embraced the mass medium of their day. Interviews with and information provided by these individuals reveal that radio was ubiquitous and that the listeners tuned in to Spanish-language radio when it was available. Why did they listen? In general, they have reported that they listened to Spanish-language radio for language maintenance, as was the case for my father, and they tuned in to English-language radio for acculturation purposes, as was the case for Joe Bernal.[6] Most often, they listened for the sheer pleasure, and they wanted both English and Spanish. It is perhaps not surprising that they would seek out Spanish-language radio for music, as in the 1940s, Spanish-language radio was 88 percent music.[7] Interviews with the men and women of the generation reveal that, like other Americans, they had songs that made them stop everything and listen. For instance, José R. "Joe" Jasso, of San Antonio, recalled listening to Spanish-language radio from Mexico. His favorite song was "Ya me voy para la guerra" (I'm Going to War). "I knew I would be going off to war," Jasso said. "This song spoke to me."[8]

Nicanor Aguilar, 1946. Courtesy of the U.S. Latino & Latina
World War II Oral History Project.

Radio's Golden Years

The 1930s and 1940s were the golden years of radio, as more stations began
transmitting in the United States. In 1940 a total 846 stations were in operation.[9] But listeners weren't limited to stations licensed by the federal
government. They could also tune in to stations outside the U.S. boundaries, capitalizing on the sky-wave effect of radio waves. Some particularly
powerful radio transmitters, most notably the "border blasters" along the
U.S.-Mexico border, could transmit at up to 500 kilowatts. Those stations

could serve as cultural lifelines to people like my father, serving far away from others who could speak Spanish.

Spanish was only one of the "foreign" languages heard on U.S. radio waves, a fact that raised the hackles of those who felt that English should be the official language of the country. Ironically, the diffusion of different languages via the new medium came at a time of loud demands for Americans to adopt a common language and common traditions and values.[10] Latinos/as were not the only non-English-speaking Americans who felt the sting of the nativists' attacks.[11] In fact, foreign-language radio was the subject of complaints to the fledgling Federal Communications Commission—even while 200 of the United States' 846 licensed radio stations in 1940 broadcast some portion of their programs in a language other than English.[12]

Concentrated in the southwestern part of the United States, on land that only a century earlier had been Mexico, Mexican Americans formed a critical and very visible mass, as well as a devoted target audience.[13] It is worth noting that they were listening to Spanish-language radio at the same time that they were prohibited from speaking Spanish on school grounds—and were punished for doing so, sometimes harshly.[14] In interviews for the U.S. Latino & Latina World War II Oral History Project, participants said they were aware that their use of Spanish was being discouraged and even prohibited. But the pervasive discrimination didn't dampen their enthusiasm for Spanish-language radio. Californian Henry "Hank" Cervantes, in fact, recalls his Mexican-born grandmother shaking her head at the inherent contradictions:

> She would often say, "What a strange country—they punish kids in grammar school for speaking Spanish, and in high school they hire teachers to teach them the language." That's essentially what the problem was, but that [Spanish] was our home language. But we spoke it, not so much at school, because we were afraid of the repercussions. But of course our parents only spoke Spanish, so we had no other choice.[15]

The embrace of Spanish-language radio did not necessarily imply a rejection of English. It is more accurate to say that Spanish and English coexisted for many of these men and women and that radio was an important part of their lives, as it was for other Americans.

Radio extended Americans' horizons beyond their immediate surroundings. For instance, before the advent of radio, the world of Hank Cervantes, who grew up in California's Central Valley, was limited to the agricultural fields. Like many others, Cervantes and his family followed the *pisca*, the harvest. He recalled sleeping on "gunny sacks filled with corn husks":

> My brother and I would often fall asleep listening to the braceros and the men of the family sitting around the campfire singing songs like "Las mañanitas," "La paloma," "La cucaracha," "La golondrina," "El rancho grande." Those are the songs that I recall from that time period.[16]

One of his aunts, María Rincón, owned a Victrola record player and "three or four records." But then radio came. Cervantes was enthralled:

> Time went on and we acquired a thumbnail-shaped radio, and the program that my parents would mostly listen to was *Los madrugadores*. They came out of Los Angeles and they were led by Pedro González. And occasionally from Texas, we would catch Lydia Mendoza, who was billed as "La Alondra de la Frontera" [Meadowlark of the Border]. And that's when we began hearing songs like "Guadalajara," "Estrellita," "Siete leguas," "Cielito lindo," "Adiós, Mariquita linda" . . . We would get up as close as we possibly could. My mother would have to make my brother and me back off so other people could get somewhere near it. It didn't have the volume . . . that later on other radios had. They were rather limited.[17]

For Cervantes, a music lover, radio represented an introduction to a greater variety of music, in both Spanish and English—a far wider selection than his Tia María's few records and the campfire sing-alongs of the farmworkers. In the years to come, he and his brother would remain glued to the radio set, tracking the English-language hits of the day, wanting, he would suppose later, to "fit in" with the Anglo kids in the area.[18]

Radio in the 1930s and 1940s

Radio's role in World War II has been the subject of several articles and books. The Armed Forces Radio Service, for instance, was developed as a morale booster for fighting men in Europe and the Pacific. The relations of AFRS with the British Broadcasting Corporation have been well documented.[19] There has also been important research on adjustments made by the AFRS to include entertainment more palatable to African Americans, by developing "Jubilee Radio," for example—a program that included songs by Billie Holiday, Billy Eckstine, and others.[20] The inventiveness—and irreverence—of Americans in the Pacific has also received some attention: the string of radio stations was referred to as the "Mosquito Network" and had programs like the *Atabrine Cocktail Hour*. It reminded the men and women stationed in the malaria-infested jungles to take their daily dosage of antimalarial Atabrine tablets.[21]

Still other writings about the role of radio in World War II have considered the development of broadcast journalism, and in particular the contributions of pioneers like Edward R. Murrow, Eric Sevareid, Howard K. Smith, and Charles Collingwood. That generation of resourceful journalists had started in newspapers and were learning, on the job, to develop their skills on the airwaves, while using the immediacy of radio in covering major breaking events.[22]

But little has been researched regarding how World War II men and women enjoyed the "DXing," or distance listening, capability of radio. For an untold number of U.S. Spanish speakers, the sky-wave effect of AM radio waves was a boon that began in the 1920s and continued into the 1950s and beyond.[23] It contributed significantly to listeners' ability to hear Spanish-language radio, and thus it deserves some attention here.

Gene Fowler and Bill Crawford have described the "sky-wave or ozone-skip effect," which enabled radio waves to "bounce or skip off the atmosphere surrounding the globe in much the same way as a rock skips across a smooth pond." Fowler and Crawford write that people as far away as New Zealand became familiar with the border blasters.[24] Some border radio stations were high-powered enough, under specific atmospheric conditions, to reach as far away as the Philippines and the Aleutian Islands.

The most colorful high-powered stations on the border were established by entrepreneurs whose programs had been banned from U.S. airwaves but who found a haven in Mexico, along its border with Texas. Their offenses centered around fraudulent advertising, as well as slander. They founded stations like XER and XERA in Villa Acuña (across from Del Rio), XEPN in Piedras Negras (across from Eagle Pass), XEAW in Reynosa (across from McAllen), and XENT (twelve miles south of Laredo).[25] There, the Mexican government was less stringent in governing content, except for requiring the U.S. stations to broadcast one-quarter of their airtime in Spanish.[26] The Americans gladly complied, inadvertently becoming important to Spanish-speaking Latino soldiers and others. The border blasters became hugely popular with Mexican Americans throughout the Southwest, and they helped create Mexican American recording artist celebrities, giving U.S. Latinos/as their own home-grown stars, rather than singers and musicians in Mexico and further south.

Those border-blaster stations could not have come into being at any other time in history. In the earliest days of radio, there were few laws specifying what could not be aired: standards and regulations were being established as the needs arose. An early law, the Radio Act of 1927, promised there would be no censorship. For enterprising and unscrupulous entrepreneurs, it was a green light to proceed at full throttle. Two Americans who seized the opportunity were John R. Brinkley and Norman Baker. Brinkley, originally of Kansas, had a $100 diploma from the Kansas City, Missouri, Eclectic Medical University, a diploma recognized in eight states.[27] "Dr." Brinkley was best-known as the "goat gland surgeon," for his trademark surgical procedure to replace a man's prostate gland with a goat prostate; thus, Brinkley claimed, the patient would be imbued with renewed vigor. In 1930 the Federal Radio Commission revoked his KFKB broadcasting license in Kansas, accusing him of defrauding the public with false promises of medical cures.[28] After losing a court appeal, Brinkley moved his operation to Villa Acuña (now Ciudad Acuña) in 1931 and was given a license to broadcast, first at 75,000 and later at 500,000 watts.[29] His station, XER, operated until 1934 and resurfaced the following year as XERA, which lasted until 1941.[30]

Norman Baker received a license to begin broadcasting in 1925 via the 500-watt KTNT (Know the Naked Truth) in Muscatine, Iowa. Baker sparred with many, including physicians. The medical profession regarded him as a "cancer quack" because, since 1925, he had claimed to have a cure for cancer at his Baker Institute in Muscatine.[31] The Federal Radio Commission in 1931 declined Baker's application for a license renewal, on several grounds, including claims that he used the airwaves to attack individuals, corporations, and organizations, that KTNT's programming consisted largely of selling Baker's merchandise, and that the station used obscene language.[32] Two years later, Baker set up shop twelve miles south of Laredo, at the 150,000-watt XENT. That station continued to broadcast until 1944, when Mexican authorities refused to renew its broadcast license.[33] Baker returned to the United States in 1940 to serve four years in federal prison on fraud charges.[34]

Despite their notoriety, stations like XER and XENT played a role in introducing the World War II generation of Latinos and Latinas to such singers as Lydia Mendoza. A San Antonio–based singer, Mendoza was first introduced to listeners of a San Antonio station around 1932.[35] In short order, Mendoza recorded songs on the Blue Bird label, and these were played on Brinkley's XER in Villa Acuña—reaching Hank Cervantes in California and Ramón Rivas in Alaska. Years later, Mendoza would associate her songbird nickname with this airplay:

My voice and my songs on those Blue Bird records were heard all along the border, and I believe that the idea of calling me "*La Alondra de la Frontera*," the Lark of the Border, was born from that. Because they only listened to me along the border, they didn't know of me in Mexico.[36]

Mendoza's reference to her popularity on the U.S. side of the border recognizes how the border blasters promoted recording artists like her and contributed to the emergence of regional Mexican-American music. While Spanish-speaking recording artists benefited from the exposure—giving them greater renown—the stations did not always play fair. Mendoza's promoter, Ramiro Cortés, said that a mail-order business at XER sold photographs of Mendoza without her permission and without sharing any profits with her:

In Del Rio, there was a big, strong, very strong radio station; they tell me that you could hear this radio station all over the world. A Dr. Brinkley was the owner of that station. He used to advertise the glands, he was transplanting glands, a lot of bull, you know. There was a program there, every day, that played Lydia's records. And then this fella, somebody, not Brinkley, but another guy who rented some time from this radio station, he was advertising, he was selling Lydia Mendoza's photos for one dollar. "Mail me one dollar, and I'll mail you an autographed picture of Lydia Mendoza." He made, like a million dollars. He made it rich, because the dollars would come in the mail by the thousands every day, by the thousands. But still, Lydia didn't get nothing from that.[37]

Mendoza's second husband, Fred Martínez, recalled that he first heard her voice over the border blaster stations. His experience underscores that Mendoza's fans made some sacrifices to tune in—particularly during the graveyard shift, when the stations carried the Spanish-language programs:

I heard Lydia sing for the first time in 1937. That was after I had married my first wife. Lydia used to come on the radio from Piedras Negras at about three o'clock in the morning. My father-in-law used to like to listen to her, so he used to get up about three o'clock in the morning and make some coffee, smoke cigarettes and listen to Lydia Mendoza on the radio.[38]

Henry "Hank" Cervantes also tuned in to the Del Rio station and recalled hearing Lydia Mendoza. Years later, Cervantes described her music as guitar-heavy. In an interview, he dismissed the notion that the Spanish broadcasts were necessary to reinforce his identity:

> I don't know about anyone else, but I've always been Mexican. And I didn't need any songs to remind me of that. It's ingrained in me, as well as many other people. And the sound of Spanish just captivates your attention. . . . Then, too, it was our home language. My mother only spoke Spanish. And she taught us how to read and write in Spanish and taught us little poems in Spanish.[39]

Listeners could also pick up the stations farther in the interior of Mexico. Armando Flores grew up in Corpus Christi, Texas, and tuned in to Spanish-language radio locally, as well as from Mexico City stations. His sisters were "hooked" on the radio *novelas,* or soap operas. "They kicked me out of the room whenever they would listen to them," Flores recalled.[40]

In smaller towns throughout the country, English-language radio stations also aired a portion of their programming in Spanish. For instance, Nicanór Aguilar of Grand Falls, Texas, remembered picking up KIUN from Pecos, Texas, fifty miles away. This station carried mostly American popular music, but it also played some Spanish-language music. About 20 percent of the content was Spanish-language, he recalled. Aguilar said it was the only station that could be picked up in his area.[41]

Radio in the Spanish-Speaking Community

Interviews with the World War II–era Latinos and Latinas reveal that they sought music and some news and drama on radio, both in Spanish and in English. They were likely listening to programs airing on blocks of time that individuals had bought from the station. In the early days of radio, Jorge Schement and Félix Gutiérrez have found, Spanish-language programming was limited to station time bought by these brokers, who then sold sponsorships to local businesses.[42] The first full-time Spanish-language radio station in the country owned by a Latino—at least in the continental United States—was founded in San Antonio by Raoul Cortez.[43] His station, KCOR, went on the air in 1946.[44]

Vicente Ximenes, from Floresville, Texas, thirty miles southeast of San Antonio, recalled tuning in to radio when he was in the Civilian Conservation Corps. Between 1939 and 1941, he cleared brush in Floresville and Seguin, forty miles north of Floresville. He recalled:

Armando Flores (*the soldier in bed*), 1942. Courtesy of the
U.S. Latino & Latina World War II Oral History Project.

When we came back to the camp, most of the people that were in my camp were *mexicanos* from El Valle [the Texas Rio Grande Valley]. . . . But the Mexican music was always our way to relax, and to work, but more to relax when you got back to camp. You had a little place there [at the CCC camp]. It was just a little piece of the barrack—it wasn't even an apartment—but we always had a radio there, listening to Mexican music.[45]

Ximenes' recollections of working with Mexican Americans from other places in Texas, and listening to Spanish-language radio with them, signifies how the music formed a link between the young men. They may have been strangers from different parts of Texas when they arrived in the barracks at the camps, but they had a common language and could appreciate music on Spanish-language radio. That served to unify them.

Use of Spanish in the United States in the 1930s and 1940s

A recurring theme in interviews conducted for the U.S. Latino & Latina World War II Oral History Project is the use of Spanish. Many interviewees report that their parents spoke only Spanish, some because they were immigrants from Mexico, but others because it was possible to survive easily with little or no English in the Mexican American enclaves throughout the Southwest. My father, for instance, was the youngest of eleven children. The Rivas family could trace its lineage to Texas for eight generations. Interestingly, my father's family had operated largely outside of English-speaking circles.[46] Even though he attended public schools, going up to what he surmised later was the fourth grade, his English was rudimentary at best when he enlisted in the army in 1941.

The experience was not limited to rural Texas. In the northern New Mexico town of Las Vegas, Miguel Encinias joined the New Mexico National Guard when he was sixteen. Most of his friends in the company, he said later, spoke no English; it was, for all intents and purposes, a Spanish-speaking company. He was terrified before he joined, Encinias said, that he might be put into a unit where he wouldn't be able to communicate with men who spoke no Spanish.[47]

From the hundreds of enclaves of Spanish-speaking Americans, listeners of the World War II generation tuned in to Spanish-language radio with their own peculiar needs and desires, sometimes ignoring prevailing socialization efforts that would have them forsake their mother tongue.

Forbidden Tongue

In considering Spanish-language radio in the World War II era, one would be remiss not to address the anti-Spanish sentiment prevalent at the time, and how speaking Spanish came to be considered as un-American. The "Americanization" movement that developed at the turn of the century, writes historian Guadalupe San Miguel, was "a three-fold program of agitation, protection, and education of immigrants in the English language and in citizenship training." The instruction applied to both U.S.-born and foreign-born residents and they were all to learn about basic American "ideals." These ideals were to be encouraged, not forced upon them.[48] San Miguel notes that after World War I the Americanization movement took on a darker character. Immigrants were to forsake their own culture and language and adopt the "American" way of life.[49]

Consistent with the Americanization trend, the Texas state legislature passed a law in 1918 that made English the exclusive language of public school instruction, applying not only to teachers but also to school administrators and even school board members. And, to give the law teeth, the legislature criminalized the instruction of any language besides English.[50] Teachers in both public and private schools could legitimately argue that they were only doing their jobs by imposing English on the hapless Spanish-speaking students.

The Spanish-speaking population did not accept this. In Joe Bernal's family in San Antonio, for instance, the children were expected to learn perfect English. But they also addressed their parents in Spanish and were surrounded by Spanish in their communities. As an adult, Bernal would reassess the practice of prohibiting Mexican and Mexican American children from speaking Spanish. He came to believe that being punished for speaking Spanish amounted to "a rejection of your culture": "That's something that [I understood] after some hard study and information coming through in the '60s and '70s . . . the thought was new in my mind, that it was a put-down and that it was a denial [of culture]."[51]

People like Nicanór Aguilar, of Grand Falls, Texas, chafed at the discrimination in the form of inferior schools and the prohibition of speaking Spanish. He was adamant about his rights: "Spanish has been spoken in the United States for three hundred years. People have always tried to take away Spanish, but you can't fight nature. And Spanish is very natural here in the United States."[52]

Joe Bernal, 1945, after his induction. Courtesy of the U.S.
Latino & Latina World War II Oral History Project.

José R. "Joe" Jasso, 1944. Courtesy of the U.S. Latino &
Latina World War II Oral History Project.

Tuning In after the War

Spanish-language broadcasting gained greater visibility and demand after
the war when a few returning Latino veterans became broadcasters. Among
them was Pete Moraga, a native of Tempe, Arizona, who served in the navy.
Moraga used the GI Bill to earn a degree in advertising from the University of
Arizona and then got a job at a startup station in Phoenix, KIFN—Arizona's
first all-Spanish-language radio station.[53] When KIFN first went on the air on
23 November 1949, its slogan was "La Voz Mexicana" (the Mexican Voice).
Moraga began to fill a void by covering news in the Mexican American community: "I felt an obligation to be able [to] . . . cover more about the Hispanic
community than what was being covered at that time, because there were a
lot of real good stories going on."[54]

Pete Moraga, aboard the USS *Ocelot* at Ulithi, 1945. Courtesy of the U.S. Latino & Latina World War II Oral History Project.

Moraga built an illustrious career in journalism, working in the 1980s as the news director at the Spanish-language Los Angeles KMEX and helping to polish young journalists such as Jorge Ramos and María Elena Salinas, two of Univision's best-known and most respected national primetime anchors.

Conclusions

The World War II generation of U.S. Latinos and Latinas were coming of age at the same time that radio was emerging as a mass medium. They chose English sometimes, and often they chose Spanish-language broadcasting, hungering in some cases for their home language, the language that "spoke" to them. They did this at the same time that society rejected Spanish, prohibiting them from speaking it and punishing them if they did. Several reported being told to speak English or "go back to Mexico."

They also used English-language radio to navigate more successfully in the United States. But even then, they actively retained the language and tuned in to Spanish-language radio before, during, and after the war. For that generation of individuals, which has not been adequately recognized for its agency, the loyalty to the mother tongue indicates an independence of thought and a deeply held conviction that language is a key part of identity that must not be treated lightly.

The very act of listening to Spanish-language radio was an act of resistance for them. In spite of the efforts to make these Latinos and Latinas reject their language, they persevered. "Language can't be denied," said Nicanór Aguilar. "It makes up your culture and who you are as a person."[55]

Hank Cervantes, 1945. Courtesy of the U.S. Latino &
Latina World War II Oral History Project.

✹ *3* ✹

"Now Get Back to Work"

Mexican Americans and the Agricultural "Migrant Stream"

▬

DIONICIO VALDÉS

The Mexican immigrant fills the requirements of farm labor in California and the Southwest as no other laborer could. He withstands the high temperatures and is adapted to field conditions. He goes from one locality to the other as the season's activities require his service. He takes care of the highly perishable products as they demand picking. He does heavy field work, which other laborers do not desire and are unsuited to perform. His migratory character makes him fit into the needs of each locality for transient and mobile labor. —R. G. RISSER, manager, Crop Production Department, California Vegetable Union, 1928

There isn't much you can do for these people. They all have large families which they can't support; they can't educate . . . that have been on relief and all that for generations. . . . I know in this area there's Mexican families that had never been off relief except during the war, when they made them get off and go to work. —WILLIAM CRODDY, California orange grower and director, Orange County Farmers Incorporated, 1971

As a child, Hank Cervantes was oblivious to the self-serving assessments by growers like R. G. Risser and William Croddy that portrayed Mexicans as inherently predisposed to agricultural labor and capable of little else. Born in Fresno, California, on 10 October 1923, Cervantes worked the crops with his family for many years until shortly after the United States entered World

War II. His dreams already aspired upward. He fancied becoming a pilot after he read a poem his third-grade teacher gave him. Soon afterward, while harvesting prunes with his family, he saw three military planes overhead and told his mother of his dream of flying. Years later, he remembered her response: "She smiled and she said, 'Good for you. Now get back to work.'"[1] For Mexican migrant workers, the dreams of little boys flying airplanes seemed utterly unattainable; better to keep one's head down and tend to the task at hand.

Cervantes began working with his family during the Great Depression, a watershed in the history of agricultural labor in the United States, characterized by a nationwide migrant stream, or route. In contrast to earlier and later eras, the migrants of this generation were overwhelmingly U.S. citizens, an ethnically diverse group composed mostly of European Americans, African Americans, and Mexican Americans.[2]

This chapter describes the migrant phenomenon of the 1930s and 1940s through the use of recollections of the Mexicans who participated in it. It examines the profound changes taking place that led to a recovery of agricultural industries in the later years of the Great Depression and World War II and how those changes affected Mexican workers. It is concerned with how Mexican workers became involved in migratory agricultural labor, how their experiences reflect continuity and change, and how they were affected by and reacted to broader changes in the industry as well as their immediate conditions. Although researchers have conducted many local and regional case studies of the migrant phenomenon, none has addressed the national issue of Mexican agricultural workers on the basis of their own accounts.[3] This chapter first discusses factors underlying the unfolding of long-distance migratory labor and how it affected Mexican workers. It then examines individual and family work experiences in their two major migrant streams before, during, and after World War II.

Migration and Agricultural Labor

Observers who focus exclusively on the broad decline in agricultural employment during the twentieth century miss sharp fluctuations that are evident in the history of farm labor. The surplus of workers associated with migratory labor, for instance, often reflected the varying patterns of public investments in irrigation, research on different crops, and changes in production and distribution techniques. At the same time, the sharp decline in demand for industrial and service workers at the end of the 1920s and early 1930s, along with the reorganization of production in several major crops resulted in a sharp increase in surplus labor that reduced costs for agricultural employers, encouraging higher production. With the outbreak of World War II in Europe, the demand for food encouraged still greater output while the labor market tightened.[4] A reliance on workers of Mexican origin accompanied the expansion of agriculture and the growth of farm employment.

The cotton industry of the Southwest represented the nation's single most important employer for the tens of thousands of Mexican immigrants and their children who entered the United States during the first half of the twentieth century.[5] In contrast to the Deep South, where landowners contracted African Americans and European Americans primarily as sharecroppers and tenants, employers in the Southwest hired Mexicans, mostly as wage workers. Tenants and sharecroppers rented the land they tilled in a single location whereas laborers often traveled long distances to find jobs, particularly in cotton chopping and picking. Employers preferred wage labor in cotton over sharecropping once the industry began operating on a large scale in South and Central Texas, the newly irrigated sections of the Rio Grande Valley in West Texas and New Mexico, the Salt and Gila river valleys in New Mexico and Arizona, and the Imperial, Coachella, and Central valleys of California. The differences in labor patterns between Texas and California became somewhat blurred following the decline of sharecropping, which further accelerated during World War II.[6]

The next major employer of Mexicans, the sugar beet industry, was concentrated in California, Colorado, the intermountain West, the Great Plains, and the Great Lakes Midwest. Commercial sugar beet production skyrocketed in the 1890s and early 1900s, and Mexicans became the dominant laboring group in the aftermath of World War I. They typically worked in a single area for the entire season, but by the 1930s mechanization had reduced labor demands and compelled workers to travel more frequently and greater distances to find seasonal employment.[7]

The commercial fruit and vegetable producers scattered across the country also increasingly turned to Mexicans, but they did so unevenly. Beginning during World War I, the rapidly expanding citrus industry of Southern California and South Texas attracted thousands of Mexican workers, who dominated picking.[8] By the end of World War II, concentrations of Mexican workers were evident in the coastal valleys of California, the Willamette Valley of Oregon, the Yakima Valley of Washington, the Western Slope of Colorado, the Lake Michigan coast of Michigan, and the Lake Erie coast of Ohio.[9] Because vegetable production was so widely dispersed across the nation, employers typically hired Mexicans in settings where they were already numerous, especially along the U.S.-Mexico border that included California, Arizona, and Texas.[10] In other locations, particularly in the Great Lakes, Great Plains, the Rocky Mountains, and the Pacific Northwest, Mexican laborers moved into other nearby crops after completing their work and becoming unemployed.[11]

The Great Depression was characterized by the massive presence of people in temporary and seasonal agriculture as migratory workers. While migrant labor in commercial agriculture had an earlier history, the Great Depression witnessed unprecedented growth, fairly clear patterns of interstate migration that covered much of the nation, and the numerical dominance by U.S.-born workers of various backgrounds. Federal government researchers identified three major streams, or corridors, of migration, each with several branches.

The East Coast stream extended northward from Florida and the Deep South along the Atlantic Coast into the Carolinas, the mid-Atlantic states, New York, and New England. The midcontinental stream ran from Texas and neighboring states northward into the Midwest, Great Plains, and Rocky Mountain states. A smaller but still substantial number of workers from Texas also joined the Pacific Coast stream, whose principal base was in Southern California. It extended into the central part of the state, particularly the coastal valley and Central Valley systems, and the Pacific Northwest.[12] Mexicans from Texas also entered South Florida, their first important presence along the East Coast, in the mid-1950s. Although there was no universal experience for migrant workers, a large portion established permanent homes in the southern sections of the nation, working local agriculture during the late fall, winter, and early spring. In the spring or early summer, they traveled northward, "following the crops." Researchers agree that U.S. citizens of Mexican origin became an important part of the midcontinental and Pacific Coast streams during the latter years of the Great Depression. In relative and absolute numbers, their presence increased during World War II and the 1950s as fewer African Americans and European Americans worked in agriculture.[13]

Four general groups of agricultural wage laborers can be identified based on their migration status: local workers, intrastate migrants, interstate migrants, and international migrants. Great variation was evident within each group, and individuals moved frequently from one status to another. Thousands of small farmers, including owners, renters, and sharecroppers, for instance, moved in and out of wage labor. Migration patterns were complicated but can be understood more clearly with a closer look at individual Mexican farmworkers from their two major home bases, South Texas and Southern California.

Oral history projects from California State University, Fullerton, and the University of Texas at Austin have generated narratives that offer ground-level insights into the experience of migratory agricultural labor. The Mexican American History Collection at the Center for Oral and Public History in Fullerton contains interviews conducted between the late 1960s and early 1980s and provides a basis for understanding individual lives in the agricultural communities of Southern California, especially Orange County, and elsewhere in the state and the Southwest. The collection is enriched by interviews with growers, community leaders, and managers, as well as workers of diverse backgrounds. A second corpus of documents comes from the U.S. Latino & Latina World War II Oral History Project in Austin, an effort that began in the late 1990s. While much of its focus is on South Texas, its oral narratives cover a broader geography than the Fullerton collection. Moreover, it focuses on Latinos and Latinas and the central experience of the World War rather than on communities or relations among different groups of people. Although the contents of the two collections are not always comparable because the emphasis, interview protocols, interviewing experience, and interviewer training varied, the oral narratives provide an unmatched source of information on the lives of Mexican agricultural laborers.

Working in Texas

The largest labor reserve existed in Texas, especially along its border with Mexico, the initial crossing point into the United States for a majority of Mexican workers between the military conquest of the mid-nineteenth century and the 1950s. By the 1920s their most important employer in the state was the cotton industry, while significant numbers also worked in the winter vegetable industry.[14] Workers from San Antonio traveled to the cotton fields located in the Dallas area to the north, Karnes City to the west, and the Gulf Coast region. Further south, Mexicans from the Rio Grande Valley were heading toward the Panhandle area, particularly Lubbock County, by the 1930s.[15]

Mexican workers in Texas traveled often and over great distances between the 1930s and 1950s. For workers like Gonzalo Garza, "cotton picking was our life." They lived in a highly segregated world that restricted their interaction with the Anglo-American community in the schools, in the neighborhoods, and at work. Garza recalled that Anglo-American employers set the tone in social relations by caring only for the number of workers that they could secure. Their primary concern was for *"cuantas manos tienen"* (how many workers they have).[16]

A small portion of the workers had once owned small farms, including the family of Beatrice Escudero Dimas, born in El Paso in 1923. Her family raised cattle and grew crops for home consumption on the outskirts of the city. When the hardship of the Great Depression started, however, Dimas' father began selling their animals in order to eat. They even lost their home. In 1935 they had no choice but to answer the call of the labor recruiters. "There was nothing else," Dimas said. Her family traveled eighty miles to Clint, Texas, to pick pima cotton. Dimas found the change especially difficult because she could no longer attend school, which she loved. She continued working in the West Texas cotton fields with her family until she married in 1942.[17]

Eliseo López also came from a family of small farmers near Ganado, north of Victoria. They were poor, he recalled, but always had plenty of meat and vegetables to eat. Then his father died in 1941, forcing him to quit school to help his brother on the farm. In contrast to the Dimas family, the war influenced their lives directly, for his brother was drafted in 1942 and he himself entered the service a year later. With the departure of key earners in the family, "so went the farm."[18]

The majority of Mexican small farmers in South Texas were renters and sharecroppers in the 1920s and 1930s, including Henry Falcón, whose father worked a small farm on the outskirts of Austin for several seasons.[19] Candelario Hernández' parents were also sharecroppers outside Austin in the 1930s, producing corn, cotton, and sorghum.[20] Sharecropping was tied mostly to cotton, which formed the center of working life for thousands of Mexican families, including that of Peter, Otis, Paul, and Narciso Gil, whose parents were also born in Texas. Paul boldly asserted his family's station in life: "We were all cotton pickers."[21]

Augustine Lucio, born in 1922 outside San Marcos, Texas, worked the land his family sharecropped and attended school only three to five months each year. Since their earnings on the farm were insufficient, the family traveled seasonally to West Texas to chop and pick cotton until Lucio joined the military in 1941. His experience of hard work in agriculture served to ease the physical strain of the transition from civilian to military status. He stated that basic training was very difficult for the other recruits who were not used to hard work, but it "was routine for me."[22]

Gonzalo Garza, 1946. Courtesy of the U.S. Latino & Latina World War II Oral History Project.

Candelario Hernández, ca. 1941. Courtesy of the U.S. Latino & Latina World War II Oral History Project.

Ester Arredondo Pérez, born in Needville, sixty miles east of Houston, also came from a sharecropping family. Her father planted cotton, corn, and other crops from the 1920s until immediately before the United States entered World War II. Work prevented her from starting classes until October each year, yet she managed to graduate from high school, a rare feat for young rural Mexicans in those days. Because of her success, her father preferred that she did not stay at "*el rancho.*" She went to Houston to live with an aunt and briefly obtained a job in sales, then went to San Antonio, and in 1942 obtained employment in engine repair at Kelly Field. Later she was transferred to Sacramento and to Honolulu.[23] The expansion of the military during the war enabled her to use her talents to achieve a degree of upward mobility.

Baltazar Villarreal was born in 1920 and grew up on a cotton-producing ranch north of Edinburg, Texas. Like other sharecroppers, his family devoted a portion of the land to the family's consumption of corn and other vegetables, hogs, chickens, and cattle. And like other local sharecroppers, they

(*Left to right*) Ester Arredondo Pérez, Henrietta Delgado, Catalina Sierra, and Beatriz Ovalle, 1949. Courtesy of the U.S. Latino & Latina World War II Oral History Project.

typically cultivated about forty acres for themselves. This was not sufficient for the family to survive, so they had to migrate for part of the year to nearby farms or towns. Villarreal started working on the family farm at six years of age, and like other local youth, he began working away from home at around age fourteen. He earned between 50 cents and $1 per day, plus meals, prior to his military induction in 1941.[24]

Robert Zepeda, another youth from a sharecropping family, was born in Bay City, Texas, in 1916 to parents originally from San Luis Potosí. The family raised cotton as a cash crop and, for home consumption, planted cantaloupes, onions, garlic, celery, lettuce, tomatoes, turnips, cucumbers, bell peppers, eggplants, and corn, as well as sugarcane for their mules, horses, cows, goats, and hogs. Zepeda and his brothers also hunted doves, quails, armadillos, and rabbits. In the late 1930s and early 1940s they would travel with neighbors to places including Crystal City, Austin, and Waxahachie, Texas, and across the Red River to chop and pick in Louisiana. Zepeda recalled that Bay City schools were segregated and that the local movie theater owner assigned Mexicans and African Americans to the balcony. Zepeda worked in agriculture until he was drafted into the army shortly after the Pearl Harbor invasion. Like thousands of other veterans, Zepeda refused to return to migrant labor after the war.[25]

While a large number of Mexican families enjoyed modest upward mobility made possible by the war, others experienced instability and downward mobility. This was especially the case among workers affected by the collapse of sharecropping. Benito Morales was among them. His parents were from San Luis Potosí, but he was born in Flatonia, Texas. Morales attended school in the morning, then came home and changed clothes to work on the farm, plowing land and chopping and picking cotton. This continued until he was fifteen years old, when his family "couldn't make it anymore." His father had to sell everything—the farm equipment, cows, and mules. Morales moved to Chicago with the hope of benefiting from the wartime economic boom, as his sister and father had already moved there. However, he was drafted in 1943.[26]

Prior to World War II, many Mexican and Mexican American families also worked as "hands," residing for extended periods on ranches and farms where they were employed. Among them was Apolonio Pardo, born in Goliad in 1923. As a teenager he worked on the Ramsey Ranch, cultivating and harvesting cotton, corn, and beans. Pardo moved to Elsa where he found a job with another farmer, for whom he worked until 1944 when he was drafted into the Army.[27] Ascención Cortez, on the other hand, worked and lived at Rancho Colorado, near Laredo, which she described as a plantation. Her sons worked in the onions, tomatoes, and anything else that was available.[28]

A larger number of Mexican Americans, including Herlinda Mendoza Buitrón Estrada, resided at home and traveled to neighboring farms for work. Born in 1930 in Bastrop, Texas, Estrada and her family went to nearby fields to pick cotton between July and the second week of September. Although she remained in school, the incentives of extra rationing stamps for food and shoes from the local Office of Price Administration encouraged her to continue working on the farms.[29] Even young people from the middle classes participated in farmwork, including Tomás Cantú, the son of a small businessman from Robstown. During the 1930s and 1940s, he recalled vividly, "in this part of the world, Mexican Americans were not treated equal with Anglo Saxons. . . . We all picked cotton."[30]

Many Mexican agricultural workers from South Texas, San Antonio, and El Paso joined the migratory stream because their parents had been displaced from more stable jobs. Mexicans often expressed the memory of displacement as an experience of inequality. Calixto Ramírez recalled that while Mexicans faced hardship during the Great Depression, Anglo-Americans from the North began heading to Texas in greater numbers in response to the ready availability of jobs.[31] Santos Vásquez also remembered that Anglo-Americans from neighboring states moved into the Rio Grande Valley to fill skilled jobs as packinghouse workers, tractor drivers, and machine operators that Mexicans had been performing in the 1920s.[32] As a result of the hard times, Anglo-Americans were willing to take jobs they had previously refused, intensifying social inequality as Mexicans remained concentrated in the lower-skilled jobs on local farms or were compelled to turn to migratory labor.

Although large numbers of individuals and families were deported or willingly returned to Mexico during the Great Depression, Victoria Guerrero's parents remained in Texas. The family, however, was forced to migrate in order to survive. Guerrero was born in 1924 in La Feria, a small town in the Rio Grande Valley, where the schools were segregated. Early in life, she resided on the small farm where her sharecropping father grew cotton and vegetables, including spinach, potatoes, and carrots. When she was in the sixth grade, however, the family started traveling to find work, first to nearby Raymondville, then farther north to the area around Corpus Christi and Robstown. Later, they migrated as far as Lubbock in West Texas, often with the families of her uncles and her grandmother. To survive as a migrant, Guerrero said, "was very hard": "I remember we were living under a great big tent that farmers put up for us." She recalled that despite the difficult conditions, there were many happy moments "because we shared with each other." Her favorite memories were of Sundays, when each family took turns making chicken dinners, and when her grandmother "would sit in the center of a circle and tell stories to all her cousins": "She told stories in Spanish. We loved to hear her tell stories."[33]

The parents of most youth came from Mexico, including those of Joseph Alcoser, who entered Texas from Piedras Negras, Coahuila, in the early 1920s. When he was an infant, his family moved to Melvin, where he recalled that they paid rent with their labor. Alcoser started migrating at age five. His family's early participation in migratory labor resulted from the periodic release of his father by the Works Progress Administration, a government-sponsored work assistance program. Government officials consistently released their Mexican employees at harvest time, which compelled them to work for local farmers in the cotton harvest. In the spring and summer they moved from farm to farm and lived in camps with no facilities: "We lived under trees."[34]

Calixto Ramírez, 1945. Courtesy of the U.S. Latino & Latina World War II Oral History Project.

Joseph Alcoser, ca. 1946. Courtesy of the U.S. Latino & Latina World War II Oral History Project.

When the cotton bolls opened up, the entire family was transported to Taft and Sinton in the southeastern part of Texas and to Lubbock and Plainview in the west and north. Hundreds of people slept on the side of the road, in part because police sometimes prohibited them from staying within the city limits. Alcoser's family lived under a tarp his father had purchased, which became a tent when strung under a tree. According to Alcoser, migratory work became a way of life for Mexicans: "That was typical of all Mexicans that were farmworkers—even people that owned a little bit of land would be trucked from farm to farm." He recalled that because picking the dry cotton plants scratched their hands, "we wore gloves, but they wore out and we would tape our fingers." They also faced much discrimination on the road. At the end of the cotton harvest, Alcoser attended school, where "in spite of everything else, I concentrated on learning as much as possible." He attended the segregated school in Melvin until two teachers, Guadalupe Pérez and a Señora Rentería, organized a public demonstration against discrimination. The school closed down as a result of the protest, and Alcoser enrolled in a new one that had originally been built for Anglo-Americans. He and his brothers continued working in agriculture until they entered the military, which ended his work history in agriculture. After the war, Alcoser found employment in Lubbock as a barber until he moved to California.[35]

Big cities like San Antonio were an important part of workers' lives, primarily because they served as points of congregation and recruitment. The city's West Side was a major recruitment site where local residents like Jesús Herrera left school early to pick cotton. His family went south to Karnes City and then north to Temple and Byron, returning to San Antonio long after the new school term began.[36] Other San Antonio youth, like Pete Prado, born in 1921, picked cotton in the northern part of the state. Upon his return to the Alamo city, Prado worked on the streets, selling vegetables, fruits, and newspapers.[37]

Corpus Christi, Texas, was also a hub of activity during the cotton harvest. Armando Flores spent brief but pleasurable weekends on Leopard Street among thousands of people who arrived in trucks from neighboring communities, farms, and ranches to purchase groceries and clothes, go sightseeing, visit with other families, and head to the beach to swim or fish. Large numbers of working families gathered during the harvests. As Flores related, "You can't even walk down the street because of the multitude of people walking up and down. It was a big deal to come from all over to the big city. . . . It was a fun place."[38]

From Texas to the Midcontinental Stream

The small towns and cities of South Texas formed the largest single source of Mexican workers in the midcontinental migrant stream before, during, and after World War II. Labor migration that had earlier been taking place in conjunction with the sugar beet industry practically ceased with the onset of the Great Depression, then was renewed on a greater scale beginning in the late 1930s, when recruiters once again combed the towns of South Texas and arranged truck transportation to the fields up north.

Recruiters lured the family of Herminia Guerrero Cadena to Michigan. Born in 1933 near Falls City, southeast of San Antonio, she moved to Mercedes, Texas, in 1940, and the following year took her first trip to Michigan to work in the sugar beets, along with her parents, four brothers, and a sister. They were contracted to hoe, block, thin, and top sugar beets until their return to Texas in late November. The family went to Michigan again in 1942, when her parents decided to remain there and send her to a small rural school near Caro. In 1945, Cadena married, although she continued to work alongside the local women and children recruited to meet the rising wartime demand for sugar. After her family settled in Michigan, they maintained contact with workers migrating from Texas. Cadena remembered that her parents were very generous and, when others were in need, would give them "whatever we had." She also recalled occasions when migrants came to her home to clean up while her mother prepared bean-and-egg tacos for them. In one instance, they permitted a young married couple to live with them for several weeks without paying rent.[39] Cadena noted that many people continued to experience hard times during the war but survived the worst through the assistance of others who were making a gradual transition out of the migrant stream.

While most of the Mexican families who participated in the migrant stream were experienced in Texas agriculture, others were new to the midwestern fields. This was the case with Henrietta López Rivas. She recalled that her stepfather, who was born in Mexico, was dismissed from his job of twelve years at Duncan Field in San Antonio. He believed it was because he was not a naturalized citizen, but Rivas said he was told it was because he was ill, which she denied years later. Her mother was too proud to accept charity or to go to the soup kitchens, so "we had to leave . . . though she didn't know what a hoe was, she didn't know what a rake was, she knew nothing about fieldwork." They worked briefly for Belgian farmers in Texas until they were recruited for jobs in the Great Lakes sugar beet region of Michigan and Ohio.[40]

Herlinda Estrada also recalled that her father lost his job in a dairy at the end of the war because he was not a U.S. citizen. In 1946 she, her father, sister, and two brothers who had just completed their tours of duty in the army went to Michigan to work in the beet fields. Unlike many ex-servicemen, they could not enjoy the luxury of refusing to work in agriculture, but like many others from Texas, they soon settled out and became part of the growing Mexican neighborhood in Saginaw.[41]

Workers were commonly motivated to join the migratory trail because they were informed that job opportunities were better in the Midwest than in Texas. This is why George Vásquez left Texas with his family for the sugar beet fields of Minnesota. Recruiters and fellow migratory workers had told them that they could make "big money" outside Texas.[42] Even government investigators and scholars of the era repeated the story that there was better money to be made in the beet fields.[43] This did not mean, however, that the racial division of labor was evident only in Texas. The tales belied an unspoken but widespread understanding among agriculturalists that Mexicans were more suitable for fieldwork because they could be made to accept lower standards, as Anglo-Americans rarely topped sugar beets in the Midwest or picked cotton in South Texas.[44]

George S. Vásquez, 1945. Courtesy of the U.S. Latino &
Latina World War II Oral History Project.

The migrant stream that took shape in the late 1930s also attracted people like Eliseo Navarro, who did not travel with relatives. Born in the segregated town of Asherton, Texas, in 1925, Navarro recalled that almost the entire local Mexican population would leave during the summer to work in the fields, either to sugar beet country or to Taft and elsewhere in Texas to pick cotton. Although he did not consider his family very poor, he joined the migratory workforce as a single worker at the outbreak of the war in Europe. He and his friends worked in the sugar beet fields near Lansing, Michigan, for $11 per acre.[45]

Victoria Guerrero, whose family worked in Texas agriculture for many years, first traveled with them to the Michigan sugar beets in 1941. She remembered an experience common to migratory workers—the tuberculosis tests required in midwestern states like Michigan. Individuals who tested positive could not work, saving the state the cost of hospitalization required for all people diagnosed with the highly contagious and deadly disease. Guerrero's family traveled the long road north on semitrucks in 1941, 1942, and 1943, working from June to the end of October. On weekends, local farmers drove the workers to the nearby town of Fairgrove to shop and socialize and even watch outdoor movies that the farmers arranged for them. Guerrero recalled meeting German prisoners of war who also worked in the fields: "They didn't work as long as we did. They weren't allowed to work those hours by the government."[46] George Graham, who was in charge of housing and distribution of German prisoners of war for Southern California orange growers, confirmed her observation that their workload was light and that they usually finished by noon because government regulations stipulated these work arrangements.[47] No such regulations protected Mexican American children.

Working in Southern California Agriculture

The migrant stream originating in Texas and traveling to the sugar beets was preceded by an earlier migration out of New Mexico, promoted by the beet industry in California and the Rocky Mountain and Great Plains states.[48] Agricultural labor migration from New Mexico declined sharply during the 1930s and did not recover significantly afterward. By the end of World War II, migrants from Texas dominated the sugar beet harvest in the intermountain West and the Great Plains.[49] Prior to the Great Depression, Mexicans had established themselves in several California agricultural settings, some of which formed the major bases for seasonal migration into the Central Valley and neighboring locations.

A clear majority of the migratory workers from Mexico to California during the early twentieth century had come through Texas, especially El Paso. Joe Venegas was among them. He was born in Chihuahua in 1912 and crossed the border with his family seven years later. Each person paid two cents to enter the United States, but not before they were placed in a big room to be bathed and vaccinated. They were immediately recruited to work in the cotton harvest around Phoenix, after which they moved to Orange County.[50] A large number of children like Rubén Casillas were born to the Mexican immigrants who crossed at El Paso. He recalled that it was common for Mexican families like his own to work in agriculture because they could find no other gainful employment.[51]

The dramatic expansion of agriculture in places like the Imperial Valley in Southern California attracted the family of Felícitas Noriega. She was born in Sonora, and while she was still a child, her family moved back and forth across the border between Sonora and Arizona, where her father worked in the mines. The family also worked in Blythe, California, where one of her grandmothers had arrived earlier "to pick cotton" as a *reganchada*, or contracted worker. In the early years, Noriega recalled, the important commercial crops were cotton and hay, and "everybody used to pick cotton." She regularly went out to the fields with her brother, but "I don't think we were good cotton pickers," she said. "We used to make about $15 to $20 a week both, together, picking cotton to support our family."[52]

The work was difficult and affected the schooling of the children, according to Noriega. She started working in the fields at nine years of age and completed only the second grade, partly because she did not attend school regularly and lost interest. Noriega never learned English well. She described her family's hardship in another way. She had only one pair of shoes "because you couldn't afford to have more." She added that families of cotton pickers constructed shacks on the farmer's property and paid him rent. While picking cotton, Noriega also started working "a little bit in the houses of ladies": "I used to wash and iron for a living to help my mother." In the early 1940s, the war offered her an opportunity to leave agriculture permanently when she obtained a job as a waitress. Then in 1951, when Mexican braceros, or contract workers, began coming to the Imperial Valley, she opened a small restaurant. Her regular clientele of about twenty braceros allowed Noriega to maintain her small family business. But her memories of the years in the fields were not happy: "I try to forget them, but I can't."[53]

The Southern California citrus industry also offered work to thousands of Mexican immigrants and their children.[54] Before World War II, some citrus employers sought to maintain a resident workforce by providing permanent housing for the working families. Workers also rented houses in local communities. They were attracted by job security in the form of extended periods of employment and greater residential stability than most agricultural workers, but it often came with a price. They commonly lived in tightly controlled settings in camps or employer-controlled towns, whether working on extensive operations like the Bastanchury ranch, which had more than three thousand acres planted in citrus by the late 1920s, or on modest-sized ranches or holdings as small as the ten-acre orchards that had been established as homes for middle-class Anglo-American families. Workers lived near the orchards and offered a stable labor supply to the ranch and to collaborating citrus growers and packinghouse owners.[55]

The owners of local independent citrus packinghouses and representatives of grower associations controlled the industry and made decisions pertaining to production, distribution, and labor relations.[56] The associations or packinghouses arranged work schedules and transportation to the fields and provided clippers for the pickers.[57] With a delay of about eight years for trees to reach maturity, the heavy tree plantings during the boom of the 1920s resulted in a marked increase in citrus production throughout the Great Depression, when Mexican migration to the United States had already subsided.[58]

Citrus leaders portrayed the industry as an ideal employer because it could provide relatively steady work. The winter navel orange yield lasted from November through May, spring Valencias were harvested from May until November, and lemons were picked three or four times per year.[59] In theory, employers could coordinate picking to provide nearly year-round employment for some, but weather, uneven production, failure to coordinate according to the workers' needs, and employer desire to maintain a surplus of workers reduced opportunities for stable jobs. While men dominated work in the local citrus orchards and tomato harvest, Mexican women picked strawberries and worked in the plants that packed fruits and vegetables.[60]

Mexican citrus workers in Southern California did not consider their opportunities as favorably as did their employers. As a youth, Chaoi Vásquez, born in Fullerton soon after the end of World War I, picked oranges because "that's all there was around here." He recalled that about 90 percent of citrus harvest workers were Mexicans: "They were all poor and they were all laborers." Vásquez recalled that most Mexican people during the late 1930s and the 1940s "had big families and their fathers' wages were real scarce, so a lot of these folks would load their kids and take off and go up north to work." He picked oranges until he got married and secured employment in construction.[61]

Dan Muñoz, whose grandparents came from New Mexico and Chihuahua, recounted experiences that point to how grower associations and owners of packinghouses and large ranches dominated politics in the small citrus communities. Muñoz was born in San Fernando and grew up in a *vecindad* (building complex) called Pico Court, owned by Sunkist and composed of cabins with outdoor toilets and dirt streets. He observed that "we were immediately programmed to go to the fields," meaning that local Mexicans had few other options than to become citrus workers. In the 1930s Muñoz' family moved from the *vecindad* to the city of San Fernando, where they were surrounded by orange and grapefruit orchards. The town, controlled by the local growers, maintained segregated neighborhoods, schools, and services, including a Mexican theater that showed Mexican movies. The Mexican school also served Filipinos and the few Blacks who lived on the fringes of town, west of the tracks, which "we could not cross after six p.m.," Muñoz remembered. Local police enforced geographic boundaries by making sure that persons did not violate the lines of segregation. Muñoz concluded that "we were tightly controlled."[62]

In the citrus town of National City, where Lauro Vega was born in 1923 to parents from Jalisco and Sinaloa, the influence of the company was also pervasive. His father worked in the lemon orchards and vegetable fields surrounding the town. The family lived in a company-owned cabin and maintained a garden plot to help make ends meet. After work, Vega's father tended the tomatoes, onions, sweet corn, string beans, and nopales, or prickly pear cacti, "which helped us in those days." To further support the family, Vega collected discarded food behind local stores and picked oranges and loquats in East Park. The Mexican neighborhood and elementary school were on the West Side, the Anglo-Americans lived on the East Side, and the few White youth residing among Mexicans attended their own schools a mile away. The town had a single school for White children in the sixth grade and beyond, while Mexicans were assigned to a separate ungraded classroom. Despite the lack of formal signs to designate the lines of segregation, Vega recalled, "they had us pretty well controlled."[63]

Grower efforts to control Mexicans included repression of labor organizing, as Garland Coltrane, a former police chief in the town of Orange, acknowledged. His responsibilities included keeping out labor organizers, especially leftist leaders who challenged the grip that growers maintained over Mexican workers. He reasoned that the organizers "were registered Communists that were laboring under this Communist, Marxist indoctrination," and he lamented that the "apathetic public" was not sufficiently alarmed.[64]

Daniel Muñoz, ca. 1951. Courtesy of the U.S. Latino &
Latina World War II Oral History Project.

Jane Deming, the daughter of an Orange County ranch owner who headed
the local orange growers' association, also recalled that Coltrane "loathed
communism with a passion": "They [Communists] were active with the
labor groups and he fought the very best way he knew how . . . along with
some other people, obtained a restraining order to prevent the Communists
from being on the ballot."[65]

Despite actions by authorities like Coltrane to suppress political activity, Mexicans openly expressed their dissatisfaction with segregation and
inequality. Alfredo Esqueda, who grew up in the Fullerton area and picked
oranges, lemons, and grapefruit there until 1948, recounted one of the major
organized challenges to grower control, the 1936 citrus strike. He recalled
that workers were upset about unfair deductions, as the associations charged
workers 15 to 20 cents for rides to and from work, and additional sums for
clippers and other necessary equipment. In addition, inspectors made exces-
sive demands on workers with the aim of weeding out organizers and union

sympathizers while reducing wages, until "they were only paying six cents a box and people weren't making any money at all." Esqueda remembered that workers "were down in the dumps so it got to a point when I don't know just who it was but they organized a union" run by Margarita Hernández. The police, according to Esqueda, sided with the growers, and "every once in a while the officers would come around and try to break up the strike" by raiding union headquarters. Workers defended themselves in several skirmishes, and in one instance, in La Habra, a police officer was shot, and "one of the fellows who had done it took off to Mexico and we never did hear from him." After several weeks, Esqueda joined other hungry strikers who traveled north to pick grapes "to alleviate themselves." Esqueda noted another concern, that the government-sponsored migrant camps of the San Joaquin Valley were unsanitary, only outdoor toilets were available, there was "no running water," the "bedding was all hay," and "the kitchen was filthy inside." In addition, "the children did not attend school."[66] For many of the workers who had led fairly stable lives in the citrus communities, the 1936 strike marked a turning point, the first time they had to migrate up north to find work.[67] Opportunity for employment in the citrus industry declined only gradually, and local Mexican Americans continued to find work in the groves during the war and postwar periods.

The Expanding California Migrant Circuit

The Central Valley of California became an increasingly important site of seasonal employment for Mexicans following the expansion of the massive irrigation networks during and after World War I. The system of labor recruitment and distribution, however, broke down in the early 1930s as a result of the infamous repatriation campaigns and grower reactions to a wave of Mexican labor organizing, highlighted by the Central Valley cotton strike of 1933.[68] Cotton growers sought replacements, particularly among Anglo-American workers from the dust bowl region of the upper South, many of whom had recently lost their small farms or their jobs as sharecroppers.

Growers again began welcoming Mexican workers from Southern California in the late 1930s. Albert Rangel, like many others, responded by traveling with his family annually from the Los Angeles area—starting just prior to the U.S. entry into World War II—to pick grapes, peaches, apricots, and other fruit. He recalled that workers frequently complained about the conditions, but employers "never paid no attention to them." Manuel Guilin, who crossed the border in 1928 at fourteen years of age, worked around Calexico picking and packing lettuce and melons and making boxes until entering the military in 1942. After returning from the war, he became a crew leader for a melon packing company that followed a seasonal migrant circuit from the Mexican side of the border, through Blythe, Mendota, and Firebaugh.[69] The war marked an interlude in his life as an agricultural worker.

The family of Gonzalo García, born and reared in Southern California, left each season for "what we would call up north" to pick figs around Fresno and grapes around Delano and to harvest string beans and prunes around San Jose. Born in 1933, he recalled that families made the decision to migrate on the basis of information obtained through word of mouth. When neighbors returned from Fresno in 1938, they convinced his father that he should take the family the following year. García reasoned that "in our case it was a matter of economics": "My father used to make $20 a week," while the entire family "would average $80 a week." Normally his father and the four boys would pick, "and then when the crop got real good, then my mother would help us." García recalled that when the school year ended, "we would pack our few kitchen utensils and our few things that you would ordinarily take when you went camping, only in this case it was a matter of utility." The only item the rancher provided was a tent in "what we would call camp, and the tents were put right up in the orchard where we would work." Those living in the camp "were all Mexicans."[70]

García added, "We'd have to go out and scrounge around for an old oil-can and cut a hole in it and make a stove. And every year when they would prune the trees, they would stack the wood up next to the orchard, and this was our fuel supply." Despite the difficult conditions, workers managed to find respite. García noted that after work the youngsters would always find "a creek or river or something and we'd always come back and go down and play in the river or play baseball or hide-and-seek or something until we got called to dinner." In the evening, he recalled, "the next-door neighbors, next tent over, they would come over and we would sit around and talk and listen and sometimes ask questions and it was like one big family." García added that "we enjoyed it tremendously," especially on Saturdays when his father "would give us 10 cents every week when we were up there, and of course he would take us to the show."[71]

Andrew Aguirre and his family entered migrant agricultural labor in the 1930s. He was born in 1925 in El Paso and moved to Chula Vista with his family at age three. His grandfather had been a herder in Jalisco, and his father, who "never got beyond stoop labor," found work in the Chula Vista and San Diego area, cultivating and harvesting vegetables for local Japanese farmers. Aguirre started working celery, string beans, tomatoes, and other crops. Around 1938 his father and an older brother took their first trip together on the migrant circuit into Northern California. Aguirre joined his father and eight siblings in 1939 and 1940 for the trip to the San Joaquin Valley in an old truck. Piecework—payment on the basis of the tray, the row, and the bucket—meant that even the youngest could make a contribution. They worked in the San Jose plums, Gilroy tomatoes, Madera grapes, and Fresno cotton. On their return to Chula Vista, Aguirre spent little time in school because "it seemed like nobody cared whether I went or not." He continued to work locally for Japanese farmers and soon advanced to driving a caterpillar and trucks, until he enlisted in the Marine Corps in 1941. Like many other Mexican American veterans, Aguirre refused to work as a stoop laborer after the war.[72]

Rudy Acosta, born in El Paso in 1923, began his story in 1934, when his parents divorced and his mother took the children to join her married sister and work on a ranch at the San Gabriel Mission, outside Los Angeles. The family later joined another aunt who had signed up with a labor contractor for the cotton harvest near Delano. They found the work unpleasant and soon signed up with another labor contractor for the prune harvest, riding on a flatbed truck through Bakersfield, Los Banos, Hollister, and Gilroy. Acosta recalled a season when they resided in a prune orchard camp next to an arroyo. They constructed a lean-to with a roof of tree branches, and his mother cooked on a stove made from a fifty-gallon drum. Work involved picking up the plums, dumping them into trucks, unloading them into cleaning tanks, and placing the clean fruit on four-by-eight-foot slats to dry. In one season, the family, which included three sons between twelve and eighteen years of age, cleared $350. This enabled them to pay rent in advance for a home in Los Angeles and leave agriculture permanently. Although the family did not experience significant upward social mobility, their work experience served other purposes, particularly because the aunts were able to save enough to move to the city and keep their families in proximity.[73]

Conclusion

A critical watershed for mid-twentieth-century agricultural labor in the United States was the articulation and expansion of the nation's migrant streams. The appearance of the migratory workforce stemmed from several factors, including the rise in massive unemployment and changes in production for several labor-intensive industries, spurred in part by mechanization as well as the expansion of production in new parts of the nation. Long-distance migratory patterns also arose from efforts by employers to contain struggles initiated by workers in several parts of the nation to achieve stability and a greater degree of control over their lives. Employers preferred politically weak seasonal workers with distant roots who were not likely to challenge their authority collectively, whether over segregated schools in Texas or wages and working conditions in California.

Thousands of people who had been engaged in relatively stable agricultural work were displaced, along with an even greater number of young adults and youth, particularly children of Mexican immigrants who were reaching adulthood during the Depression and World War II. They were compelled to migrate increasing distances to find work, and as they gained visibility, they soon became identified with the nation's migrant streams. According to workers' own stories, World War II did not introduce appreciable change, except that many entered military service.

Facing extremely high levels of structural unemployment, Mexican workers became an important segment of the expanding migratory agricultural labor force during the Great Depression. This continued during subsequent decades. But as their stories of the 1930s and 1940s confirm, they were not predisposed to being agricultural workers or migrants, as growers and agricultural experts claimed, and they did not become part of a permanent Mexican agricultural underclass. The vast majority of them did not engage in seasonal migratory labor for extended periods, and eventually most of them were able to settle permanently in urban areas and obtain nonagricultural employment. Even while away from home they were able to create social, recreational, and cultural outlets and to find new work opportunities.

The broad patterns that produced the major migratory labor streams for Mexicans based in South Texas and Southern California reveal important parallels. Both were composed primarily of a generation of children of immigrants from Mexico who came to the United States to work in agriculture during and in the aftermath of World War I. While a large portion of the earlier generation enjoyed comparatively stable employment during the season, some were already migrating prior to the Great Depression.

The economic downturn marked a disruption in their earlier employment patterns, highlighted by mass repatriation of Mexican immigrants and the deportation of their children and their replacement in their former jobs by Anglo-American and African American workers. A system of migrant labor began again later in the 1930s and expanded during World War II, turning again to workers of Mexican origin and far surpassing in scale that of the previous generation. It marked an uneven but consistent trend toward greater reliance on wage labor and increasing residential instability for workers. Despite the demand for more agricultural products stimulated by the war, the rapid decline of small Mexican farmers continued. Many individuals who were small farm owners and operators relate stories of losing their land when young men in their families were drafted. Workers in many settings where wage labor had been relatively stable, including the citrus orchards of Southern California, were compelled to travel more and work shorter periods in a greater variety of locations and crops. Finally, citizen agricultural workers in both home bases were affected similarly by the Mexican Labor Program. Their stories do not mention disruption or job displacement by Mexican contract workers, or braceros, during World War II. Yet after the war and particularly during the 1950s, the displacement of U.S. citizens became a widespread complaint among workers from South Texas and California, who were compelled to migrate even greater distances to find employment in agriculture.

Hank Cervantes was a rarity as an agricultural worker who achieved his youthful dream of becoming a pilot and a military officer. Most of his contemporaries achieved much more modest occupational mobility, and most continued to work for wages. Their transition out of agricultural labor reflected a shift in the broader structure of the nation's labor force that affected people of all ethnic backgrounds. Most realized their dream of not returning to agriculture after military service ended, because employment in other sectors was expanding. But their stories confirm the recent assessment that although they recovered from the worst of the Great Depression, systematic prejudice and discrimination limited their collective opportunities and upward mobility relative to that of the majority population. In sum, the experience of Mexican agricultural workers before, during, and after World War II was mixed, conferring on them neither significant upward mobility nor a stagnant position as a permanent underclass.

4

THE LATINAS OF WORLD WAR II
From Familial Shelter to Expanding Horizons

JOANNE RAO SÁNCHEZ

Women played a significant role in helping the United States win World War II. Approximately 350,000 females served in the military. Another 18.61 million worked at the home front, some 6.5 million of them newly employed because of the wartime labor shortage. They worked in defense industries and helped fill vacancies caused by departing servicemen.[1] By war's end, the proportion of women in the workforce had risen to 36 percent, up from 25 percent in 1941.[2] Others on the home front served in the Red Cross, worked in Civil Defense, or performed for the United Service Organizations (USO). Women also participated in letter-writing campaigns to boost the spirits of American GIs. They wrapped bandages, collected scrap metal and grease, bought war bonds, and planted victory gardens. With the advent of rationing, they learned to do without and to creatively maintain their families' nutrition. While their spouses, siblings, boyfriends, and other loved ones served in the war, they grappled with worry and loneliness as they maintained morale on the home front and became more self-sufficient and confident in their daily affairs. Many scholars also contend that the war was a "major watershed in the lives of American women."[3] It changed their social expectations and their perceptions of self, especially of their worth. It also increased the number of married women—and the percentage of all women—who entered the workforce on a permanent basis.[4] Moreover, it provided women their first opportunity to serve as regular members of the armed forces.

Although we know much about the home front experience of women during the Second World War, important questions remain unanswered. This is especially evident in the case of Latina women, one of the least studied groups in U.S. history.[5] According to Christine Marín, "the contributions made by Mexican American women . . . have yet to be reported or recognized in their proper historical perspective."[6]

Sherna Berger Gluck included two Mexican Americans in her seminal 1987 work, *Rosie the Riveter Revisited: Women, the War, and Social Change*—an inclusion notable for its rarity among historians at that time. Gluck told how the war work produced opportunities for Mexican American women to socialize with Anglos. She notes, "Despite the nature of the social contacts between the races, a significant breakthrough had been made. The social worlds of these working class women had been expanded, and many of the women acknowledged the significance of this."[7] Richard Santillán made an important contribution to the subject with his article "Rosita the Riveter: Midwest Mexican American Women during World War II, 1941–1945." He concluded that while the wartime experience "modified the social and political attitudes and behavior of many Mexican American defense workers regarding their roles in the home and community," it also provided the women a "training ground . . . [in] leadership and organizational development."[8] Santillán called for additional research, as his study did not extend to female workers outside the war industries.

Vicki L. Ruiz's works also filled some of the void. In *Cannery Women, Cannery Lives: Mexican Women, Unionization, and the Food Processing Industry, 1930–1950*, she demonstrates how, especially during the war years, a few Latinas were able to assume leadership positions in organizing and bargaining for cannery workers in Southern California.[9] Ruiz's subsequent study, *From Out of the Shadows: Mexican American Women in Twentieth-Century America*, is an exemplary social history of Mexicana women, spanning the entire century. Ruiz found that some Mexican American women started to improve their socioeconomic status in the 1940s as a number of them "began to break into lower white-collar occupations" as clerks or in sales positions. She describes "cultural coalescence," as second-generation Mexican American women blended cultural norms in the 1950s and the restrictive practice of chaperonage fell largely into disuse.[10] In their brief discussion of the World War II period, Teresa Acosta and Ruthe Winegarten added that Tejanas began entering government service and earning better salaries.[11]

These examples notwithstanding, the inattention of scholars continues. For instance, a 2003 publication that purports to examine the general topic of Texas women in World War II fails to include Tejanas among the twenty-

seven women who are profiled.[12] Emily Yellin's *Our Mothers' War*, an otherwise excellent and comprehensive study, also fails to mention Latinas,
although it does include a chapter on African Americans and another on
Japanese Americans.[13] A number of questions emerge from the incomplete
literature on women. How did gender and racial/ethnic discrimination affect the wartime experience of Mexican American women, and how did their
experience differ from that of other women? Also, in what ways did Latinas
contribute to the war effort, and did the war mark a watershed for them?

This chapter seeks answers to these and other questions. It is based primarily on interviews with twenty-one Latinas who served on both the home
and war fronts.[14] Like most American women, Latinas contributed to the
war effort, despite the discrimination that they faced in their male-dominated communities and the general society. Discrimination denied them equal
opportunities in the more lucrative defense jobs.[15] In contrast to the gender
and racial discrimination on the home front, Latinas generally encountered
friendly and supportive relationships in the military. Some of them also felt
that they had gained acceptance in home front employment areas like nursing, defense, and civil service. Wartime employment often provided them
the opportunity to make their first significant contact with Anglos. A few of
the women who were interviewed even married Anglo-Americans. The new
military, defense, nursing, and civil service jobs that some were able to secure during the war years improved their earnings and enabled them to travel and live beyond their families' supervision. For some, wartime job training
paved the way for postwar employment or gave them the confidence and
funds to pursue additional schooling. Improved employment opportunities
for themselves and their husbands also helped several of them to move into
the middle class.

Reinforced by U.S. consumer culture, the employment of Latinas fostered cultural change and helped break down the confines of familial control
and chaperonage.[16] Dancing and socializing with GIs and going to wartime
canteens became acceptable activities, even for some Mexican American
women.[17] The crisis of the war was an extraordinary time in which the social
climate changed for all women, but more so for Latinas.

The remainder of this chapter is divided into five parts. The first discusses
the socioeconomic characteristics of the interviewees on the eve of the war,
while the second examines their prewar social and employment experiences.
The third part addresses the women on the home front, and the fourth examines the ones in military service. The final section illustrates the interviewees'
postwar social and employment experiences. And, in the conclusion, I examine the impact that the war had on their lives.

Socioeconomic Characteristics

On the eve of the war, the women who were interviewed were young, were predominantly from Texas, and most claimed U.S. citizenship. One of the women was born in Mexico, seventeen in Texas, one in Kansas, one in New Mexico, and one in Puerto Rico. Twenty women were of Mexican heritage. Eleven were second-generation Americans; that is, they were born in the United States, and at least one of their parents was born in Mexico. The women who reported their parents' educational background noted an average attainment level of six grades. Although four parents had no formal schooling, two had college degrees. Five of their fathers engaged in farm labor, one owned a small farm, five were nonfarm laborers, one was a jailer, and one was a toll collector at an international bridge. Two mothers were widows and heads of households who supported their families with domestic work. Five families, on the other hand, could be classified as middle class, since three heads of household were small-business owners, one was a public official, and one was a teacher.[18] While most of the women described their mothers as housewives, the mothers also performed other work, including housekeeping, laundry, sewing, migrant or farm labor, managing the family business, working as a jail matron, and teaching in a public school.

At the time of the attack on Pearl Harbor, the women were between nine and twenty-five years of age, and their average age was seventeen. At least thirteen of them had one or more siblings in military service during the war. All but three of their husbands or future husbands also served in the military. One of the women married before the war, ten during the war (nine of these to servicemen), and ten after the war. Their ages at marriage ranged from fifteen to twenty-nine, with the median and mode being twenty-one. This is slightly higher than the figure recorded by all females in the country, which averaged slightly over twenty between 1947 and 1950.[19] This difference conforms with Karen Anderson's contention that "many [Mexican American women] were deferring marriage while they contributed to the support of themselves and others."[20]

Prewar Social and Employment Experiences

As with the larger population of women, the hard times of the Depression had a profound effect on the Latina interviewees.[21] While millions of Americans lost their jobs and their property, Mexican Americans were especially hard-hit because most worked in rural, low-paying jobs without insurance or significant savings. Anti-Mexican ideas also became more evident as jobs became scarce. Many Americans felt that the Mexicans were mostly immigrants who were threatening to take jobs from "real Americans" and were straining the ability of federal relief programs to care for the U.S.-born. As Francisco Balderrama and Raymond Rodríguez have pointed out, "Regardless of their place of birth, it became fashionable to blame Mexicans for the country's economic ills."[22] At this time, public health entities depicted ethnic Mexicans as a diseased group that burdened social services: "The image of sick and diseased Mexicans also provided a strong justification for deporting Mexicans and for constructing them as outside US social membership."[23] These anti-Mexican beliefs resulted in the deportation and repatriation of approximately one million men, women, and children (many of whom were U.S. citizens) between 1931 and 1938. This represented the loss of approximately one-third of the Mexicans and Mexican Americans in the United States.[24] Federal, state, and local government agencies were involved in the campaigns to rid the country of Mexicans, as well as in denying them help through public works projects.[25]

Accusations of illness could also be used as an excuse to lay off or fire Mexican workers during the Depression. Henrietta López Rivas of San Antonio recalled the hard times. In 1934 her family lost their home, and her stepfather, Juan Luna, lost his job at Kelly Air Force Base (then called Duncan Field). Her stepfather's supervisors alleged that they had sent him home because he was ill. Years later, the stepdaughter disagreed: "He wasn't fired, he was laid off because they said he had a cough, but he wasn't sick. . . . They gave him a pension of $29 [a month]. . . . [My parents owed] $1,200 [on their house] and they couldn't make the payments."[26]

The family moved to a house without electricity or indoor plumbing, where they lived for the next year. Then, like thousands of other Mexicans, Juan Luna and his family joined the migratory labor force in Texas that ballooned to about 400,000 Mexican and Mexican American workers during the Depression years.[27] Rivas described the experience in stark terms: "[It was] horrible. . . . There was a lot of suffering doing fieldwork."[28]

Beatrice Escudero Dimas lived in El Paso, and she too remembered the difficulties that Mexicans endured during the Depression. When her parents lost their dairy farm in the mid-1930s, the family moved to Flint, Texas, to work in the cotton fields. Dimas loved school and regretted having to drop out in the eighth grade to help her family pick cotton.[29]

Plácida Peña Barrera of Guerra, Texas, also remembered her family's suffering. Before the Depression, authorities accused her paternal grandparents of not paying their taxes and took possession of their homestead and ranch

Alfred Dimas and Beatrice Escudero Dimas, ca. 1945. Courtesy of
the U.S. Latino & Latina World War II Oral History Project.

Plácida Peña Barrera, 1948. Courtesy of the U.S. Latino &
Latina World War II Oral History Project.

property. The foreclosure caused her grandparents to move to the northern
Mexican state of Coahuila. After they returned to Starr County, Texas, a tor-
nado in 1933 destroyed her grandmother's small house, where all of Barrera's
family lived. These two misfortunes—the earlier loss of their ranch and the
destruction of her grandmother's house—made life "especially hard" during
the Depression.[30]

A number of the interviewees shed further light on the difficulties of the
Depression. "In those days," recalled Theresa Herrera Cásarez of Austin,
"people just piled up, with two families or maybe three . . . living in the same
home because they didn't have the money to pay rent."[31] Cásarez and several other women told similar stories, including accounts of mothers feeding
and housing strangers who typically went door-to-door, asking for food or a
place to sleep.

Some of the women spoke of attending segregated schools. The "Mexican ward schools" were little more than one- or two-room shacks, and the teachers and administrators often had low expectations for their students.[32] María Isabel Solís Thomas, who was born in Veracruz, Mexico, offered a poignant example of low expectations involving a teacher who told her, "You'll never make it because you are a Mexican. You're going to be nothing but a housemaid. You're no good, nothing but thieves."[33]

Educators who were primarily interested in Americanizing the Mexican children also created problems. Herminia Guerrero Cadena, of Falls City, Texas, lamented that Mexicans at her segregated school were frequently punished for speaking Spanish. Cadena and several of the other interviewees also remembered how frustrated and belittled they felt when teachers changed or Anglicized their names.[34]

The discrimination that the Latinas experienced had a lasting effect on them. Sallie Castillo Castro, for instance, is still pained by it: "[Mexican Americans] could not join the Red Dragons, the drama club at Austin High School . . . no matter how talented you were. . . . You felt left out. . . . It stays with you the rest of your life."[35] Castro regretted that Mexican Americans were not allowed to play on the Austin High football team even after their parents protested.[36]

Henrietta López Rivas, from the south side of San Antonio, likewise recalled that Mexicans were not allowed to play football or to attend high school football games. Rivas described another discriminatory practice that belittled Mexicans: elementary teachers expected Mexican children to sit "in the back of the room."[37] She also remembered that the teachers would rarely encourage them to participate in classroom activities: "We would raise our hands, but we were never called."[38]

Name-calling and harassment also occurred, and the teachers allowed them. A student who called Rivas and her brother "dirty Mexicans," for instance, went unpunished.[39] Many of the interviewees noted that Mexican food was also the object of ridicule during school lunchtime: "We'd take tortillas and they [Anglos] would hide them, and . . . laugh."[40] Because of this derision, sometimes Mexicans would forgo lunch or try to hide what they were eating.

Discrimination and segregation also occurred outside the schools. Ventura Terrones Campa, of Newton, Kansas, remembered that her father refused to go to the movie theater because Mexican Americans had to sit in the balcony. Moreover, she reported that she was not allowed to eat at the counter of the local drugstore.[41] The refusal of service in public establish-

María Isabel Solís Thomas and James Thomas. Courtesy of
the U.S. Latino & Latina World War II Oral History Project.

ments was a common practice, according to several of the interviewees. Many reported that when they received service in restaurants, they often had to enter through the back door and take their food home. In some communities, public pools were off limits to Mexican Americans, so they had to swim in rivers and lakes instead. Martha Ortega Vidaurri of Austin recalled how much her six brothers wanted to be Boy Scouts, but they were not allowed, even though their Methodist Church sponsored the troop.[42] Hospitals also segregated Mexican Americans. Gloria Araguz Alaniz, of McAllen, was saddened because they put her dying mother in the damp basement of a hospital, a segregated unit. She added that by 1945 things had changed. When her brother was hospitalized, he was not sent to the basement, since the hospital no longer practiced segregation.[43]

Latinas also faced gender discrimination within their families, primarily involving what Vicki Ruiz calls "the reins of constant supervision."[44] Since family honor rested on the preservation of the virginity of young unmarried women, parents required chaperonage and supervision. Some Mexican American women obeyed; others rebelled in various ways.[45] Several of the women in this study recalled the sheltered and male-dominated lives that they led before the war, and a few shared their responses to the constraints. Delfina Luján Cuellar of Albuquerque said that she was not allowed to date, and that she was kept from going to high school: "Girls did not go to high school. . . . In those times, they would not let us. They thought that we'd be too free."[46] Concepción Alvarado Escobedo, of Southton, Texas, described a similar situation: "My mother would take me to the dances, because in those days you'd have a chaperone." She was allowed to leave the Southton area only once before she joined the military.[47]

Unlike her brothers, Apolonia Muñoz Abarca, of Mission, Texas, was not permitted to work in the family meat market, because her father believed that "girls should not work."[48] Apolonia nevertheless secured a weekend job, without her father's permission.[49] Ventura Campa told of her "very strict" father, who "wouldn't let us go anywhere." She recalled that her parents would not allow her to attend business school. She was expected to stay home and help her mother. Ventura eventually managed to circumvent authority by announcing that she was going to "sewing class" and used this opportunity to see the man who was to become her husband, Diego Campa.[50]

As Vicki Ruiz highlights, when faced with such strict and sheltered family life, Mexicanas could give in and "accept the rules, . . . they could rebel, or they could find ways to compromise or circumvent traditional standards."[51] Many of the women in this study chose the latter route.

Diego and Terrones Ventura Campa, ca. 1944. Courtesy of the U.S. Latino & Latina World War II Oral History Project.

Edelmiro Vidaurri and Martha Ortega Vidaurri, ca. 1944. Courtesy of the U.S. Latino & Latina World War II Oral History Project.

Concepción Alvarado Escobedo, 1944. Courtesy of the U.S. Latino & Latina World War II Oral History Project.

Daily Lives

The war permeated the daily lives of the Latina interviewees. They worried constantly over the welfare of their loved ones in the military. Henrietta Rivas reported that after her brother enlisted, "There was not one young man left [in the neighborhood], and many of them were killed. It was a horrible time for us. You could hear . . . the women crying for their sons."[52] Martha Vidaurri experienced the war in a more intimate way. Her six brothers served in the military. One was killed in the Normandy invasion, and another was imprisoned by the Japanese and forced to join the Bataan Death March.[53] Apolonia Abarca also remembered the pain of having her brother overseas: "It was very traumatic, because we were a very close family. His plane went down in France . . . and we didn't hear from him for six months."[54] Delfina Cuellar spoke about the time when her mother received notice by "V-mail" that her brother had been wounded in action.[55] Two of Ventura Campa's brothers and her husband also served overseas, and she recalled, "All I did was worry. I did not want them to be killed."[56] Theresa Cásarez also had two brothers at the war front, the oldest of whom had five young children. She remembered that it was difficult to go long periods without hearing from them or to receive letters that the censors made practically unintelligible.[57]

With husbands, boyfriends, fiancés, and siblings at the war front, the women learned to be self-sufficient. Latinas and Anglo women endured rationing, nutritional concerns, child-care and financial responsibilities, the upkeep of their homes, wartime travel, and even work outside the home. For Latinas, however, financial difficulties and sheltered upbringings sometimes exacerbated conditions. The women in this study who were raising families typically stayed with their in-laws or their parents, at least part of the time. They were often without their husbands, even for milestone events like the birth of a child. Some were able to visit their own families, but traveling alone with a child presented a special challenge.[58] Beatrice Dimas related that she learned to travel alone by train with her baby to visit her injured husband in a West Virginia military hospital.[59] Ascención Cortez of Laredo, on the other hand, told of her husband's long and painful rehabilitation after a grenade severed his right hand.[60] Like Dimas and Cortez, four other women in the study learned to cope with the fact that their husbands were disabled in the war. After the war, they helped their loved ones recover from their injuries.

As with their Anglo American counterparts, many of the women acknowledged that the war contributed to their personal development. Theresa Cásarez, for example, observed, "I think that the war . . . matured people in my generation because . . . we learned to do without things that we never dreamed we would."[61] Numerous others echoed Sallie Castro's sentiments: "[The war] made us mature . . . a lot faster . . . than we would have otherwise. It made us aware that we needed to grow up, and because so many boys [were] gone, there were a lot of jobs that . . . the women had to take care of."[62]

The Latinas made substantial contributions to their families and society, even though some were still teenagers. Although 66 percent of the adult female population did not work outside the home during the war, all but three of the twenty-one women in this survey earned wages, underscoring the importance of their income to the economic welfare of their families.[63] Six of the women worked in the health care industry. Delfina Cuellar was a housekeeper before the war but, at the age of thirteen, became a receptionist for a Mexican doctor after the war began. Sallie Castro was fourteen at the time of the Pearl Harbor attack but worked at Seton and Brackenridge hospitals in Austin. She collected tin in her spare time.[64] Gloria Alaniz, of McAllen, also worked in a hospital, primarily as a nurse's aide.[65]

Apolonia Abarca and Elena Tamez De Peña, of San Benito, Texas, became public health nurses. De Peña said that nurses were "much in demand" because "doctors were scarce during the war."[66] Abarca had been interested in nursing since high school, when she helped a nurse take handicapped children to Moody Hospital in Galveston. Both Abarca and De Peña were trailblazers in their field, as they were the only Hispanics in the first year of their nursing programs. While attending nursing school, they lived away from home for the first time. They found themselves integrated with Anglos, many of whom had little experience with Mexicans. Abarca related her initial encounter with her roommate, an Anglo from Virginia, who had "never been around Latinos": "She had heard that Mexicans . . . have knives and they'd kill you. . . . That first night, she didn't sleep." In spite of this experience, the two became good friends, and soon her roommate "wanted to date only Latinos."[67] Abarca saw "lots of discrimination in the hospital wards." In the charity wards, for instance, Latinos and Blacks were placed in segregated units—away from Anglos.[68] Despite the extent of discrimination in her workplace, none was directed at her: "I think because I was a little White, I didn't have any problems. They thought that I was Anglo." Her explanation of how she was spared the discrimination underscores the importance of color in the discrimination that both Blacks and Mexicans faced during the war years.[69]

Upon completion of nursing school in 1944, Abarca obtained a job at the newly opened Corpus Christi Memorial Hospital, where she helped establish the operating and emergency rooms. Soon the U.S. Public Health Service offered her the position of director of nursing services at its Public Health Service venereal disease clinic, which treated "Victory girls" (wartime prostitutes). She took the job because of the pay.[70] She went from earning $175 a month to $250 a month.[71] This can be best appreciated by considering that the military paid its soldiers in the seven lowest ranks a monthly salary that ranged from $50 to $138 in 1943.[72]

Because Abarca enjoyed volunteer work, she offered her services at the Corpus Christi Community Settlement House, initially run by the Corpus Christi Council of Church Women, a group that included various faiths. The purpose of this and other settlement houses was to Americanize recent immigrants and offer them social services, such as immunizations, nursery school, showers, and recreation, as well as classes in English, hygiene, first aid, sick care, midwifery, child care, home economics, vocational occupations, and a variety of arts and crafts. The stated goal of the Corpus Christi Community Settlement House was to lead their clients to "self-reliance, good health, and better citizenship."[73] There, Abarca taught home nursing in both English and Spanish. She enjoyed helping the less fortunate and having the opportunity to teach for the first time.

In 1946, Abarca returned to Corpus Christi Memorial Hospital as the director of services for the outpatient clinic, which served mostly Latinos and the very poor. She was the only Latina professional employed at the clinic at the time.[74] Abarca felt fortunate to have had administrative positions, since most Mexican Americans were relegated to lower-paying and more physically arduous work. "I've always ended up with administrative jobs. I never had to do bedside nursing, which is very unusual, especially for a Latina," she said.[75]

De Peña's first nursing job was at the State Health Department in Edinburg, Texas. After she married in 1942, she moved to Corpus Christi and continued to work for the same agency as a public health nurse. Unlike Abarca, she noted some important changes in the occupational standing of women, especially Latinas, during the war years: "There were not too many professional women at the time [in the early 1940s]. As years progressed, you [saw] more Mexican American, Latin American nurses and teachers."[76]

Although most Mexicans worked in unskilled or semiskilled jobs, some of them managed to secure skilled, professional, and white-collar occupations. Relatively few of them, around 5 percent of the entire Mexican workforce in Texas, found employment in the wartime industries, which included manufacturing plants in munitions, oil refining, aircraft construction and repair, smelters, and shipbuilding.[77] In contrast, roughly 10 percent of all female workers worked in defense plants during the war.[78] Only seven of the 95 women interviewed by the U.S. Latino & Latina World War II Oral History Project managed to secure employment as higher-paid and higher-skilled workers in defense industries.[79]

Henrietta López Rivas says that the war was "the best of times and the worst of times"—the best "because we quit our jobs [as migrant farmworkers]," and the worst because so many lives were lost. After she left migrant work early in the war, Rivas was employed as a housekeeper for $1.50 per week and subsequently became an interpreter for Civil Defense, a job that required "perfect English and perfect Spanish."[80] Later, she worked at Kelly Field in San Antonio, where she learned to repair airplane instruments. The move from housekeeper to interpreter and then a technical position was significant: "I was getting $90 a month for that. That was a heck of a lot of money . . . From $1.50 a week [as] a domestic to $90 a month!"[81] Rivas, the only woman in her work group, continued to move up, eventually becoming an assistant supervisor. Upward mobility also brought important psychological gains: "I think it made me feel like I was equal. [It made me feel] more intelligent because what I did, very few Anglos could do."[82]

Josephine Kelly Ledesma Walker had similar work experiences. She was working in Austin as a sales clerk for Lerner's Shop, a clothing store, when the United States entered the war. Ledesma signed up to study aircraft repair at Randolph Field in San Antonio and became the only woman in the training program. Once her training finished, Ledesma requested a transfer to Bergstrom Field in Austin, to be with her husband and son. At Bergstrom she was the only Mexican American woman among three female mechanics on her shift. Ledesma had important responsibilities. She remembered signing a liability waiver to test-fly the aircraft that she repaired. Ledesma drew much satisfaction from her work, primarily because she was making a meaningful contribution to the war effort—"by taking one place . . . that would be another place for a boy to go [to the front]." She went on to say, "Oh, I loved it. . . . I thought I was doing a real big thing. . . . It was . . . very rewarding knowing that you could do something to make that aircraft go. Our motto . . . was to keep 'em flying."[83] Ledesma and her husband eventually moved to Big Spring, Texas, so that he could also work in aircraft repair. There they grew to appreciate even more the new wartime opportunity to secure work in war industries. While they were in Big Spring, a café owner refused to serve her husband. They moved back to Austin.[84]

María Isabel Solís Thomas wanted to be a teacher or a nurse, but with nine other children in her family, there was no money to reach her goal. When

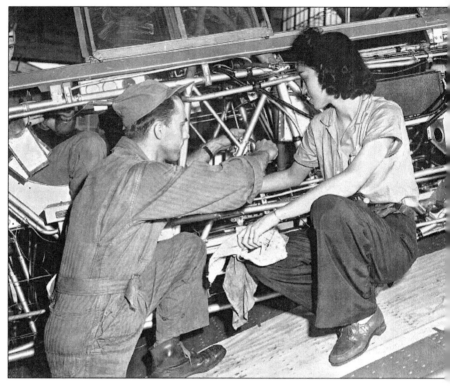

Josephine Kelly Ledesma Walker, training another mechanic. Courtesy
of the U.S. Latino & Latina World War II Oral History Project.

the war started, she was eighteen years old. Thomas attended a dermatol-
ogy school in San Antonio, worked at a Walgreens pharmacy, and lived with
one of her married older sisters. She and a sister applied for a job and were
selected to work at the Kaiser Shipyard in Richmond, California, near San
Francisco. At its peak, Kaiser employed more than ninety thousand people.[85]
The jobs in shipbuilding were especially difficult and dangerous and were
reserved for men until 1942. By 1943, however, women made up 10 percent
of the nation's shipbuilding workforce.[86] Shipbuilding involved strenuous
lifting and welding, and the workers had to endure loud noise, frigid temperatures, and the risk of burns and electrocution.[87] Nevertheless, by 1944
women at Kaiser constituted "nearly a quarter of all production workers, and
seventy percent of all laborers, the least skilled classification in the yard."[88]
The female production workers averaged $42 a week.[89]

María Isabel and her sister benefited from the opportunity to work with women of different social backgrounds. María Isabel recalled that the women, who came from "all over," lived together in a dormitory and "shared with one another as if we were one big family."[90] Although few Latinas entered war industries or worked alongside Anglo women in both war industries and in the military, she reported that "at least 40 percent of the girls there were Mexican."[91] The work was difficult but rewarding, according to Thomas. She and her sister began their shift at six in the morning and welded pipes for eleven hours, a job that required great precision. She had to crawl under parts of the ship and squeeze into small spaces. "I was so proud because . . . I did [it] just exactly the way they wanted me to. They said, 'Hi, Shorty. You did pretty good.'"[92]

Working in a war industry brought other important changes in the lives of these two Mexican workers. While employed at the shipbuilding plant, María Isabel and her sister both married Anglo servicemen of the Methodist faith. This caused some "shock" for their parents, who were Catholic and accustomed to traditional ways that included chaperoned relationships before marriage. They had not known that their daughters were dating. María Isabel added that before meeting James Thomas, she had dated only Mexican men. As the war came to an end, Kaiser discharged her. She then took a "sad train" to Indiana to live with her husband's family while she awaited his return from the Pacific theater.[93]

The effect that these jobs had on women like Thomas was considerable. They received significantly higher wages than they had previously earned. Their salaries offered them financial independence and gave Thomas and her sister an opportunity to live on their own, far away from familial restrictions. Their work helped to challenge preconceived notions of what women and Latinas were capable of doing, and it gave them and many Anglo defense workers newfound confidence. At war's end, many female defense workers regretted having to give up their positions to the returning male GIs.

Rivas, Ledesma, and Thomas obtained some of the more lucrative jobs in the war industries, but they were not the only ones who benefited from improved job opportunities during the war. Civil Service jobs, often in military establishments, also provided Latinos and Latinas the means for occupational advancement. For instance, Aurora González Castro, of San Antonio, landed her first job after high school at the State Department of Public Welfare, where she took dictation for social workers. She recalled that Kelly Field offered opportunities to "Hispanics or people who were not well off . . . to work for the government. They paid $100 a month."[94] Castro took a job as a secretary at Kelly and became a supervisor in charge of military service records. Now, after thirty-nine years in the Civil Service, Castro acknowledged the transformative effect of her work at Kelly:

> It did change our lives. We didn't have money [before the war]. . . . We didn't have a . . . nice house. We had an outdoor toilet. We never knew the other world. I never knew the other world. We didn't have a car. We didn't have a radio. . . . But how has it changed my life? . . . I feel like we're a middle-income family, lower middle-income. . . . We have everything we need now.[95]

Ventura Campa also worked on the home front; however, she was not able to obtain a job in a war industry or in the Civil Service. Campa raised her family at the same time that she graded eggs and dressed chickens in an egg packing plant in Newton, Kansas. She reminded her interviewer that the improvements in the occupational standing of Mexicans must be weighed against the segregation and discrimination that existed in prewar Newton. Mexican Americans had to sit in the balcony at the movie theater, and they were forbidden to sit at a soda fountain counter. This continued until the war's end. She and her infant daughter lived with her parents while her husband, Diego Campa, fought in Europe and the Pacific. Although her work paid less than most urban-based jobs, Campa saved enough money to make a down payment on a house, which the couple purchased with a GI loan when her husband returned.[96]

Although some of the women in this study were still in school, they worked on the home front. Herminia Cadena, for instance, was a migrant worker in Michigan when she was only nine years old. Later, she worked as a theater usher and a housekeeper.[97] Plácida Barrera, fifteen when the war began, helped on the family farm and worked as a clerk at the post office in Roma, Texas, on weekends. Barrera attended Texas A&I University in Kingsville, Texas, for a short while but had to leave school to help her family financially.[98] Theresa Herrera Cásarez worked as a teacher's aide, and as a sales clerk in an Austin department store on Saturdays. During her senior year, she became part of a dancing and singing group, made up mostly of students from the University of Texas. They performed traditional Mexican dances at the university and with the USO at Camp Swift in Bastrop, Texas.[99]

The three interviewees who worked in their homes were Ascención Cortez, Beatrice Dimas, and Martha Vidaurri. Homemakers contributed to the war effort in a variety of ways. If their husbands were in the military, the women were expected to care for their children, homes, and finances without worrying their spouses. They were also expected to keep up their husbands' morale as well as the morale of other GI relatives and friends. Cortez came from a family of farm laborers who lived on a ranch near Laredo. After her father died in a farm accident and her brother was killed in action in the war, she married Hernán Cortez when she was just fifteen. Within a few months he enlisted and was sent overseas. To make ends meet and for companionship, Cortez moved in with her mother-in-law and awaited the birth of her first child. She spent much of her time writing letters to her husband and attending daily church services with her mother-in-law to pray for her husband's safe return. Shortly after her daughter's birth, Cortez got word that a grenade had severed Hernán's right hand. For the rest of the war, Cortez assisted in her husband's rehabilitation while at the same time raising their daughter.[100]

Many war wives traveled around the United States to provide moral support and companionship to their husbands who were stationed at various bases across the country. Beatrice Dimas and other military wives faced common difficulties. Dimas learned how to travel long distances alone by train to places where her husband, Alfred, was stationed. She went to Fort Benning, Georgia, and to Fort Meade, Maryland; then to Phoenix to live with her in-laws until her daughter was born; and later back to Fort Meade. When her husband was injured in a parachute accident, she and her baby made the journey from Fort Meade to the hospital in West Virginia to visit him. Because of the difficulty of traveling with her baby daughter, she formed a group of mothers to help one another while traveling.[101]

Letter writing was especially important to boost GI morale, and Latinas joined in this activity.[102] Martha Ortega Vidaurri spent much of her time writing letters to her six brothers who were stationed overseas, to her husband, Ed, who was stationed in Iceland, as well as to other GIs from her church. In attempting to evade the censors, she devised a code so that she and her husband and brothers could communicate more freely. Vidaurri also collected scrap metal to aid in the war effort.[103] Whereas Cortez, Dimas, and Vidaurri were married and contributed to the war effort as wives and mothers, some of the women were single and made their major contributions by joining the military.

Latinas in the Military

Rafaela Muñiz Esquivel of San Antonio, who worked shelling pecans and sewing handkerchiefs in the 1930s, also moved up from the unskilled ranks into the nursing field. In 1939, her father took out a loan to pay her $60 nursing school tuition at Robert B. Green Memorial Hospital. Sending Rafaela to nursing school represented a major sacrifice for the family, since her parents had twelve other children to support. The decision, however, made a big difference in the young woman's life and in the economic well-being of the family. When she finished her nursing program in August 1942, Rafaela joined the Red Cross. Later she enlisted in the Army Nurse Corps and fulfilled a dream that would not have been possible before the war—she "always looked forward to traveling."[104] During her basic training, Esquivel was a charge nurse at Brooke Army General Hospital in San Antonio in the women's and obstetrics wards. Her contribution to the war effort involved more than skill; it also entailed hard work. She described her twelve-hour shifts as "pretty hectic" and remembered that there were so many patients that "sometimes we had some of the women [being cared for] . . . in the kitchen."[105]

Unlike African American men and women, Mexican Americans served in integrated military units.[106] This afforded them the opportunity to meet and associate with Anglos from all over the United States. Esquivel's recollections are instructive. She remembered that her friends in the Army Nurse Corps were Anglos. Among them was an Anglo nurse who became her best friend. Based on her recollections as well as those of others, integration usually involved work settings with few Latinas. Their small number may have facilitated the integration. The military camaraderie, as well as the lack of a policy of segregation, no doubt explains much of the integration. Latinas, however, may not have reached a sufficient number in certain occupational categories in the military to provoke the fear and distrust often associated with segregationist behavior among fellow workers.

Esquivel's experience as one of seventy-six thousand military nurses also demonstrated that Latinas, although few in the nursing area, contributed significantly while at the war front.[107] Shortly after her arrival in France, she was sent to the 101st Evacuation Hospital in Luxembourg, an assignment that required "the most stable nurses," as evacuation hospitals were set up just a few miles from the war front. She recalled that they did not bother to change into pajamas to sleep, as they were often roused from their beds to care for the wounded: "They used to bring them [the wounded American and German soldiers] by the loads. [We were] always on the go. . . . Most of the time, we were dressed. . . . Of course, when we had our baths, if you want to call them that, we took them out of helmets."[108]

Like Esquivel and her Anglo colleagues, war nurses sometimes served behind enemy lines and faced considerable danger. From Luxembourg, Esquivel was sent to Germany, just five miles from Patton's Third Army, to a former monastery that had been turned into a hospital. With the sound

Rafaela Muñiz Esquivel. Courtesy of the U.S. Latino
& Latina World War II Oral History Project.

of bombs nearby, the nurses stayed in combat clothing all of the time: "We
were busier . . . in Germany because . . . they were coming in droves, due
to the bombing in nearby villages."[109] They treated soldiers and civilians, including women and children. In recognition of her exemplary service, Esquivel was promoted to the rank of first lieutenant in France in May 1945.[110]

While women in the military "never quite received the same pay, rank,
or benefits equal to that of their male counterparts," the Latina interviewees
and other women nevertheless found military service a very positive experience in personal development.[111] They spoke of the many skills they learned
and the new places they saw, as well as the work alongside Anglo Americans,
which altered their perspectives.[112] Some also noted how the military pay
helped them and their families. Cármen Contreras Bozak of Puerto Rico,
for instance, underscored the importance of military pay by describing her
family as "very poor."[113]

Bozak's recollections offered other direct and indirect allusions to government and military service as a rewarding experience. She pointed out, for
example, that in 1941 the government acknowledged her abilities by assign-

ing her to work as a payroll clerk for the War Department. This experience as well as the hope that she would "get to travel" persuaded her to enlist in the Women's Army Auxiliary Corps (WAAC). She traveled to Iran, where she met General Dwight D. Eisenhower. Military service, however, involved some sacrifice, according to Bozak. Although she never faced discrimination, women at home had the impression that WAACs were "smokers and drinkers." On the other hand, Bozak was able to use her bilingual abilities in Spanish and English. This led to her being selected for the first company of WAACs sent overseas. She served as a Teletype operator in the Signal Corps in Algeria and in Italy until 1946. The war changed her life in a more profound way. As Bozak noted, "I met and married my husband" and made a life that "was completely different from the sort of life I led up to that point." Theodore J. Bozak was a Polish American. Intermarrying contributed to other important changes in her life after the war. She experienced "almost a change of ethnicity" and never spoke Spanish again.[114]

Concepción Alvarado Escobedo also credited military service for major changes in her life, although she emphasized patriotism and poverty as motivating factors for joining the war effort. She was a civilian air raid warden for the Civil Defense early in the war, making sure that all persons in her assigned area had their lights turned off after dark. Not satisfied with her home front contribution, Escobedo reasoned, "If I could play some small part in the war, I would do it."[115] In 1944 she enlisted in the Women's Army Corps. Whereas Anglo-American women's primary motivation to enlist was patriotism, Escobedo, like many other Mexican Americans, cited financial need as a major factor in her enlistment. She recalled, "I would send my mother... $5 or $10 a month. That was another reason why I... join[ed]."[116]

Military life for Escobedo meant that she had to travel a great cultural distance between a sheltered life and the promise of opportunity outside the home. Since her mother did not want her to join the military, Escobedo asked to be stationed close to home, at Randolph Field in San Antonio. She was sent to Georgia instead for basic training but, afterward, to Randolph. In the military, Escobedo acquired important skills and experienced an entirely different life, serving as a file clerk and then a baker. She observed, "There weren't any [other Mexican Americans], I don't think."[117] In contrast to the discrimination that Mexicans often faced at the home front, Escobedo pointed out, "I was never treated badly. We were all the same." When asked how military service had affected her, Escobedo called attention to the experience of integration and cultural contact with Anglos, including the benefits that she gained as a result:

Cármen Contreras Bozak. Courtesy of the U.S. Latino
& Latina World War II Oral History Project.

I believe that it opened up my mind to a lot of things. . . . [It enabled me to]
learn more about people and about [my]self. You learn how to get along
with other people. . . . We always lived where mostly Mexican people lived.
I didn't have much experience with . . . Anglos or any other nationality
or ethnic group. When I was at Randolph Field, a lot of the women who
were close to me were from the East—New York, New Jersey . . . northern
states. . . . At Randolph Field, I didn't have any Mexican friends.[118]

Felícitas Cerda Flores, born and raised in Houston, Texas, also recounted
the major contrast between her civilian and military lives. She had already
worked outside her home as a helper and a typist in a day care center. Flores
and her father also showed their support for the war by collecting scrap
metal in their spare time. In 1943, when she was twenty-two, she enlisted in
the WAAC. She was sent to Louisiana and then to Aberdeen, Maryland, where
she was a typist for the quartermaster. When asked about her experience in

the military, Flores responded, "It was beautiful. . . . I just fit in real good with the girls, girls from all over the United States."[119] Flores learned about life in the rest of the United States through these conversations. She added that she was the only Mexican American in her unit. Flores, however, noted that her Methodist church had given her the opportunity to interact with people of different races and ethnicities. Underscoring the importance of church as a site of cultural change for Mexican Americans, she explained, "They . . . put it in my head that we are all American, and I learned to get along with other people outside of my culture. That helped me in the service." While in the military, however, Flores appreciated the camaraderie: "Nobody looked down on me. I was one of them. We were all the same, even the captains. . . . No one ever called me Mexican."[120]

Postwar Experiences (1945–1959)

The twenty-one Latina interviewees underwent important changes in their socioeconomic status and place of residence after the war. Although the cultural image of female domesticity is often applied to all women in the 1950s, and especially to Mexican women, only four of them remained in their homes to raise their children.[121] Moreover, while 29 percent of all American women were in the labor force in 1950,[122] 81 percent of these Latinas worked outside the home. More than a third of them worked in highly skilled occupations, some of which they retained from the war years. Furthermore, the four housewives also experienced upward mobility through their husbands. They were married to a leatherworker, a small-business owner, a master sergeant in the army, and a police officer. While there is ample room for additional research, it is instructive to note that thirteen of the Latinas were members of the middle class in the early postwar period. Only five of them had this classification in the prewar years.[123] Five Latinas, or 23.8 percent of the total, worked in the professional or technical fields in 1950, whereas the figure among all Latinas in the Southwest was 4.6 percent. Nine Latinas, or 42.8 percent of the total, were in various clerical positions, including bookkeepers and accountants. This percentage compares favorably with the 23.9 percent registered by all Latinas in the Southwest in the same year.[124] Only three of the Latina interviewees remained in farm labor, factory labor, or janitorial jobs.

Social advancement may be measured in other ways. Eight of the women, for instance, noted that they became homeowners during the early postwar period, most likely with their husband's GI Bill benefits. This was an impor-

Emma Villareal Hernández. Courtesy of the U.S. Latino
& Latina World War II Oral History Project.

tant development, since most of the women had previously lived with relatives. The group also exceeded the six-year schooling average registered by
their parents. By war's end, most of the Latinas had graduated from high
school, two had graduated from college, and another had a year of college.
They were slightly more educated than the average female in 1950; 66.7 percent of the Latinas had high school diplomas, and 61 percent of the general
female population did.[125] In the early postwar years, seven of the Latinas
obtained additional formal education, perhaps as a result of their improved
economic situation and increased confidence. One of them completed high
school, two graduated from business college, two attended college for a year
and a half, one completed a nursing degree, and one earned a master's degree. Three of the five veterans in the group (60 percent) used their GI Bill
benefits, in contrast to the 35 percent overall of female GIs who did so.[126]

The twenty-one Latinas recorded other important accomplishments.
Apolonia Abarca, for example, helped open the first eye clinic and the first
cancer clinic in Corpus Christi. She also became the first director of the

Planned Parenthood program in the city. Elena De Peña earned a master's degree and became the first Mexican American nurse for the Corpus Christi Independent School District. Theresa Cásarez and Sallie Castro were awarded scholarships by the League of United Latin American Citizens (LULAC). Both became members of LULAC, and in the late 1940s Sallie served as treasurer of LULAC Council 85. In 1950 this civil rights organization asked Theresa to be the first Hispanic observer to work at the polls at Palm Elementary School in Austin. The two women later obtained jobs at the Internal Revenue Service, where Theresa worked as an accounting supervisor.

Emma Hernández chose not to work outside of the home for many years but served as the treasurer of a Veterans of Foreign Wars Auxiliary. Rafaela Esquivel became the president of the Parent Teacher Association at her daughter's school. At the time of this writing, she remained the only woman and only Latina in her Veterans of Foreign Wars post. Cármen Contreras Bozak started a chapter of WAC veterans in Fort Lauderdale and later founded a chapter of military widows.[127] After passing her General Education Development test, Beatrice Escudero Dimas worked for five years for the U.S. Department of Housing and Urban Development and then earned her associate's degree in 1985. From their myriad accomplishments, one can see that many of the women continued to be trailblazers well into the postwar period.

Conclusion

The Second World War altered women's lives in a number of ways. While the total number of women in the workforce declined briefly after the war, they continued to enter the labor market at an increasing rate. For the first time, married women became more than half of the female workforce, and the percentage of married women in paid employment continued to increase. Women could serve in the regular army and obtain veterans' benefits for the first time in American history. Wartime saw women proving themselves in male occupations and gaining confidence in various new roles on the home front, without the help of their husbands. Wartime jobs and responsibilities no doubt increased their feelings of self-worth, independence, and accomplishment.

The twenty-one women in this study benefited significantly from wartime opportunities. They learned new skills, obtained better-skilled and higher-wage jobs, gained personal freedom and independence, and broadened their experiences outside their homes and traditional Latino culture. The difficulties that they overcame and the psychological pain that they suffered helped them to become more independent, to mature, and to gain a sense of security from their achievements. The service they rendered the United States—whether in the military or on the home front—improved their financial situation, demonstrated their patriotism and made them proud to be part of the war effort. Though some lost their wartime jobs, others continued in their newfound careers. A number of them went on to obtain additional education and higher-level careers after the war, enabling them to enter the middle class. This brought great benefit to their families as well.

Although many welcomed the personal freedom they had gained, most returned to their hometowns at war's end. They returned changed. The leadership that several of these women exercised in the postwar period might not have been possible without their wartime experiences. Government assistance in the form of their spouses' GI Bill benefits made it possible for many to buy new homes. While some experienced personal setbacks and discrimination in the 1950s, it was impossible to completely overturn the transformation they underwent during the war. This most likely fostered their resolve that their children's personal and professional development would exceed their own. The Latinas in the study included a few more middle-class members than was the norm in the prewar period. Eight of them moved into the middle class from the working poor or working classes.

Additional research on Latinas during World War II is still needed. However, some significant conclusions can be drawn from this study. As with Anglo women, the war was a watershed for Latinas. Indeed, the war seems to have brought more changes for Latinas than for Anglo-American women, since prewar Latinas were most often employed in low-paying jobs, often experienced racial and ethnic discrimination, lacked much knowledge of the world outside their communities, and were considerably more sheltered than their Anglo-American counterparts. Although the war did not eradicate discrimination, Latinas made inroads in employment. Working with Anglos in the military, defense plants, nursing, and civil service jobs enabled Latinas to build the necessary friendships and respect that began to break the barriers that kept them separated from mainstream America.

AUTHOR'S NOTE: I would like to thank Paula Mitchell Marks, Maggie Rivas-Rodríguez, my husband, Mario L. Sánchez, Brenda Sendejo, and Emilio Zamora for their assistance. Special gratitude to St. Edward's University for a 2000–2001 sabbatical to work on this project.

☀ 5 ☀

MEXICAN NATIONALS IN THE U.S. MILITARY
Diplomacy and Battlefield Sacrifice

▬▬

EMILIO ZAMORA

Two of Mexico's best-known contributions to the war effort came from a squadron of air fighters that joined the Allied forces in the Pacific theater and more than 300,000 contract workers, or braceros, who worked in U.S. agriculture and the railroads. Lesser known but equally important contributions included binational agreements that made available critical war supplies such as rubber, tungsten, and copper for the U.S. industrial machine and allowed Mexico's security-sensitive neighbor to build naval bases, airfields, and radar installations in Mexican territory. Another reciprocal agreement allowed each country to draft for military service the citizens of the other who were living within its borders. Mexico did not call up U.S.-born persons; the United States, on the other hand, registered Mexican nationals and eventually called up 15,000 of them to serve in the military.[1]

This chapter examines the registration and conscription experience of Mexican nationals in the United States. My goal here is twofold. I hope to offer a better understanding of the new set of improved yet still troubled intergovernmental relations that emerged during the Second World War. I also wish to acknowledge the contributions of the 15,000 Mexican recruits as a neglected topic in the history of Mexican-U.S. relations and Mexicans in the United States.

On the first point, the reciprocal military agreement of 1943 was originally meant as a strategic demonstration of unity and cooperation consummated between the two most important cobelligerents in the hemisphere. The accord, however, quickly turned into a delicate diplomatic issue as critics in Mexico branded it a concession of major magnitude. In response, the administration of President Manuel Avila Camacho tried to save face with a potent public advocacy campaign on behalf of the Mexican recruits. To further complicate matters, Mexico's diplomatic campaign fortified a larger interventionist effort in defense of Mexicans in the United States. Clearly, the normalization of relations that materialized during the 1940s was not without serious problems in adjusting wartime differences. It did not, for instance, remove doubts when the U.S. State Department subsequently declared that it would extend the hemispheric focus of its Good Neighbor Policy into the domestic arena. More cooperative relations also failed to allay fears that the United States would continue to pursue a hegemonic purpose even as its diplomats promoted the inter-American system of cooperation and goodwill.

Regarding the role played by the Mexican nationals in the U.S. military, I have based my analysis on data gathered by the Mexican and U.S. governments, primarily with surveys among Mexican draft registrants and recruits. The focus is on Mexican nationals from Texas, primarily because they contributed the larger share of the total Mexico-born registrants and recruits from the Southwest and represented a convenient and robust sample for the study. The data suggest that they were longtime residents by the early 1940s and that the positions they filled in the occupational structure were more highly skilled than those filled by the majority of Mexican nationals and U.S.-born Mexicans. Some of them, perhaps the majority, welcomed the opportunity to use military service to secure U.S. citizenship or to express their support for the war effort, while others lamented and even protested their conscription. Their complaints of discrimination, on the other hand, emboldened the critics of Avila Camacho and prompted Mexico's consular corps to act decisively and publicly on their behalf.

Mexican-U.S. Relations

From a diplomatic standpoint, the most significant challenge associated with the registration and induction of Mexican citizens into the U.S. military involved the numerous complaints of discrimination received at the Mexican

Embassy, Mexico's Foreign Affairs Ministry (Secretaría de Relaciones Exteriores), and the numerous consulate offices throughout the Southwest. In many instances, grievances involved the strict enforcement of registration and conscription regulations and the official U.S. penchant for interpreting the constant back-and-forth movement across the border as attempts by Mexican nationals to evade the law. In some cases, Mexicans may have encouraged U.S. draft board members and immigration officials to take this view by failing to register and answer the call to arms because they were not sufficiently informed about the responsibility that had been suddenly thrust upon them. Others may have interpreted military service in the United States as a rejection of their Mexican heritage and citizenship. Although most administrative difficulties that gave rise to misunderstandings were resolved to satisfy the declared need for cooperation, intergovernmental deliberations revealed the political tightrope that Mexico was forced to walk as it sought to make common cause in defense of the Americas.[2]

As previously noted, Mexico's protests of discrimination against its citizens in the United States provided the backdrop for the story of Mexican soldiers in the U.S. military. At the same time that Mexican officials were noting their concern over Mexican registrants and conscripts, they were making use of Mexico's position as the United States' principal ally to redouble their interventionist efforts. The U.S. State Department, on the other hand, expressed concern over the public and diplomatic attention that the Mexican government drew to racial discrimination, but U.S. officials eventually realized that they had to address the problem as a hindrance to cooperation and goodwill in the Americas. The interagency effort was led by the Office of the Coordinator of Inter-American Affairs (OCIAA), which was responsible for promoting the Good Neighbor Policy in Latin America. By 1942 the OCIAA had established the Division of Inter-American Affairs and the Spanish and Portuguese Speaking Minorities Section to oversee the government's unprecedented initiative in favor of racial understanding. Although the effort did not make an appreciable dent on discrimination, the Mexican consulates, often in collaboration with Mexican organizations in the United States like the League of United Latin American Citizens, led a spirited public campaign in support of the civil and labor rights of Mexican nationals and U.S.-born Mexicans. The public discourse and diplomatic communications over Mexican nationals in the U.S. military was part of this larger story of an expanded Good Neighbor Policy and racial discrimination as an emerging issue in Mexican-U.S. relations.[3]

Redefining intergovernmental relations often created contentious diplomatic moments around issues like trade, military collaboration, and racial discrimination, but the overriding concern for hemispheric unity against the Axis powers dictated cooperation and reciprocity. This was evident as the war clouds loomed large over Europe in the late 1930s, and the administration of President Lázaro Cárdenas faced major difficulties in building common cause with the United States. One of the complicating factors was the widespread and virulent anti-U.S. feelings among Mexico's public. Long-time resentments associated with the 1846–1848 war and anger over the more recent deportations of hundreds of thousands of Mexicans, beginning in the late 1920s and continuing through the Depression years, increased in the wake of the famous oil crisis.[4] Cárdenas' 1938 decision, backed by the courts and a special commission, to expropriate foreign petroleum companies in the aftermath of a bitter labor dispute had also sparked rancorous debate in the United States. The outcry included demands to call in Mexico's debt, reduce the purchase of Mexican silver, and even intervene militarily in defense of the oil companies. Bellicose proposals incensed the Mexican public even more. Most points of contention, however, were settled with the start of Avila Camacho's administration in 1940, when the growing threat of war convinced both governments to define their wartime relations in more cooperative terms. By the time Mexico declared war on the Axis powers—in May 1942—Mexican officials had mustered the necessary political capital to win public support for a full alliance with the United States.

Soon after his inauguration, Avila Camacho committed Mexico to oppose military aggression against another American nation at the same time that his administration announced that it would cooperate fully with the United States on the condition that "pending" issues were resolved. The Japanese attack on Pearl Harbor on 7 December 1941 led Avila Camacho to convert what Blanca Torres has called Mexico's "feigned neutrality" into a more open policy of cooperation. Two days after the attack, Mexico broke diplomatic relations with Japan, and on 11 December Mexican officials severed relations with Germany and Italy. By the middle of January 1942, Mexico and the United States had initiated a more determined plan for economic and military cooperation with the signing of the Mexico-U.S. Commission for Mutual Defense agreement. In response to U.S. security concerns on the Pacific coast, Avila Camacho also established the Pacific Military Region under the command of former president Cárdenas. Moreover, Mexico demonstrated its commitment to war readiness by establishing a military service requirement for able-bodied men, military instruction in public schools, and an Office of Defense. By the middle of 1942, Ezequiel Padilla, Mexico's foreign minister, began making stronger appeals throughout Latin America for a wartime alliance with the United States. On 22 May 1942, after the sinking of two Mexican tankers in the Gulf of Mexico, Avila Camacho declared war on the Axis powers and aligned Mexico solidly with the United States and the Allied cause in the Americas.

Although an increasing number of Mexican citizens appeared to support the administration's preparedness activities and war policy, widespread opposition was also evident throughout 1941–1943. When the tide began to turn, around May 1942, hundreds of Mexican youth began to congregate regularly in front of the U.S. Embassy to volunteer for military service. Mexican public opinion clearly turned in favor of the war, thanks in large part to the belligerent German gunships in Gulf waters. Whether one sees Mexico's decision to enter the war as a reckless feint, an authentic expression of the will of the people, or some of each, Mexican officials risked major, disruptive political divisions with their bold actions. Moreover, they committed the nation to a war whose human costs and threats to national sovereignty they could not possibly predict.[5]

Soon after Mexico declared war, a diplomatic issue emerged that was to result in the reciprocal military agreement of 1943. The problem began with Mexico's new status as a cobelligerent and the accompanying understanding that committed its nationals to service in the U.S. military if they resided on the northern side of the international border. U.S. registration and conscription requirements acknowledged this understanding. With the 1940 passage of the Selective Training and Service Act, the U.S. Congress required that all males between the ages of twenty-one and thirty (the requirement was later changed to ages eighteen to forty-five) residing in the United States register with their local draft board. The act also announced that foreign-born persons who declared their intention of becoming citizens would be subject to military service. Mexicans who filed a Selective Service Form 301 (an application for relief from military service) were granted a nonresident status and a Class IV-C designation, which exempted them from military service. The alternative was to fill out Form 302. Filing that form made the applicants subject to the military draft with a I-A classification, but it also secured them U.S. residence and assured them U.S. citizenship upon their completion of military service.

Up until the passage of the Selective Training and Service Act, the Mexican Embassy and individual consulate offices had been advising Mexican nationals to seek exemptions from the draft by filing Form 301. Some draft boards continued to honor the exemptions after May 1942. An undetermined number of Mexican nationals who were otherwise exempt from military service under the 1940 Selective Training and Service Act and who submitted a Form 301 nevertheless were drafted, and they served. Draft boards, in other words, did not always grant the registrants the option of refusing to agree to be drafted despite the numerous complaints that Mexican consular offices received and made known to U.S. authorities.[6]

The decision by the United States to unilaterally introduce Mexican nationals into the U.S. military, regardless of the choice that they were offered, became a sensitive issue for the Avila Camacho administration. The president had managed to gain popular support for his policy of cooperation with the United States in large part because he had promised that Mexicans would contribute to the war effort as workers on the home front and not as soldiers on the battlefields. Avila Camacho and members of the Mexican Congress, however, decided to accommodate U.S. policy if a condition was met that would allow Mexican officials to claim a measure of negotiating independence and save face with the Mexican public. They asked that Mexico retain the right to draft U.S. citizens on Mexican soil. This understanding of reciprocity was included in the 22 January 1943 agreement.[7]

The complaints by Mexicans in the United States, some of which reached the Mexican press and fueled the ongoing critique against the Avila Camacho administration, prompted the Secretaría de Relaciones Exteriores to give added attention to the work of the Mexican consulate in the United States. Mexican consuls were directed to redouble their efforts to ensure that their nationals understood their responsibilities and rights. They were to encourage Mexicans of draft age to register, and to advise the young men that military service in the United States did not mean a loss of a birthright, unless they elected to become U.S. citizens upon completion of military service. The possible loss of Mexican citizenship was nevertheless a major concern for many prospective recruits, some of whom evaded registration and the draft by returning to Mexico. This placed added pressure on Mexican officials who also had to advise them on how to resolve their registration and draft problems with the U.S. government.[8]

Not all of the Mexican registrants saw the trade-off as a choice between service in the U.S. military and the loss of their birthright. The registration form asked that they declare whether they wished to be subject to the draft, with the understanding that if they did, the government would give them the opportunity to become U.S. citizens. Many interpreted the act of registration as well as military service to mean an automatic loss of Mexican citizenship, but others understood it as a welcome option for U.S. citizenship and all the privileges and opportunities they believed that this represented. Framing the choice in these terms offers a better explanation for the decision by most of the 15,000 Mexican nationals who served in the U.S. military. Their record of sacrifice on the battlefield—1,492 dead, injured, imprisoned or disappeared—also attests to the power of wartime propaganda and the might of individual volition to exercise options for citizenship.[9]

At the same time, clear signs of dissent appeared in Mexico, especially after the United States announced a lottery draft in August 1942. In some cases the opposition held demonstrations and even threatened armed action. The major concern was that Mexican soldiers would be required to fight on foreign soil under U.S. command. This is the reason why Mexico continued to tread carefully in devising collaborative plans with the United States, especially in the area of military cooperation. The Avila Camacho administration, on the other hand, wished to do more than assure the United States that it could be counted on to assist with home front production and that it was militarily capable of defending the hemisphere's southern flank. Mexican officials also wanted Mexican soldiers to participate directly in the fighting to improve Mexico's standing as a cobelligerent and, according to Cárdenas, "to hold its head high" in the postwar planning for peace and renewed intergovernmental relations.[10]

The decision to train, equip, and deploy Mexico's air squadron, El Escuadrón 201, eventually met the need as a wholly Mexican military force that would see three months of action in the Pacific in 1945 under U.S. command—as members of Mexico's air force but not as U.S.-conscripted troops. Waiting until almost the end of the war to deploy El Escuadrón 201 underscores the difficulty that Mexico faced in openly agreeing to deploy troops. The lag could also be explained by a delayed realization that Mexico could capitalize on the romanticized reputation that military tradition gave air squadrons. Ground troops simply did not lend themselves to the kind of publicity bonanza reserved for fighter pilots. This explains why the 15,000 Mexican nationals in the U.S. military did not figure in the discussions over "symbolic" military contributions before the Mexico-U.S. Commission for Mutual Defense that resulted in the deployment of El Escuadrón 201. The agreement that established the squadron, consequently, must be seen as more than another important contribution to the war effort. It was also a more agreeable act of military collaboration that necessarily emerged out of a contentious process that took around four years to unfold.[11]

Soon after the signing of the reciprocal agreement of 1943, Foreign Minister Padilla asked for the first installment of information on the soldiers. The request was made largely to placate critics in Mexico who considered the agreement in direct contradiction to their country's promise that Mexicans would not serve in the U.S. military. George Messersmith, the U.S. ambassador to Mexico, understood the political significance of the request and successfully intervened with military officials who, as a matter of practice, typically rejected such security-sensitive requests from other countries. The reports that the U.S. Office of the Adjutant General released between 1943 and 1945 in response to Mexico's requests are the single most important source of information on Mexican nationals as well as U.S.-born Mexicans in the U.S. military.[12]

Mexican Nationals in the U.S. Military

According to one report, 6,499 Mexican nationals entered the U.S. military between November 1940 (two months after the U.S. Congress passed the Selective Training and Service Act) and January 1943, when the reciprocal agreement was signed. More than half of those recruits joined during the last two months of 1942, most probably in response to Mexico's declaration of war against the Axis powers and the United States' subsequent announcement that nationals from cobelligerent nations were subject to the military draft. The attention that the media gave the wartime initiatives and the stepped-up recruitment activities by local draft boards no doubt encouraged Mexican nationals to register for the draft and to report when called to serve.[13]

The consular records at the Secretaría de Relaciones Exteriores demonstrate that Mexican nationals embraced the war effort as was the popular sentiment of the day. The majority who responded to the mail survey administered by the Mexican government in July 1944, for instance, agreed with the Allied cause and their country's alliance with the United States. The steady number of recruits who continued to register and join the military between 1943 and 1945, as well as the hundreds of young volunteers who were turned away by the U.S. Embassy in Mexico, offer added proof of support for the war. Although some of the would-be volunteers may have entertained the possibility of obtaining U.S. citizenship, the Mexican press characterized the popular acts as evidence of growing support for the United States in the Allied cause. At the same time, the consular records as well as articles in newspapers like *La Prensa* (San Antonio, 1913–1955) and interviews with veterans and family members indicate widespread claims of discrimination on the home front. Complaints noted that draft boards disregarded conditions of financial hardship and made unfair charges of evading conscription against Mexicans who visited relatives across the border. The majority of the Mexican nationals who registered and served, however, focused on the U.S. citizenship status that they were going to earn, on a belief in the just cause of the war, and on their military duty as representatives of the Mexican nation.[14]

The July 1944 survey generated quantitative information that allows us to begin constructing a profile of Mexican nationals in the U.S. military. The survey instrument sought birth date and immigration and occupational information and encouraged the recruits to volunteer personal opinions about their experiences in the military. The following analysis is based on a sample of 231 respondents recruited in Texas. The sample represents 30.7 percent of the total number of 709 persons who returned the questionnaires between 1944 and 1945. Neither the respondents nor officials of the Secretaría de Relaciones Exteriores who administered the questionnaire explained why some recruits submitted the questionnaires while others did not.[15]

Two of the most striking characteristics revealed by the data were the young age of the recruits when they crossed the international border and their consequent long residence in Texas prior to joining the military (table 5.1). They averaged slightly more than five years of age when their families migrated. Their average age of arrival decreased from 1903 to 1930, in large part because birth dates before 1903 and after 1930, the earliest and latest recorded birth dates, made potential recruits too old or too young to meet the military's maximum and minimum age requirements. They had crossed the border into the United States in growing numbers at the same time that overall immigration from Mexico was increasing markedly. The majority of them, for instance, immigrated during the 1910s and 1920s, that is, during the Mexican Revolution and immediately after World War I. They also claimed an average of 25.2 years of residence in Texas and a mean age of almost 30 years in 1945, making them significantly older on average than most military personnel at the time (the average age for all personnel across services was 26).

The record of long residence in the United States—a result of their early age at the time of crossing the international border—strongly suggests that the more recent arrivals from Mexico avoided military service to a greater extent than longer-term residents. This finding also points to a group of Mexican recruits who may have been more socially and culturally similar to

Table 5.1. Mexican Nationals Recruited in Texas into the U.S. Military, by
Birth Date, Age at Arrival, Years in United States, and Age in 1945

Birth Date	Number in Sample	Percentage of Total Sample	Average Age at Arrival	Average Years in U.S.	Average Age in 1945
1903–1905	9	3.9	8.3	32.1	40.4
1906–1910	44	19.1	8.0	28.7	36.6
1911–1915	40	17.3	6.3	25.7	32.2
1916–1920	77	33.3	3.9	23.0	20.9
1921–1925	59	25.5	3.9	18.9	22.7
1926–1930	2	0.0	0.5	18.0	18.5
Total or average	231	99.1	5.2	25.2	28.6

SOURCE: "Mexicanos reclutados (en el) Ejército Norteamericano," part 2, 1944–
1945, Archivo Histórico Genaro Estrada, Secretaría de Relaciones Exteriores,
Mexico City. The data are drawn from questionnaires sent to Mexican nationals
serving in the U.S. military. A total of 709 questionnaires were returned in 1944
and 1945. The sample for this analysis is drawn from 238 respondents living in
Texas at the time of their induction. The data submitted by 7 of those respondents were incomplete and were omitted from the analysis, bringing the total
number of cases analyzed to 231.

U.S.-born Mexicans than to their immigrant counterparts. Although they
were Mexican citizens and American immigrants, the Mexican soldiers had
typically spent their early formative years in the United States and could have
served as a proxy for the U.S.-born Mexican population of the second and
third generations. Their position as the "1.5 generation" suggests they had a
greater opportunity for incorporation into U.S. society than their Mexico-
born parents had. The degree of the soldiers' social integration can be de-
duced by examining the relationship between their record of long residence
and their standing in the occupational structure. This assimilationist hypoth-
esis considers that immigrants' length of U.S. residence correlates with their
attainment of better-skilled jobs.[16]

The soldiers' extended stay in the United States is clear from the data; a positive correlation with their occupational standing is not (table 5.2). The occupational data do not suggest that the age at arrival and the length of residence in the United States had a determining effect on the soldiers' occupational standing. Across all the general jobs categories, the conscripts consistently claimed an average of approximately 23–24 years of residence. Those in the white-collar category reported a slightly higher age upon arrival and a consequent higher age in 1945. The students, largely because of their youth, represented an anomaly, with a later age at arrival, a shorter stay in the United States, and a younger age in 1945. Nevertheless, the record of long residence among most of the conscripts suggests that in each of the occupational categories, recent arrivals were underrepresented in the U.S. military. These data also suggest that length of residence in the United States did not necessarily guarantee the recruits better-skilled jobs on the home front, possibly because of the generalized nature of racial discrimination. On the other hand, some self-selection may have occurred among 1.5-generation members, who were more disposed than the newer arrivals to see military service as a way to obtain U.S. citizenship.[17]

Corresponding occupational data from the census and registration records of foreign-born persons from Texas provide yet another basis for analyzing the significance of long-term residence and developing a fuller profile of Mexicans in the U.S. military (table 5.3). The 1930 and 1950 columns are based on census occupational data for Mexicans in Texas, while the column for 1943–1944 registrants contains occupational figures culled from the 1940 and 1943 registration forms filled out by Mexican nationals in Texas in response to the Selective Training and Service Act. The conscript data originated in the questionnaires administered by the Mexican government.[18]

In order to appreciate the relative occupational standing of the registrants and the conscripts, it is first necessary to comment on mobility trends evident among the general Mexican population (including U.S.-born and Mexico-born Mexicans) in the census reports of 1930 and 1950. The increased proportion of Mexicans in skilled and semiskilled occupations and their corresponding decrease in the unskilled category, particularly among the farm laborers, point to upward mobility. Wartime opportunities, in other words, allowed some Mexicans to recover from the hard times of the Depression years as they moved out of agricultural and into nonagricultural employment. Underscoring this trend is that two-thirds of the entire Mexican workforce in Texas filled unskilled occupations in 1930, while less than half remained in this category in 1950. This trend continued beyond the immediate postwar

Table 5.2. Mexican Nationals Recruited in Texas into the U.S. Military, by
Occupational Category, Age at Arrival, and Age in 1945

Occupation	Number in Sample	Average Age at Arrival	Average Years in U.S.	Average Age in 1945
WHITE COLLAR	33	6.9	24.7	32.3
Professional, technical, and kindred workers	3	7.7	26.0	33.7
Managers, officials, and proprietors	7	9.0	22.57	31.6
Farm owners and managers	23	3.9	25.5	31.6
SKILLED	62	4.6	24.4	29.0
Craftsmen, foremen, and kindred workers	43	4.6	25.2	29.8
Clerical and kindred workers	19	4.5	23.6	28.1
SEMISKILLED (operatives)	41	5.0	24.4	29.4
UNSKILLED	83	5.6	23.6	29.2
Service workers	24	7.6	21.3	29.0
Laborers, except farm and mine	47	4.7	24.9	29.6
Farm laborers	12	5.0	24.6	29.1
STUDENTS	12	7.9	14.4	22.3
TOTAL OR AVERAGE	231	6.0	22.1	28.4

SOURCE: "Mexicanos reclutados (en el) ejército norteamericano," part 2, 1944–1945,
Archivo Histórico Genaro Estrada, Secretaría de Relaciones Exteriores, Mexico City.
The data are drawn from questionnaires sent to Mexican nationals serving in the U.S.
military. A total of 709 questionnaires were returned in 1944 and 1945. The sample for
this analysis is drawn from 238 respondents living in Texas at the time of their induction.
The occupational data submitted by 7 of those respondents were incomplete and were
omitted from the analysis, bringing the total number of cases analyzed to 231. Twelve of
the respondents classified themselves as students.

Table 5.3. Occupational Distribution of Mexican-Origin Persons in Texas, 1930–1950

Occupations	1930	Registrants, 1943–1944	Conscripts, 1945	1950
		PERCENTAGE OF MEXICAN-ORIGIN PERSONS		
WHITE COLLAR	11.0	9.8	14.3	9.9
Professional, technical, and kindred workers	1.9	1.8	1.3	2.7
Managers, officials, and proprietors	0.5	3.2	3.0	4.4
Farm owners and managers	8.6	4.8	10.0	2.8
SKILLED	10.1	26.1	26.9	21.8
Craftsmen, foremen, and kindred workers	3.9	16.7	18.6	6.8
Clerical and kindred workers	6.2	9.4	8.2	15.0
SEMISKILLED (operatives)	11.3	14.9	17.8	19.4
UNSKILLED	65.5	49.3	36.0	46.8
Service workers	22.0	21.1	10.4	20.0
Laborers, except farm and mine	13.0	19.0	20.4	10.1
Farm laborers	30.5	9.2	5.2	16.7
UNREPORTED	0	0	5.2	1.7
TOTAL	97.9	100.0	100.2	99.5

SOURCES: Mario Barrera, Race and Class in the American Southwest: A Theory of Racial Inequality (Notre Dame, Ind.: University of Notre Dame Press, 1979), 132; "Registration Forms for Mexican Nationals, 1943–1944," National Archives and Records Administration, Southwest Region, Fort Worth, Tex.; "Mexicanos reclutados (en el) ejército norteamericano," part 2, 1944–1945, Archivo Histórico Genaro Estrada, Secretaría de Relaciones Exteriores, Mexico City. The columns corresponding to the 1930 and 1950 occupational structures for Mexican workers were prepared by Barrera with the use of data from the U.S. Bureau of the Census. The present author used the occupational data from the second and third sources to prepare the columns for registrants and conscripts. A total of 902 Mexico-born registrants for 1943–1944 constitute the Texas sample used in this study; all of the registration forms included occupational data. The archives at the Southwest Region of the National Archives and Records Administration did not have a count for the number of Mexico-born registrants in other states. The total of 1945 conscripts is 231, after omitting 7 respondents who had missing occupational data. There is no 1940 column because that year's census did not provide comparable occupational data for Mexicans.

period. At the same time, however, Mexicans moved up the occupational ladder at a slower rate than the rest of the workforce, leaving them concentrated in the lower-skilled jobs. Occupational inequality, in other words, persisted despite the upward mobility rate evident among workers, including Mexican workers. The generally better occupational standing of our sample of Mexican registrants and conscripts (relative to the larger Mexican population) suggests that they fared better in making use of mobility opportunities. To state this differently, the draft boards seem to have taken greater notice of Mexicans in the higher-skilled jobs.[19]

The skilled workers registered at rates that exceeded their proportional numbers in 1930 and 1950, while the unskilled, like their less numerous white-collar counterparts, registered at lower rates than their proportional numbers in 1930 and 1950. Skilled workers, in other words, registered to a significantly higher extent than their counterparts and unskilled workers registered at significantly lower levels. The numbers of semiskilled workers who signed up for the military draft were impressive, but only in relation to their representation in the 1930 occupational structure. The recruitment rates, especially when compared with the registration record, also reveal clear patterns.

Although the unskilled represented two-thirds of the entire Mexican workforce in Texas in 1930, and one-half of the registrants and one-half of the total number of workers in 1950, they made up only one-third of the conscripts. The unskilled, in other words, registered for the draft and joined the military at a consistently lower rate than other workers. On the other hand, semiskilled workers and especially the white-collar workers joined at a faster rate than they registered. The skilled workers were the only ones who registered and joined at almost equal rates. We can infer from this that all classes of workers except the unskilled joined the military in numbers that equaled or exceeded their record of registration. The lower rate of induction among the unskilled was especially marked among farm laborers. The 5.2 percentage figure suggests that draft boards were reluctant to call them into military service, possibly because they did not want to deplete the farm labor supply or recruit workers with a lower literacy rate, which was usually associated with farmworkers. The members of the 1.5 generation who were in agriculture also may have entered the military at a lower rate because many of them joined the rural-to-urban migration and escaped the attention of the farmers who often filled positions on rural-based draft boards.[20]

The profile that emerges from the registrant and conscript data is that of an older soldier with longtime residence in the United States who could claim a better-skilled position in the Mexican occupational structure than the typical Mexican national and possibly the usual U.S.-born Mexican. The claim over the U.S.-born might seem exaggerated if we disregarded that the 1930 and 1950 occupational figures included both Mexican nationals and U.S.-born Mexicans and if we did not take into account that the Mexican registrants and conscripts represented the 1.5 generation, the middle group in the process of incorporation. The middle group, which our sample of Mexican nationals represents, may reflect experiences with registration, induction, and occupational mobility that were shared across generations. Higher-skilled Mexicans, in other words, were most probably inducted into the military at a higher rate than their lower-skilled compatriots.

The conscripts in 5 percent of the cases took the opportunity to express their views in the commentary section of the survey questionnaire. Although these twelve conscripts constitute a small portion of the total number of respondents, their comments are reliable sources of information because they reflect similar views expressed in documents authored by Mexicans in the United States archived elsewhere in the Secretaría de Relaciones Exteriores. Also, the respondents may have been more motivated than other Mexican nationals and thus may have provided fuller and more representative accounts. Moreover, they were probably among the more literate.[21]

The comments varied. Some of the respondents spoke about joining the U.S. military as a way to demonstrate that Mexicans supported the worldwide effort against totalitarianism. Some expressed concern that they might lose their Mexican citizenship and asked the embassy to intercede on their behalf, while others embraced the idea of earning their U.S. citizenship. Still others claimed extreme hardship, as they were the sole providers for the families they had left behind. At least one-fourth wrote in English, demonstrating a high level of acculturation more typically associated with second-generation U.S.-born individuals.

Others volunteered opinions about U.S. citizenship. Manuel Bustamante Martínez from El Paso and José Procopio Martínez from Laredo, for instance, announced with a sense of accomplishment that they had become citizens before they joined the military. Private Deodoro Mejía noted that he had naturalized his immigrant status in the military; Private Simón Medrano stated, "My wish is to become a citizen of the United States if possible as soon as I have the opportunity."[22] Private Prisciliano A. Martínez was the only conscript who complained of difficulties in obtaining U.S. citizenship, although he too made his wishes clear. Martínez had unsuccessfully applied for his naturalization on four occasions during his sixteen months in the military. Although the Mexican government could not possibly argue on his behalf, Martínez did not hesitate to express his displeasure: "They cannot yet decide that I am worthy of becoming a citizen of the country."[23]

Some of the conscripts expressed concern that draft boards had disregarded their conditions of hardship when they were called for military service. Private Reynaldo Gonzales Martínez, for instance, claimed that he was the sole provider of a family that included his mother, his wife, and his sister. He was especially concerned that the draft board had not taken into account that he would be leaving his wife with the responsibility of providing for his ill sixty-year-old mother and his blind sister. Private Juan Pablo Melendez also complained that he was "unjustly" inducted, given the death of his father and his position as the sole provider for his elderly mother. Melendez did not contain his anger: "These damned Gringos drafted me after I told them that my elderly mother was losing her eyesight. These damned whites are so terrible."[24]

Antonio Mancilla, residency and rank unknown, offered a more measured view of life in the United States. He criticized racism but acknowledged the need for a united front among the peoples and governments throughout the hemisphere. Mancilla joined willingly and without any rancor against the government. He did, however, blame local authorities "who abuse and trample the constitution . . . , who do not like Blacks or us."[25] Still, Mancilla added that the U.S. government could not be blamed, because the problem of discrimination was "very difficult." The Mexican consuls, on the other hand, should continue working on behalf of their nationals. Mancilla concluded with a patriotic flourish: "If I should lose my life defending the continent on which we live, I ask that my people and my nation unite themselves."[26]

Conclusion

Mancilla's distant and solitary wish from the battlefield of World War II called for a unified continental defense against the Axis powers. The allusion to his own possible death and his previous observations regarding racial prejudice, discrimination, and the Mexican consuls give added meaning to his statement. Mexicans, he seemed to suggest, could build national unity on the basis of the sacrifice of Mexican nationals in the U.S. military and could use this unity on behalf of Mexican rights in the United States. The comments by other conscripts as well as the numerous letters to the Secretaría de Relaciones Exteriores from aggrieved Mexicans in and out of uniform corroborate this view. Although some protested their induction or expressed concerns about serving in the U.S. military, the conscripts and the letter writers consistently embraced the Allied cause and called on the Mexican government to act against discrimination and inequality in the United States. These popular concerns and their corresponding government policies underscore the importance of the war in reshaping Mexican-U.S. relations.

Mexico and the United States repaired their relations primarily as a security measure, but rapprochement also meant that the United States renounced military intervention and established long-term collaborative ties that granted Mexico greater negotiating independence on binational issues. The United States' security concerns and Mexico's impressive cooperation in building the wartime alliance in the Americas were largely responsible for the newfound diplomatic opportunities. This does not mean that relations underwent fundamental change or that the change was limited to security concerns. The United States continued to dictate the general terms of the new state of cooperation, and relations remained relatively unequal between the two countries. On the other hand, the prior history of significant distance and suspicion changed, and Mexican officials used the opportunity to test the limits of the new political freedom, all the while contending with critics in Mexico who questioned these new relations. The case of the 15,000 Mexican nationals in the U.S. military provides a previously unexamined basis for understanding Mexico's balancing act between the general framework of wartime cooperation with the United States and the controversial issue of its nationals serving in a foreign army.

Mexico's wartime commitment to the Allied cause and its pledge to cooperate with the United States compelled it to seek a reciprocal agreement whereby Mexican nationals were made subject to the draft. Mexico was honoring wartime understandings, but other factors at work revealed the limits of the new wartime relations. U.S. officials largely dictated the terms of an unequal agreement with conscription rights that were exercised only by the U.S. military and included offers of U.S. citizenship as inducements to serve. Although there is no evidence that U.S. negotiators intended a one-way route to military service, they knew that Mexico preferred to contribute to the war effort in the area of production and that it most likely would not pursue an independent military option. Also, U.S. officials were clear about requiring that Mexicans serve in the military if they wished to apply for U.S. citizenship and, in effect, renounce their own birthright.

The limits to the new wartime relations were also evident in the relatively higher political price that Mexico paid in justifying the military cooperation, including the reciprocal agreement. Avila Camacho and Padilla had already been harshly criticized for their seemingly quick embrace of the United States and its leadership in the inter-American alliance. The president and his foreign minister were able to secure the necessary support for their plan of cooperation with justifiable claims against an Axis threat and the credible proposal that the war offered a historic opportunity to improve relations with the United States. Mexican officials, however, also reneged on their promise to citizens that Mexicans would never serve in a foreign army. They upset their critics even more during the open debates of 1943 and 1944 when they admitted, albeit reluctantly, that the United States was encouraging Mexicans to give up their citizenship and that the conscripts were facing discrimination in the military.

The Mexican nationals who served in the U.S. military complicated the story of binational cooperation in other ways. Their sheer numbers spoke volumes for support of the Allied cause and the desire to obtain U.S. citizenship. They added their voice to the wartime spirit of cooperation that engulfed the continent at the same time that they seized the opportunity to incorporate themselves further into U.S. society. The abundant response to military service also placed Mexican officials in the difficult position of playing down the large number of Mexican soldiers and their choice of U.S. citizenship while simultaneously seeking to gain diplomatically by claiming the contribution of those soldiers as Mexico's response to the war. The officials' reluctance to disturb national sensibilities led them to insist that the United States either provide data on the conscripts or allow the Mexican government to collect information itself. This demand amounted to a feeble gesture toward appearing independent in an otherwise unequal relationship with the United States.

Although it may suffice to say that intergovernmental relations improved while tensions and inequality remained relatively unchanged, the story would be incomplete without giving closer attention to the Mexican recruits who lived and died on the battlefields of World War II. Their sacrifice makes this act of historical recovery necessary. The findings that emerge from the data on the Mexican soldiers also help us understand that the history of relations between Mexico and the United States involved more than policies emanating from Mexico City and Washington, D.C., and more than the national debates these policies sparked. The new order also included local, ground-level experiences that the policies reflected and reinforced.

There is much that we still do not know about the Mexican soldiers. Until the voluminous records of the Secretaría de Relaciones Exteriores are thoroughly analyzed, we will not know the extent to which the possibility of U.S.

Pete Gallego and Elena Peña Gallego. Courtesy of the
U.S. Latino & Latina World War II Oral History Project.

citizenship or the fear of losing Mexican citizenship influenced them to join
or avoid military service in the United States. We are also unable at this point
to be more precise in suggesting that U.S.-born Mexicans reflected the age
and occupational patterns registered by Mexican nationals. Interviews that
the U.S. Latino & Latina World War II Oral History Project conducted with
veterans like Rudy Acosta, the son of immigrants, and Nicanór Aguilar, the

son of U.S.-born Mexicans, could provide a basis for a more extended generational analysis that includes the notion of the 1.5 generation.[27] The extent to which discrimination affected the lives of the Mexican recruits and their families also calls for more research. Interviews with veterans like Nicanór Aguilar and Felix Treviño, as well as civilians like Elena Peña Gallego and Aurora Estrada Orozco, reveal that the problem was widespread throughout Texas and that Mexicans protested its practice before, during, and after the war.[28]

Mexican recruits spent a relatively long period of time in the United States prior to their military service, and they were moving into higher-skilled jobs when the military called them.[29] The higher proportions of Mexican registrants and recruits above the unskilled ranks, however, suggest that the military was most apt to call up the nonagricultural workers who were living in urban areas. Moreover, agricultural workers with long-term residence in the United States were just as likely as their urban counterparts to serve in the military. The upward mobility and long-term residence characteristics of the Mexican soldiers suggest that recent immigrants were not encouraged to join the military. Reasons may have included a lack of language ability and a strong attachment to Mexico and their Mexican citizenship. We could also infer from these same characteristics that the upwardly mobile, long-term residents may have been more likely to serve in the military because of their greater ability to speak English and because their identification with life and culture in the United States may have blurred their ties with Mexico. Since long-term residence was shared across occupational categories, this may not have been sufficient by itself to set the Mexican nationals on an assimilationist course. When combined with upward mobility, however, Mexican nationals may have been more apt to enter military service.

Conscription, focused as it was on the upwardly mobile, long-term residents, suggests that Mexican nationals may have experienced a "citizenship draft" similar to the "economic draft" that has been offered as an explanation for the increased susceptibility of poor citizens to the financial incentives offered by military recruiters. It also points to military service as a disruption of an ongoing process of upward mobility and social incorporation. For the returning veterans, their foxhole experience, U.S. citizenship, and benefits like the GI Bill may have encouraged greater cultural and structural incorporation. These experiences, still largely unexamined in the scholarship, would have placed them alongside their U.S.-born counterparts who also benefited from military service during this time of war.

6

THE COLOR OF WAR

Puerto Rican Soldiers and Discrimination during World War II

SILVIA ÁLVAREZ CURBELO

The United States is now fighting for Democracy, not only for American Democracy, but for Democracy as a way of life, in all quarters of the earth. The Puerto Rican negroes, true to their responsibility and conscious of their duty to the nation, are ready and willing to share their blood in the supreme effort to defend our Democratic principles; today more than ever, challenged by the totalitarian demagogues. But the Puerto Rican negro, fully conscious of his ability to defend the Democratic ideal, in the same manner that our white soldiers can, have a right to demand, on the base of the same Democratic ideals which he proposes to defend, identical conditions as the white man. —JULIO ENRIQUE MONAGAS, 1942[1]

At the same time that the Allied victory over the Axis powers was being heralded as democracy's triumph over human bondage, Puerto Rican soldiers in the U.S. armed forces were writing to leaders such as Luis Muñoz Marín, the president of the Puerto Rican Senate, with complaints of race discrimination. Letters from angry soldiers stationed in Hawaii complained that even the Japanese prisoners of war fared better than them.[2] In one of those letters, Private Miguel Mateo asked the Senate president to intervene on behalf of hundreds of Puerto Rican soldiers forced to work alongside Japanese prisoners of war in the Honolulu docks and to wash their dirty laundry with the POWs' clothes.[3] Ironically, Mateo's demand was tinged with overtones of racial thinking, which would be consistent with the anti-Japanese sentiment in American mainstream culture during the war years.

Discrimination against Puerto Rican, African American, Mexican American, and other Latino soldiers was prevalent before, during, and after the conflict. In some instances, it reached tragic proportions. Coming home to South Carolina in 1946, a recently discharged Black sergeant was attacked by a racist who gouged the soldier's eyes.[4] In Texas the family of Félix Longoria, a Mexican American killed in the Philippines at the close of the war, was denied use of the local funeral parlor. After the much publicized intercession of Lyndon B. Johnson, the junior senator from Texas, Longoria was buried with full honors at Arlington Cemetery.[5]

No other such case attracted as much public attention for Puerto Rican soldiers in the mainland United States or in the European and Pacific war theaters. However, military files and testimonies from veterans demonstrate a distinct pattern of racial profiling and discrimination against Puerto Rican soldiers during World War II. Given the longtime practice of racial segregation in the U.S. armed forces and an accompanying policy that stood until 1954, it is not surprising that Puerto Rican soldiers also experienced discrimination, especially when sent to the mainland or to the war theaters. It is also clear that their experience remains under-researched.

This chapter examines how scientific jargon and methodologies validated discriminatory and profiling practices toward Puerto Rican inductees during the Second World War. It also examines these practices in light of the Puerto Rican structure of race relations. More generally, the chapter seeks to contribute to a fuller understanding of the relationship between colonialism and racism in Puerto Rican history. An examination of the early history of Blacks and Puerto Ricans in the U.S. military provides the initial backdrop to this study.

The World of Jim Crow

In every war in which this country has participated, Negro Americans have had to fight for the right to fight. At the start of each war, military leaders have questioned the Negro's abilities and finally accepted the Negro participation under the pressure of necessity. Although 920,000 Negroes served in the Army during the Second World War, the Army didn't take most of them until manpower shortages impelled their assistance, using them for menial jobs wherever possible. These men were treated as inferiors in southern training camps. The great majority was used for arduous, dirty work overseas, but they covered themselves with glory just the same. —THURGOOD MARSHALL, 1951[6]

At the onset of World War II, the U.S. armed forces were organized under the protocols of racial exclusion prevalent since the end of the Civil War, generically known as Jim Crow laws.[7] In *Plessy v. Ferguson* (1896), the Supreme Court upheld the validity of these laws and ratified the doctrine of "separate but equal" as a valid basis for structuring race relations in the United States.[8] The court cited as precedent the Army Reorganization Act of 1866, which established separate Negro regiments in the U.S. Army.[9] Military segregation in the nineteenth century reflected a robust racial discourse.

By the end of the 1800s, a number of race theories provided "scientific" legitimacy to the prevailing arguments of Black racial inferiority sustained during the long centuries of slavery.[10] Charles White, a doctor from Manchester, England, tried to demonstrate with anatomical measurements the existence of four human species separated by degrees of perfection: European, Asians, Americans (indigenous people of North and South America), and Africans. Although White opposed slavery, he argued that Black people were more related to apes than the others. He pointed out that Africans had smaller brains and bigger sexual organs, smelled like apes, and could endure more pain.[11]

Racialist theories supported the notion that African American troops were inferior to White units on both mechanical and mental aptitudes. This meant that Black soldiers were to be assigned to domestic chores, maintenance work, stevedoring, and, on a few occasions, transport duties. They were also prevented from assuming frontline combat responsibilities. Out of 380,000 Black U.S. soldiers recruited during the First World War, for instance, only 42,000 ever saw combat.[12]

Black troops also faced an inhospitable reception in their places of training. Southern governors, for example, were fierce in their opposition to the stationing of Black troops in training camps in their states.[13] The governors often argued that Black soldiers would trigger racial disturbances in southern communities and perhaps entertain the idea of treason if shipped overseas. Notwithstanding the patriotic protestations of Black leaders such as W. E. B. Du Bois, the armed forces were reluctant to allow Black troops in the expeditionary force bound for France.[14]

The national dilemma of meeting the needed troop level requirements of the First World War at the same time that racial thinking in the military and society placed restrictions on the use of Black troops became more complicated when Puerto Ricans were granted citizenship and made subject to military service. With the Jones-Shafroth Act of March 1917, Congress granted American citizenship to all residents of Puerto Rico. By virtue of the congressional statute, thousands of Puerto Rican males were eligible for induction into the armed forces. A racially charged debate ensued over the participation of Puerto Ricans in the U.S. military.

Puerto Rico's political relationship with the United States had been the subject of debate since 1898, when the Caribbean island was ceded by Spain. Unlike Cuba and the Philippines—the other Spanish colonies acquired during the Spanish-American War—Puerto Rico had an unclear standing with the United States. The First World War changed this when geopolitical considerations prevailed over racial, cultural, and historical objections and Puerto Rico became an unincorporated territory inhabited by American citizens. The geopolitical expediency, however, did not change the perception of Puerto Ricans as "others," as culturally and racially inferior. During the congressional discussions of the Jones-Shafroth Act, Senator James Kimble Vardaman, of Mississippi, for example, confessed, "I really had rather they [the Puerto Ricans] would not become citizens of the United States. I think we have enough of that element in the body politic already to menace the Nation with mongrelization."[15]

According to Jorge Rodríguez-Beruff, the approval of the Jones-Shafroth Act by Congress in 1917 cannot be understood without taking into consideration U.S. involvement in World War I. The act did more than grant citizenship to Puerto Ricans; it also extended the draft to the island and recruited around 20,000 troops for the war effort.[16] Arthur Yager, appointed by President Woodrow Wilson to serve as Puerto Rico's governor beginning in 1913, denied any connection between the enactment of the legislation and the war. Rodríguez-Beruff, however, contends that the draft was an important reason that U.S. authorities, including Yager, supported granting citizenship to Puerto Ricans.[17]

The application of federal Selective Service laws to the territory of Puerto Rico democratized the military as thousands of racially mixed Puerto Rican males responded to the call to arms. Their presence in the U.S. military, however, set off racial concerns. The lack of suitable training facilities in Puerto Rico and the possibility of sending the troops to the mainland prompted another debate about the racialized identity of the Puerto Ricans. South Carolina was initially considered a possible site for training, but state authorities quickly rejected the idea of establishing a camp for "Negro Troops." The *New York Times* expressed a popular concern over the racial perception of Puerto Ricans and the possibility of conflict: "Porto Rican Negroes . . . are unused to the Southern view of the Negro question and should be mobilized elsewhere."[18]

In order to avoid political embarrassment, government officials decided that the training camps were to be established in Puerto Rico. Yager, concerned with reconciling the issue of segregation in the military with the participation of a new racialized group, put the matter in stark terms: how would the government negotiate the practice of segregation of the Department of War with "our race problem here"? He suggested separate units organized along color lines in part because he was concerned about the "backwardness" exhibited by the fresh recruits:

> Perhaps one-third of these men who will be accepted for service have never worn shoes in their lives; they wear nothing but a cotton shirt and cotton trousers and have nothing else to wear unless it is furnished to them, and when gotten together they will look like a bunch of ragamuffins and tatterdemalions out of which an observer who doesn't know the actual conditions here would think it is utterly impossible to make soldiers. But we know that the contrary is true, as has been abundantly proved by experience with the Porto Rico Regiment. They are good material for soldiers in spite of their looks.[19]

At the same time, Yager was angered by the suggestion made by the governor of South Carolina that all Puerto Rican troops were Black, as it "touches the sensibilities of the White people here."[20]

Camp Las Casas, the new training site in San Juan, Puerto Rico, had separate barracks and separate dining facilities for the Puerto Rico Regiment and two new "colored" regiments that were organized in the spring of 1917. The Puerto Rican troops, officially considered White, were housed separately from Blacks. Only the "White Regiment" (named the Sixty-fifth Infantry in 1920) went overseas; it was stationed in the Panama Canal.[21] The Black units were deactivated after the signing of the armistice in November 1918. The Puerto Rico Regiment returned to the island without performing combat duty.

New War, Old Racism

As in 1917, the Second World War allowed Puerto Rico to assume an important position in the wartime alliance. This time the fall of France and the Netherlands in 1940 and the threat of England's collapse made the Caribbean Basin vulnerable to Germany's ambitions. U.S. authorities feared that German submarines or even a German invasion would target the Dutch, French, and British colonies in the region. The Antilles Military Department could

William L. Hastie, ca. 1965. Courtesy of
the Eisenhower Presidential Library.

not spare continental troops, so Puerto Rican soldiers, specifically National
Guardsmen from the 295th Infantry Regiment, were dispatched to guard oil
refineries and other strategic interests in Trinidad, Aruba, Jamaica, and other
neighboring territories.[22]

At the same time that Puerto Rican troops were being incorporated into
the U.S. military, draft boards in Puerto Rico engaged in what amounted to
a "whitening" process by openly rejecting Black Puerto Rican volunteers or
assigning them to service units. A few Black draftees were serving as ste-
vedores in the local ports or as orderlies in the military camps. However,
the island's racial profiling protocol posed a problem for mainland Selective
Service officers: the "White" category handled by the Puerto Rican boards
did not always conform with the popular version of the term in the United
States. It included Puerto Ricans who were considered "White" on the island
but who would be seen as "colored" elsewhere.

In the meantime, many Black leaders in the United States saw an opportunity in the presidential elections of 1940 to impress upon the candidates

the need to address the racial situation in the armed forces. President Franklin Roosevelt, in urgent need of the Black vote in the northern states, named Benjamin Davis as the first Black general in the armed forces after it was revealed that one hundred less qualified White colonels had been promoted before him.[23] The very same day that Davis was promoted, the president named William H. Hastie, the first Black federal judge, to become a civil adjutant to the secretary of war, in charge of Negro affairs.[24] Although neither of the two appointments overhauled the racial map of the U.S. armed forces, they did have a destabilizing effect on the racial setup in the military, especially in the process of segregating troops according to race in Puerto Rico.[25]

Judge Hastie's Mission

With the war in Europe, the recruitment campaign was intensified. I remember that in 1940 we used to drive around the countryside in trucks with amplifiers and lots of pork chops. People were hungry, and many young peasants would sign in order to bring meat to their families. Poverty was the main motivation to enlist. More than 3,000 men became soldiers in this way. Later, we did not know what to do with them. —SERGEANT MAJOR NICOLÁS CHICLANA[26]

Hastie was convinced that, in matters of race, the civil leadership in the Department of War was captive to the will of the military leadership. Moreover, attempts to assess the racial situation and possibly offer a way out of the segregated order in the military usually resulted in warnings that investigations could jeopardize the war effort. This was evident six days before Pearl Harbor, when the Army Chief of Staff, General George C. Marshall, rejected Hastie's proposal to deploy soldiers without regard to the unwritten policy of racial segregation.[27]

Undaunted, Hastie initiated an in-depth investigation concerning the racial situation in the military. As part of that investigation, in 1942 he discussed with Max Egloff, aide for federal affairs to Puerto Rico governor Rexford G. Tugwell, "the matter of racial segregation in Puerto Rican Army units."[28] Out of those conversations with Egloff, Hastie concluded that there was a concerted view between the military authorities and the Selective Service regarding segregation. In a letter to Governor Tugwell, Hastie stated his views in no uncertain terms: "As I understand the present situation, the military authorities and the Selective Service authorities in Puerto Rico have agreed upon a plan under which Puerto Rican selectees are segregated on the basis of 'white' and 'colored' and placed in organizations accordingly."[29] Concerned about public opinion, Hastie asked for the governor's view on the problem.[30]

Tugwell replied that racial segregation in the island involved more than an understanding between the military and the boards. Authorities also claimed to be representing popular views: "Army and Selective Service headquarters here state that, in practicing racial segregation, they are merely observing an established local custom."[31] Tugwell further complicated things when he added, "Puerto Rican Negroes, so far as I can determine, do not resent segregation. They would be happy with a Negro combat regiment."[32]

Tugwell was a staunch liberal and New Dealer. His appointment as governor in 1941 was welcomed by Puerto Rico's liberal and modernizing Popular Democratic Party (PDP), which dominated both the local Senate and House of Representatives. The party, headed by Luis Muñoz Marín, a journalist and poet, defended a social and economic reform that would uplift Puerto Rico from poverty and stagnation.

The war in Europe provided the Popular Democratic Party with a powerful rhetorical device: reforms for Puerto Rico as a U.S. territory were presented as part of the worldwide struggle of democracy against fascism, social injustice, and exploitation. When President Roosevelt and British prime minister Winston Churchill signed the Atlantic Charter in 1941, the PDP saw it as a validation of Puerto Rico's struggle to change the conditions in the island.[33] The party stalwarts added that racial differences would need to be muted in favor of a united war effort.[34]

The Monagas Report

Despite attempts to minimize racial segregation, the discourse over race and the military emerged as a central point of contention in Puerto Rico. On behalf of Governor Tugwell, Egloff commissioned Julio Enrique Monagas to write a special report on the status of "colored" soldiers in Puerto Rico.[35] Monagas was a mulatto who worked in the Tugwell cabinet as director of sports and recreation and was also an important PDP leader.

Monagas relied on the U.S. Bureau of the Census figures for 1940, which classified 76.5 percent of the 1,869,255 inhabitants of Puerto Rico as White.[36] Monagas then compared those figures with those of the 1899 census, the first one administered by the United States. The "colored" population had represented 38.2 percent of a total of fewer than 1 million. Monagas came to the obvious conclusion that Puerto Rico had undergone a whitening process in the classification process of the federal government. The color line, in other words, was part of the American culture and largely alien to the island.[37]

Monagas followed by stating that Americans had imported racial divisions: "Puerto Rico has been for the last 44 years under the American flag, and for that very same period the Island has been suffering the bitter experience of a pretended racial division."[38] He concluded that the United States was not fully democratic if racism was integral to the American culture, and he warned against the importation of segregation: "To divide the Puerto Rican soldiers in white and colored, to start here a division of races that [has] never existed, to bring to Puerto Rico the racial prejudices existing in the Continent, would constitute a dangerous menace to the stability of the Puerto Rican people."[39]

In the outskirts of the American empire, a "colored" subaltern and colonial subject was questioning the principles of freedom and equality that the United States was proclaiming throughout the world. In the end, however, Monagas embraced the PDP's racial discourse, a reformist ideology whose origins can be traced to the abolitionist thinkers—most of them White creoles—in nineteenth-century Puerto Rico.[40] For the PDP, it was more urgent to promote reforms that would benefit Puerto Rico than to open the racial Pandora's box. Ultimately, Monagas muted his otherwise keen critique of institutional racism.[41]

Despite Monagas' failure to level a consistently strong critique, military authorities sought to discredit his views and to justify segregation. Egloff forwarded the Monagas report to military officials. An unidentified National Guard officer assumed the responsibility of discrediting Monagas' views as biased and racially motivated: "Monagas is a mulatto . . . has strong racial feelings—a case of inferiority complex; has always been conscious of the fact that he is a Negro; not so much a hater of the White man, as a hater of his own fate—of being a Negro."[42]

According to the officer, the report was misleading:

> As to his argument concerning the lack of racial prejudices in Puerto Rico, it is true that we do not have the same situation as in the southern states; it is true that Negroes have the same legal rights as whites, just the same as in the northern states, but *socially* speaking, the real whites, not the mulatto nor the near white, do not mix with them.[43]

In short, most Black Puerto Rican soldiers did not resent being assigned to "colored" units. Actually, they did not want to be integrated into White units. The officer accepted Monagas' conclusion that Black soldiers wanted to be part of combat units, but he added that this was true for many Black educated men with college degrees who sought social recognition and upward mobility.

Governor Tugwell adopted the officer's opinions in his response to Judge Hastie. In practicing segregation, Tugwell argued, the military and Selective Service authorities deferred to local custom. Negro troops in Puerto Rico did not oppose segregation but demanded equal opportunity. Jim Crow segregation in Puerto Rico was thusly legitimized—in a profoundly ironic twist, by local custom. The reformist PDP, the nationalist intellectuals, and the educated mulatto and Black Puerto Ricans such as Monagas were constrained by the "people of Puerto Rico" myth, a galvanizing nationalist discourse during the modernizing decades of the 1940s and 1950s and still a powerful fetish in the present. Tugwell, on the other hand, could not bring himself to challenge the racial order, including the military establishment.

Fitness for Duty

War put a strain on service on the home and war fronts primarily because racial ideas and culturally insensitive administrative rules continued to limit the participation of Puerto Ricans. The fitness of Puerto Rican troops became an especially important point of discussion. It involved numerous investigations by the U.S. Department of War and the Selective Service, commissioned to assess racial intelligence, linguistic proficiency, and military aptitudes among Puerto Rican soldiers. Much of the research was conducted at the University of Puerto Rico.[44] Notwithstanding the urgent need for manpower, the physical standards established during this period—for example, minimum height of five feet four inches and minimum weight of 115 pounds—and the educational minimum of eight grades of schooling put many of the potential Puerto Rican recruits out of consideration.

The differing views of local Selective Service officers and military authorities in Puerto Rico inform the issue of fitness for service. Puerto Rico Selective Service director Harry Besosa, for instance, noted two sources of discomfort among Puerto Ricans on the issue of military recruitment. One was the claim that the military did not make available a combat unit for Black Puerto Ricans. Besosa also noted the popular concern that "Puerto Rico Americans are not being called because they are not considered as good as Continental Americans."[45]

The Puerto Rico Military Department backed the federal prerequisites in part because officials were concerned about maintaining what they considered the high standards that were necessary to successfully prosecute the war. The high standards, however, did not necessarily guarantee the desired goals. Major General Thomas Handy, for instance, on one occasion complained to the commanding general of the Puerto Rico Military Department that the criteria used in the general mobilization of 1940 had resulted in "a large percentage of the peon type soldier" in the Puerto Rican military.[46] Handy favored a War Department policy "whereby the peon type can be released from the Army and the higher type, more intelligent class of Puerto Ricans can be inducted."[47]

Thomas R. Phillips, chief of staff of the Puerto Rico Military Department, explained the lack of "suitable" elements by claiming that local boards practiced favoritism and allowed some influential persons to avoid the draft. He concluded, "All the volunteers whom the Puerto Rican politicians like to talk about are the hookworm infested *jíbaro* or the feisty city slum dweller. At least fifty per cent of them are hardly out of the moron class and not over five per cent of them are fit to be in the Army."[48]

His hope was that the eligible few would satisfy the need for non-combat troops in Africa. He added a racist flourish: "They are hardy and have surprising endurance in a hot climate."[49]

The underlying assumptions that Puerto Ricans did not meet military expectations were also evident in the physical and mental standards that the U.S. military used as pretexts for legitimizing their prejudiced view of Puerto Ricans. In a letter to Governor Tugwell, Phillips expressed the familiar racialized concern over fitness when he recounted a conversation with two military generals who visited the island:

> About three-fifths of the Quartermaster Corps is now Negro, and they have encountered an insuperable problem in training them. They counted on using them for service troops but he said their progress was so slow he was unable to release them to go overseas and as a result they have inadequate service troops available for shipment. Our tests indicate that the mental level of the Puerto Rican is not much different from that of the Negro.[50]

Analogizing such perceptions of Blacks and Puerto Ricans underscored the interrelated nature of the racialization process on the mainland and on the island.

Postwar Assessments

A report on the Puerto Rican Induction Program after the war confirmed that authorities sought to limit the number of Puerto Rican inductees and to restrict troops to noncombat jobs. The report also rationalized this practice: "By the end of 1941, it had become apparent that Puerto Rican troops inducted under U.S. standards were drastically inferior to continental troops. They were inferior physically, mentally, and in other ways."[51] The view that Puerto Ricans were not suitable for combat was also apparent in the stated objectives of the induction program:

> The prime purpose of the Puerto Rican induction program was to obtain full utilization of manpower available in U.S. possessions and territories. . . . In this manner, the total Army strength could be augmented with personnel which, admittedly, was not generally suited for front line duty, but which could be valuable and necessary for their duties and services. Thousands of potential actual combat U.S. continental personnel would thereby be released from secondary services. . . . It served a third purpose in demonstrating to U.S. continental citizens that all available sources for non-father (pre–Pearl Harbor) manpower were being exhausted through Selective Service before fathers were called. . . . Finally, a fourth purpose not directly related to the actual prosecution of the war was to provide employment for many idle Puerto Ricans classified as 1-A.[52]

In another part of the report, the Puerto Rican Induction Program was labeled a "glorified" public works program associated with the New Deal, a "WPA [Works Progress Administration] in uniform." This concept of induction as relief program also appeared in a report by military intelligence:

> The induction of Puerto Ricans in the Army was based on military and political necessity. The use of Puerto Ricans as a general service replacement is limited. Due to his environment and heredity he is inferior in general to the average continental soldier. In addition, the special training he requires renders his utilization uneconomical. It is believed that the Army should contain as small a group of Puerto Ricans as it is politically expedient to employ.[53]

In contrast to these insensitive views, the Third Battalion of the Sixty-fifth Infantry Regiment served in the Maritime Alps combat zone (between Italy and France) during 1944 and 1945 in a way that belies the assumptions of Puerto Rican inferiority held by most of the military brass. The case of Agustín Ramos Calero indicates that Puerto Ricans, backed by strong command, could perform at the highest level. A native of Isabela, he was known as the "One-Man Army" for receiving twenty-two decorations and medals from the U.S. Army for his heroics, becoming the most decorated Puerto Rican soldier of the island and the second most decorated Latino in the U.S. military.

Volunteering in 1941, Ramos Calero was first assigned to the Sixty-fifth Infantry Regiment and later served in other units. The fearless rifleman received the Silver Star, the third-highest category of combat medals that the army awards. Ramos Calero fought against a squad of Nazis in Colmar, France, in 1945, killing ten of them and capturing twenty-one shortly before being wounded himself. During his military service, Ramos Calero also earned four Purple Hearts, a Presidential Citation as a member of a distinguished unit in combat, the European-African–Middle Eastern Campaign Medal with four stars representing his participation in four campaigns, the Army Occupation of Germany Territory Medal, the Victory Medal, the American Campaign Medal, and the Fourragère cord, granted by France to the Third Infantry Division in which he served. The Puerto Rican sergeant was wounded on four occasions and also served in the Korea War. Ramos Calero retired as a sergeant first class in 1962.[54]

Notwithstanding the exemplary conduct of Ramos Calero and many other Puerto Rican soldiers, few U.S. civil and military officers acknowledged their capabilities. One of those few was James Bell, a continental American officer who was stationed in Puerto Rico during the war and served as an English instructor for army recruits. In a letter to Senate president Luis Muñoz Marín, Bell described the prejudice that Americans expressed toward Puerto Rican soldiers:

I am stationed here with a very special group of Americans. It is supposed to be the most intelligent body of soldiers in the Caribbean Defense program. We teach English, four hours a day, to Porto Rican trainees.... What makes an agreeable American so offensive to a human being he does not understand?... We have a first class superiority complex. The custom in large part of the Army has been to call the Islanders, including the Porto Ricans, "gooks."... Such remarks as the following have been recorded from the words of men in my camp:... "They are ungrateful to the United States, too ignorant to take advantage of what we are doing to them. If they had independence, the politicians would knife each other and there would be hell to pay. The mixture of Black and White is bad because it brings down the level of the White race. The chief interests of the Porto Ricans are rum and women. Those who go to study in the States revert to type when they return...." And so one hears quite often, that the Porto Ricans are inferior, disagreeable, diseased, filthy, stupid, odious, contemptible, and not to be associated with even at a distance.[55]

Conclusion

In 1950, when a conflict erupted in Korea, Puerto Rican troops were hurriedly thrown into combat. The Sixty-fifth Infantry Regiment became one of the most effective units in the bloody first year of the war. What had changed for the Puerto Rican soldiers that they suddenly became eligible for combat?

Ingrained ideas about the inferiority of the Puerto Rican soldiers had persisted, but there was a strong resolve on their part to confront prejudice with superior performance. In early 1950 the Sixty-fifth Infantry Regiment was able to defeat the much-decorated Third Division in the Portrex amphibian maneuvers, held in the neighboring island of Vieques. Portrex was the largest amphibious-airborne exercise since the end of the Second World War. The army's Third Division played the "gallant rescuer" in the training exercise, and the Sixty-fifth Infantry acted the role of the "rebel enemy." By the time the war games ended, to the dismay of the Third's top brass and everybody's disbelief, the Sixty-fifth had contained the "invading force" for much of the time.[56] The unit's success earned the attention of General Matthew Ridgway, and when the Korean War started, he was the one who suggested the regiment's deployment.

The Korean War experience exemplifies the complex scenario of race relations within the U.S. armed forces. The performance of the Sixty-fifth Infantry Regiment in that war was impressive during 1950 and 1951, but the unit never received a citation for bravery. The Puerto Rican regiment saved the First Marine Division from extermination by the Chinese in December 1950, but it was the entire Third Division—the Sixty-fifth was one of the three regiments of the division—that received the accolades.

Two years later, when the war in Korea became more chaotic, with hundreds of soldiers dying for the sake of two or three yards of barren land, discrimination and prejudice resurfaced, and the Puerto Rican Sixty-fifth Infantry Regiment, as well as the all-Black Twenty-fourth, were turned into convenient scapegoats. More than ninety Puerto Rican soldiers were court-martialed in a controversial action that was eventually overturned, after an investigation revealed that the non-Latino officers of the Sixty-fifth had cut the Puerto Ricans' special rations of rice and beans and had ordered the men to shave off their mustaches. Such humiliation, in addition to combat exhaustion and the language barrier, contributed to the decision by some of the men of Company L to refuse to continue fighting. The Sixty-fifth was disbanded as an ethnic unit in 1953.[57] The official reason was the gradual, though uneven, phasing out of segregation within the armed forces, one of President Harry Truman's most admired accomplishments.

The Puerto Rican community knew better and hailed the moral resilience of its soldiers, Black and White, in the face of discrimination and prejudice. In a land that was still poverty-stricken, the military career represented for many Puerto Ricans a way out of unemployment and despair. Many of them were young men from the countryside or small towns. They saw military service as a path to a better future and fought their hearts out to provide for their typically large and poor families. The wartime performance of the Puerto Rican soldier, however, was also an example of *dignidad*, perhaps one of the most important concepts in the Puerto Rican cultural idiosyncrasy—a mixture of pride, courage, bravery, self-respect, and patriotism.

The soldiers of the Sixty-fifth genuinely believed that they were fighting for freedom and democracy, as Puerto Rican governor Muñoz Marín had told them when he bid them good-bye. Today the veterans of the Sixty-fifth, many with tears in their eyes and broken voices, still cherish the regimental colors, but they also recall with sadness and disbelief the prejudiced color of war.

AUTHOR'S NOTE: To my grandfather, Eduardo Curbelo Brito, a soldier with the Puerto Rico Regiment that served in Panama during the First World War.

7

GOD AND WAR

The Impact of Combat upon Latino Soldiers' Religious Beliefs

REA ANN TROTTER

World War II correspondent Ernie Pyle's adage, "There are no atheists in foxholes," acknowledges soldiers' entreaties to God while under the duress of battle and the threat of death. While the accuracy of Pyle's comment is debatable, veterans' narratives, army chaplaincy reports, and wartime soldier surveys substantiate his observation. León Leura, combat engineer with the Thirty-sixth Division and veteran of the Salerno and Anzio battlefields, for instance, recalled, "Many soldiers attended church services that never attended before."[1] World War II chaplains likewise noted that soldiers and sailors on combat duty attended church services and conferred with chaplains at higher rates than their stateside counterparts.[2] The immediate effect of combat upon servicemen's religious practices is well documented and convincing, but the enduring impact on their spirituality has received negligible attention.

Spirituality among Latinos

Spirituality and faith traditionally have formed fundamental facets of Latino lives and identity. Catholicism, particularly popular Catholicism, has wielded a "tremendous influence in shaping Mexicans' and Mexican Americans' religious, cultural, and social lives," according to Arlene Sánchez Walsh in

"The Mexican American Religious Experience."[3] Noted theologian Orlando O. Espín wrote that popular Catholicism not only represents the most widely practiced form of Catholicism in Latino culture but also is "a key matrix of all Hispanic cultures." It is from this cultural context that people acquired the tools and abilities to identify, interpret, and express their experiences, especially with the divine.[4] Thus, the veterans' religiosity is essential in studying their responses to war. Religious references are common throughout veterans' narratives, yet the subject of war and spirituality remains conspicuously sparse in Latino historiography of the World War II era.

This chapter examines the long-term spiritual effects of combat among eighteen Latino veterans. The memories of these men, conveyed through eighteen oral and documentary narratives, revealed that World War II produced a significant and lasting influence upon their religious attitudes. Four themes resonated consistently throughout the narratives. First, all of the veterans expressed moral and spiritual concerns about killing. Second, all reported that praying mollified the degenerative effects of fear, grief, and horror. Third, their faith in God increased as a direct consequence of their combat experiences. Fourth, they sought a meaning and purpose for their survival.

Violence and Religion

The veterans' thoughts associated with the act of killing are central to this discussion because of the combat soldiers' paradoxical situation. American social mores and religious beliefs across denominations condemn violence and killing. Yet most denominations also promote such actions as moral and patriotic duties for servicemen. The Bible commands people, "Thou shalt not kill," but killing under certain conditions is sanctified by church and state. Archbishop Charles Chaput of Denver, Colorado, explains: "Deliberate killing of the innocent or defenseless, even in war, is always gravely wrong. But in the Catholic tradition, killing in combat can be legitimate as an extension of the right to self-defense and the defense of others."[5]

George Wickersham II, a protestant chaplain who served with the marines in the Pacific theater, told soldiers concerned about killing, "We who were defending our rights and the rights of others were not transgressing God's law." World War II chaplain Elisha Atkins believed that combat soldiers were more concerned with survival than spiritual dilemmas inherent in killing: "For nearly half of them the so-called 'religious problem' did not exist, either in respect to outward observance, or inward speculative and moral dilemmas."[6] Atkins, however, did not speculate on how these "religious problems" bothered the other half.

Survival was a primary concern of servicemen who lived amid the pervasiveness of death—of their fellow soldiers, of civilians, and of enemy combatants—as well as fear of their own death. However, in spite of death's constant presence, Joe F. López, a veteran of Patton's Third Army, Eightieth Infantry Division, stated, "You never *really* get used to it."[7] Neither could the men completely inure themselves from the strain of killing other human beings, even the enemy. Survival did not negate soldiers' spiritual apprehensions about killing. "Killing is what war is all about," Lieutenant Colonel Dave Grossman wrote in *On Killing*, "and killing in combat, by its very nature, causes deep wounds of pain and guilt."[8] Soldiers' accounts attest to the veracity of Grossman's words.

Even before entering combat, Charles Trujillo, lead scout for the Twenty-fourth Infantry Division, struggled spiritually: "My biggest conflict was with religion, 'Thou shall not kill.' . . . Oh, it worried me a lot! I worried *a lot*. How do you go and kill somebody?"[9] Ceprian Armijo of the Eighty-ninth Division also was bothered by thoughts of killing others and took steps to blunt his role: "I took mortars instead of the machine guns and the rifles . . . because I didn't know what I was hitting."[10] The burden of killing usually struck soldiers during their first combat experiences, as illustrated by a Latino veteran of the Second Infantry Division: "I remember the first person I killed, the first German. I went up to him and turned him over, hoping that he would still be alive, but he wasn't. He was a young guy just like me. I was twenty. He was maybe twenty or twenty-two. I got sick to my stomach. It's crazy! You shoot to kill, and then you hope— but that is the way it is."[11]

The remorse and repugnance toward killing hit others after the war. Tony Olivas fought his way from the battlefields of Italy through Germany as a forward observer and faced no issues with killing. Yet, upon arriving home to rural Colorado, he found himself unable to assist his father in slaughtering the family farm animals. "You don't want to kill," he explained.[12] The recriminations came decades later for Ernest Montoya, who had no qualms during the war about having killed enemy Japanese: "You do a lot of thinking after you get out. . . . These killings bother me. Combat. I think about that. You know, I'm a Catholic—the Ten Commandments. . . . I wonder what That Guy's going to tell me when I go meet him. Hey! I think about that."[13]

To reconcile their religious beliefs with their combat roles, several soldiers placed killing within the frameworks of duty, work, and survival. Prior to entering the service, Salvador Valadés carefully considered his duties to

Richard G. Candelaria, 1944. Courtesy of the U.S.
Latino & Latina World War II Oral History Project.

Tony Olivas, 1943. Courtesy of the U.S. Latino &
Latina World War II Oral History Project.

his country and to God with his mother's reminder, "The Fifth Command-
ment teaches us not to kill." He said, "I could not be a conscientious objector
but felt that it was our duty to defend our country."[14] Reflecting on his combat experiences with the Ninety-fourth Infantry Division, Valadés wrote
that he did not "struggle spiritually with World War II," but he expressed
doubt about other wars: "I think we can all agree that war is unnecessary and
a complete waste. However, when a country is faced with the situation that
faced this country during World War II, we were left no alternative but to
defend ourselves and others."[15]

Equating combat missions and actions with job assignments also eased
the "guilt that might otherwise distress combat soldiers" who were involved
in killing, Gerald Linderman wrote in *The World within War*.[16] Dennis Baca,
who served with an antitank platoon in the Americal Division, said he cried
for the Japanese soldiers he killed: "I know I killed a lot of them. I hate to say
it, but it was our job."[17] Fighter pilot Richard Candelaria explained, "That's
why the training is so important. You do things automatically without hav-

ing to think about them."[18] He always framed killing in combat as "doing a job."[19] It was his job to defend bombers while on escort duty, to deplete enemy resources, to engage and destroy the enemy, and to defend himself and his fellow fighter pilots.

Ultimately, soldiers did not fight for God, country, ideology, hatred of the enemy, or even because it was their job. They killed so others would not kill them. "Self-preservation," Ernest Montoya, a veteran of the 127th Infantry Division, concluded. "That is combat in a nutshell."[20] Common among many soldiers, Charles Trujillo's hesitation about killing quickly changed when he first experienced combat: "When you're over there, and they're shooting at you, it doesn't take you long to stop your reservations—survival!"[21] Even within the context of survival, killing inflicted moral pain, as one Latino veteran with the Second Infantry Division described: "I killed a lot of Germans. . . . You tell yourself that you *have* to do it. It is either him or me. You tell yourself anything that works. But still, I killed other people. It hurts. It's a terrible thing to have to kill. You can't understand it unless you were there. And then you have to live with that."[22]

Trujillo typified the manner in which many soldiers and veterans dealt with their spiritual uncertainties about killing: what was done could not be undone, and one had to face whatever consequences might come. "When you go to war, you break about all [or] at least half of the Ten Commandments," he said. "Somebody's got to pay. . . . So come Judgment Day, somebody will have to answer. . . . Somebody is responsible. Maybe me. Maybe the government."[23]

As the veterans' narratives revealed, remorse and moral guilt about killing is a common consequence even years after the event. It is, according to William P. Mahedy, a Vietnam War chaplain and now a posttraumatic stress disorder (PTSD) counselor, "an appropriate response."[24] Regardless of the justness of any particular war, Mahedy wrote, soldiers' religious intuition senses that even though "killing enemy soldiers amounts to legitimate self-defense in a combat zone, something about it is very wrong."[25]

Reliance upon Prayer

The second theme in veterans' war narratives is their reliance upon prayer in combat. Wartime surveys of more than half a million servicemen, published in the two-volume reference book entitled *The American Soldier*, revealed that 83 percent of enlisted men in the front lines said the use of prayer helped them cope with combat to a greater extent than the usual motivations

Joe F. López. Courtesy of the U.S. Latino & Latina
World War II Oral History Project.

(not letting their fellow soldiers down; getting the job done and going home;
hatred of the enemy; and ideological reasons).[26] Soldiers realized that skills,
superior numbers, ammunition, and arms could not ensure they would make
it home alive. Soldiers depended on each other for survival, but even this
seemed tenuous as Joe F. López pointed out: "By the end of the war, out of
my battalion that first went over together, only five came back with me—out
of about 1,500 men."[27] Fellow soldiers were wounded, killed, or rotated out,
leaving men to draw upon personal resources. Luck ran out, one's number
came up, and no earthly entity could change that, so men turned to God to
contain their fears, to spare their lives, and to provide consolation amid the
ugliness of war.

The American Soldier also indicated that the use of prayer increased as the
levels of danger and fear escalated.[28] Combat induced a "paralyzing fear" in
men, according to Chaplain Atkins, "the animal fear, direct and physical,
which comes over all creatures when they know they are in danger."[29] López
remembered that kind of fear during an artillery attack in France: "I broke

down and cried once. I'm not afraid to admit that. . . . I had to learn to control my fears. If you can do that, you can do anything."[30] The best weapons, plans, and skills were of no use if soldiers could not overcome their fears, and praying was one way to manage those fears. Salvador Valadés recalled solders relying heavily upon prayer to "face the daily dangers of death. . . . Even those who had never prayed before prayed."[31] Epifanio Salazar, a paratrooper with the Eighty-second Airborne Division, affirmed this. During his first combat jump—into Sicily in 1944 at age seventeen—he recalled seeing the Germans "running everywhere and firing at us." Praying prior to exiting the plane pushed aside his fears of combat and death: "[Then I could] just think about doing my job. Jump. That's it."[32]

Men prayed just to "make it through the day," according to Frank Arellano, a Pearl Harbor survivor. "You just hoped and prayed."[33] Ernest Montoya recalled, "Everybody said his little prayer to himself."[34] Chaplain Atkins observed that "men had little recourse except prayer" when they faced combat situations in which neither action nor "any earthly help" would save them.[35] Salvador Valadés' and José Martínez' experiences illustrated this. During an attack on a wooded, hilltop fortification in Germany, Valadés was shot in the chest and left alone while his fellow soldiers continued the advance to stop the gunfire. He crawled behind a tree and gripped his M-1 rifle tightly to defend himself against a more direct German attack. When bullets hit just above his head, he "prayed to God for help."[36] Valadés believed his prayers were answered when a medic arrived to assist him. José Martínez, who served with the 200th Coast Artillery Corps, also confronted death when American troops surrendered to the Japanese in the Philippines. Martínez stood with his fellow soldiers, hands secured behind their backs with wire, and eyes staring down the barrels of enemy machine guns. He recalled that his body turned so cold that the tears falling upon his chest felt like burning matches on his skin. Preparing for death, he prayed while waiting for the burst of machine-gun fire. Inexplicably, the Japanese captors abruptly turned the Americans away from the guns and herded them to a collection point, where they began the Bataan Death March.[37] There seemed no earthly reason why they were not shot, verifying to Martínez the protective hand of God.

Soldiers prayed not only so that God would spare their lives; praying also had a soothing effect. Joseph Autobee, top turret gunner with the 448th Bomb Group, prayed for calmness and courage in the face of death during each mission. Just as his B-24 closed in on its target, he recited the Twenty-third Psalm.[38] Medic William Ornelas of the 101st Airborne experienced the

Epifanio Salazar, 1943. Courtesy of the U.S. Latino
& Latina World War II Oral History Project.

power of another kind of prayer during the Battle of the Bulge on Christmas Eve, 1944, in a little Catholic church. The church, dimly lit with candles, was a collection point for those wounded in the battle. Wounded men crowded the interior and even lay on the frozen ground outside the church, set apart from the dead. The cries and moans of the suffering soldiers filled the church. The constant flow of casualties soon depleted the supplies of medicine and bandages, leaving Ornelas and his fellow medics and nurses with no means of assisting the men, aside from giving them sips of water. In the midst of this anguish and helplessness, a French nun moved to the altar and began singing "Silent Night." A quiet calm descended.[39]

Soldiers believed that the prayers of family, friends, the faith community, and fellow soldiers enhanced their own supplications and were factors in their survival.[40] Salvador Valadés, for example, wrote that his mother's prayers helped him more than anything else. As each of her sons left for the service, she followed the same ritual: "She would ask us to kneel in front of her. She would make a sign of the cross on our foreheads with her thumb.... I felt blessed." Valadés knew he was in his mother's constant prayers: "She had great faith in God and felt that we would survive this experience somehow and that we would someday be home again."[41] Combat veteran Fred Vigil served in the navy on an army personnel transport ship during World War II and in the army with the Seventeenth Infantry Regiment during the Korean War. Throughout both wars, his mother prayed for him and kept his picture with her statues of saints. Whenever he came home on leave, "the first thing she would make me do is to kneel, and then she'd pray over me." It must have worked, Vigil concluded: "I made it through World War II without even being wounded."[42] Airman Joseph Autobee also believed that the prayers of others helped him survive the war unscathed. He told the story of his grandmother promising God to make a pilgrimage with her grandsons if their lives were spared. Both boys came home alive, and the family believed her prayers had been answered. Autobee's grandmother kept her promise and completed her pilgrimage with seemingly supernatural timing, because "right after that, she passed away."[43] Historian and Korean War combat veteran Ruben Moreno recalled that in his hometown of Tucson, Arizona, soldiers' mothers formed prayer meetings during World War II and the Korean War. His mother attended these meetings when her two sons were called to active duty during the wars: "All the Mexican mothers would promise *mandas*, take a penance to go to San Xavier Mission to light a candle for their sons, or carry out a vigil at St. Augustine Cathedral."[44] All three boys survived their wars. According to author Gilberto M. Hinojosa, "priests discouraged

William Ornelas, ca. 1945. Courtesy of the U.S. Latino
& Latina World War II Oral History Project.

the faithful from taking vows of this kind."[45] Even without the priests' sanctification, the practice persisted because the people believed in the power of *mandas* and *promesas* (promises).

Soldiers also prayed for each other, especially upon witnessing an injury or death of their fellow soldiers, according to *The American Soldier*.[46] José Martínez recalled that he and his fellow prisoners of war would "get together" and "pray the rosary" for their recovery when men were sick or injured or for their souls when they died. Martínez added that sometimes they prayed for a quick death. He related an incident when the Japanese chained a young Italian American prisoner spread-eagled between two posts. For two or three days he remained strung up in the compound while the captors "would go by and put cigarettes out on him, slap him, or hit him with a bayonet." It was "a very, slow death," Martínez recalled. "I can still hear him holler."[47] Finally the prisoners' prayers were granted, and death released the young soldier from his torment. The soldiers were powerless to do anything except pray.

Faith Forged in Battle

The abiding belief in the power of prayer was linked to a third theme in the Latino narratives: the deepening of their spirituality, their faith in God. León Leura wrote that "many soldiers change their belief in God" because of combat.[48] One war chaplain also observed that "every man, deep underneath, believes in God," but it often took "a crisis in his life to transform this belief into a living faith."[49] At the conclusion of the war, 79 percent of combat veterans surveyed in *The American Soldier* study stated that their military experiences had increased their faith in God.[50]

Many veterans' narratives corroborate León Leura's statement: "Someone up above was watching over me."[51] Their memories of pivotal, mystical experiences vivify God's direct intervention in their lives. For José Martínez, one of these events occurred when he was interned at Camp O'Donnell, a Japanese prisoner-of-war camp in the Philippines. His chronic dysentery was so bad that he was not expected to live. Consequently, he was moved to Zero Ward, where the sick were taken to die. With no medicine available, the medics could do little except watch over the patients until they died and take the men's clothes off when it was time to carry the dead out for burial. As Martínez hovered between life and death, he realized that a priest was by his side, talking softly to him, praying for him, and giving him last rites. Some time later, Martínez awoke, alert and feeling much better. He looked

León "Jack" Leura. Courtesy of the U.S. Latino &
Latina World War II Oral History Project.

around, realized where he was, and hollered at the medic, "I'm not going to
die!" To his knowledge, he was the only one who left Zero Ward alive. With
no doubts, he stated, "I'm telling you, it was a miracle. . . . I thank God I'm
alive."[52] Salvador Valadés also experienced an event that changed the course
of his life and strengthened his Catholic faith. Valadés said that he can never
forget the morning of 13 March 1945. Shot and alone, he felt for the rosary
his mother had placed around his neck just before he shipped out for overseas duty and realized "the crucifix was severed from the rosary." The medic
who eventually came to his aid noticed his concern, reached into his pocket,
and gave Valadés his rosary. "To this day," Valadés asserted, "I pray for him
and others, including Our Blessed Mother who I felt saved my life by having
the crucifix deflect the bullet enough to miss my heart. This experience has
made me more devoted to Mary, through her rosary, and I have tried to promote it in any way that I can."[53]

Richard Candelaria, a P-51 fighter ace, reported that combat rekindled his
Catholic beliefs and practices. Candelaria was a lone fighter pilot escorting

a crippled B-17 out of enemy airspace. Running dangerously low on fuel, he attempted to land at Brussels, Belgium, the closest airfield in Allied hands. Barrage balloons, however, were already up for the night, so he turned away in search of another airstrip.[54] Dense, low clouds and diminishing daylight exacerbated an already precarious and deteriorating situation. With his gas gauge needle bouncing on empty, ground control advised him to bail out immediately. However, something compelled him to stay on course and start praying, "Hail Mary, full of grace, the Lord is with thee. . . . Holy Mary, Mother of God, pray for us sinners now and at the hour of our death." Candelaria vividly recalled that as soon as he finished his prayer, a hole appeared in the cloud cover:

> Right underneath it was some sort of an airfield. . . . I touched down and landed. The engine was still turning over, so I taxied around . . . and all of a sudden, "Bump!" It stopped! . . . What a day! When you stop and think about it—out of that entire area of France, Belgium, Germany, Holland—one hole in the clouds, and there's an airfield under it![55]

Candelaria had been experimenting with different religions and had not been attending church services regularly. "But on that day in the clouds," he said, "I got my answer. . . . Somebody told me something: 'You were born a Catholic, you grew up a Catholic—you're a Catholic!' That's the way I felt from then on." He commented that many would interpret this event as happenstance, certainly remarkable but not evidence of divine intervention. He disagreed. "I don't believe it was just a coincidence," he stated. "One thing war taught me was to . . . always have faith."[56]

Martínez' and Candelaria's extraordinary spiritual experiences strengthened their faith in God, a common occurrence according to the aforementioned *American Soldier* study. Nonetheless, only 29 percent of the servicemen stated they became more religious as a result of their wartime experiences.[57] During the war, chaplains noticed this difference between men's faith and their attitudes toward organized religion. After visiting European battlefronts throughout 1941 and 1943, clergyman Dan Poling expressed concern about the "overwhelming indifference to organized religion." He found combat soldiers "sought fundamentals of faith" rather than formal church participation, and he wondered if civilian churches "would have a faith as vital as that found by men flying the lonely skies or fighting in the foxholes."[58] The experiences of trauma psychiatrist Larry Decker in counseling combat veterans verified Poling's concerns. "Survivors turn away from organized religion because it is not personalized," Decker wrote in "Including Spirituality." If deep, spiritual teaching and understanding are not provided, "the gap between the survivor's inner torment and adequate living" widens, "alienating many veterans."[59]

Charles Trujillo addressed the matter directly and clearly: "I was born and raised a Catholic, but I'm a poor Catholic compared to what I was. . . . I think it [war] made me less religious." Throughout his youth, his mother demonstrated faithful devotion and church attendance, and she expected the same of her children. But the war changed that for Trujillo. In combat, he explained, it was just God, Mother Earth, and him. During artillery attacks, for example, all a soldier could do was pray and burrow as deeply into the earth as possible: "There's nothing stronger than the earth. Ships, planes, boats, anything— they're all stopped by Mother Earth." Although Trujillo remained Catholic out of respect for his parents and his heritage, neither church attendance nor practices inspired the kind of spiritual connection he felt with nature as God's creation. He recalled a hunting trip to the Gunnison Valley of Colorado with this in mind:

> In the morning when we got up, it was really snowing. . . . We were walking along in the timber before we got out in the open. Here's this big view. As far as we could see, beautiful, white snow. The sun was just breaking. . . . That's heaven! That makes you realize what you are on this earth. Nothing! Not even a speck of dust. . . . Real beauty. That's what you get from war. At least I did. . . . [Me and God]—that's the way with me.[60]

According to World War II chaplain William D. Cleary, soldiers wanted to believe in God and hear about "a God great enough and good enough to take care of them" rather than hear "good advice about the details of conduct."[61] Men such as Joe F. López craved faith, not rules and orders: "I'm a Catholic—by words. On Easter I go to church. I don't want *no one* telling me when to go to church. I go when I want to." López' attitude toward priests also changed during the war: "I respected them, but I knew they were human. . . . I didn't know that before. That was a big step for me."[62] Viewing priests as men relaxed his sense of veneration toward them and his deference to the church, but at the same time it strengthened and individualized his belief in God.

Faith formed a fundamental aspect of the Latinos' lives even if they were not "the average Mass and sacraments" Catholics, according to author Jeffrey Burns in "The Mexican Catholic Community in California."[63] Catholicism provided the foundation for the veterans' spirituality, but war was the crucible that clarified and solidified their faith. This faith, however, was born of unprecedented suffering. Chaplain Elisha Atkins warned that an attempt "to atone for the horrible irrationality of war by insisting that it breeds religious faith is nothing short of intellectual dishonesty."[64] No one emerged from combat unscathed, and all experienced what William Mahedy has described as the "ultimate degradation of the spirit."[65]

Luis Pineda, a combat veteran of the Korean and Vietnam wars and now a lay minister for El Sendero de la Cruz Church, was well acquainted with this spiritual crisis that combat had created: "I probably killed five hundred men with the quad .50s in Korea at long range. Killing is killing, and I know I did killing. But the Lord tells us, 'Thou shalt not kill.'" Doctors could heal the physical wounds, he explained, but only God could heal the spiritual wounds. Pineda focused his present-day ministry on veterans, counseling them to confess everything to God, an act that required accepting responsibility for all one's actions and thoughts, an essential first step in spiritual healing. "You need to heal your heart," he said. "You need to heal your spirit. You need to renew your mind. . . . The Lord will forgive you. The Lord will never leave you. The Lord will always love you. . . . This is what I experienced, and it is the experience that a lot of GIs don't have."[66] According to Pineda, the next step was forgiveness—forgiving oneself and others (including enemy combatants)—and seeking God's forgiveness. These steps would facilitate the integration of veterans' combat experiences with their spiritual beliefs.

Samuel Smith, a Navajo code talker, confirmed that veterans must address the spiritual damages from war or risk suffering from a host of problems such as alcoholism and PTSD.[67] Counselor Mahedy stressed that a "theological grasp of the problem is a necessary adjunct to PTSD therapy for veterans."[68] Native American cultures understand this and conduct lengthy religious ceremonies to cleanse and heal the spirits of veterans from the contagion of war. One aspect requires veterans to relate their war experiences. Smith spent three days telling three medicine men everything he thought, did, and saw during the war. "You can't leave anything out," he said. "Then the story is out of you." He added, "Some guys never did that, and they are walking around the streets and having troubles still today."[69] Latino World War II veterans likewise sought spiritual healing. However, instead of turning to formal institutions such as the church or the Veterans Administration, they often found care from *curanderos/as*, some of whom were believed to possess spiritual powers enabling them to intervene with God and the saints on the people's behalf.[70]

A Higher Purpose

The fourth theme evident in veterans' narratives is the need to understand their experience and to develop some purpose and meaning for the enormity of suffering that World War II produced. Gabriel Valadés, a veteran of the 78th "Lightning" Division, conceded the necessity of the war but concluded that it "cost this country and others millions of dollars and wasted millions upon millions of human lives." He added, "Nobody won anything. And everybody lost something. And how do you explain to a family that lost a son or a daughter that our country won the war? Ask God to explain it to them. He's the only one who can."[71] Despite the seemingly impossible task, Holocaust survivor and psychologist Viktor Frankl maintained that it was imperative for survivors to ask: "Has all this suffering, this dying around us, a meaning? For if not, then ultimately there is no meaning to survival. For a life whose meaning depends upon such a happenstance—as whether one escapes or not—ultimately would not be worth living at all."[72]

Father Phillip G. Salois, a Vietnam veteran and PTSD counselor, explained that combat veterans possessed "a unique perspective on the meaning of life" and that "their suffering is not meaningless but can be redemptive."[73] Similarly, in their search for meaning after the war, Latino veterans acquired a sense of purpose and a desire to help others. And in doing so, they were taking another step in healing their spiritual wounds.

José Martínez saw his survival as a gift from God: "I should have died during the war. Every day since has been a gift."[74] His experiences, especially those in the prisoner of war camps, deepened his belief in God and his devotion to his faith, his family, and his circle of friends and established his priorities for the rest of his life: "I have my God. I have my wife, my family, my friends. . . . I don't have money, and I don't give a dang about it! That's it. . . . That's richness! You can't buy a family, you can't buy a friend, you can't buy God. . . . What more could I want? I don't care for anything else." Those who died remained in Martínez' memories: "I think about those other kids. They were so nice. They never made it. How come I made it? I don't know. Only God knows how or why." He added that since most people could not begin to imagine what the war was like or the suffering that soldiers endured, especially the prisoners of the Japanese, perhaps he had been spared "so I can tell my story."[75]

After the war, Richard Candelaria and Carlos Samarrón both resolved to make meaningful contributions to society. Ever cognizant of his experi-

Carlos "Charles" Guerra Samarrón. Courtesy of the
U.S. Latino & Latina World War II Oral History Project.

ence in the cockpit of his P-51 and as a prisoner of war, Candelaria has tried
to live his life more deliberately and to "try to do some good in the world in
some manner." He especially attempted to convey these goals through his
family life and his work as a businessman.[76] Samarrón, a veteran of the Third
Marine Division, also entered civilian life with a determination to better the
lives of people, especially Mexican Americans. For thirty years he worked
at the Equal Employment Opportunity Commission, ensuring that Latino
naval personnel were treated equitably. He also worked with other American GI Forum members to assist Mexican American veterans in finding jobs
and securing job training.[77]

The war instilled in Salvador Valadés the need "to get along with your
fellow man, serve your country as necessary, and, at the same time, serve
God." He believed that God had given him the gift of life, "a second chance,"
and that "what I do with it will be entirely up to me."[78] This gift was not to
be squandered or taken lightly. He noted that he had not been a particularly
good soldier, he had no wife or children at the time, and surely there were

men more deserving of life, yet he had been spared. Even after sixty years of searching and recalling the death of his soldier brother Vincent shortly after the war, Valadés wrote, "At times I still wonder 'Why me?' But I have concluded that ... my combat experience was a gift from God that has helped me in my ministries in serving Him."[79]

The veterans' pursuit of meaning and purpose illustrates Mahedy's conclusion that spiritual recovery from the ravages of combat necessitated a life transformation. Rather than being instruments of death, the veterans became bearers of life.[80]

Conclusion

The war altered the religious attitudes of Latino soldiers and the direction of their lives. Their very survival, coupled with their spiritual experiences during the war, convinced them of the power of prayer and the possibilities of divine intervention, leading to a lasting, deeper faith in God. Nevertheless, "combat raised fundamental questions of meaning for all involved," Archbishop Chaput wrote.[81] When is killing moral? What is my duty to God? What is my duty to my country? Why am I alive? Was the war worth it? Definitive answers to such questions proved elusive and would affect soldiers' perception of themselves, their roles in society, and their worldview. Their lifelong search for understanding, meaning, and purpose would reverberate beyond themselves and their families to postwar American society.

8

SILENT WOUNDS

Posttraumatic Stress Disorder and Latino World War II Veterans

RICARDO AINSLIE & DAPHNY DOMÍNGUEZ

The participation of Latinos in military service during World War II had profound effects in many areas of their lives. Some had experiences that left indelible marks, not all of them positive. The men who served on the battlefield returned to their spouses, families, and friends as different men. In this chapter we describe what these men faced after their return, as well as their struggles with reintegration. We address a significant subset of Latino World War II veterans who experienced posttraumatic stress disorder (PTSD), and we use data from the U.S. Latino & Latina World War II Oral History Project to illustrate the powerful ways in which such emotional scars also affected the veterans' relationships with their spouses, children, and others.

PTSD in History

The observation that war takes an enormous psychological toll on those who serve in the military has a long history. With respect to American servicemen and -women, reports of the emotional impact of combat service go back at least as far as the Civil War, when the war's psychological scars were termed "soldier's heart." Such symptoms have been given different names in each subsequent war: "shell shock" in World War I, "war neurosis" in World

War II, "combat fatigue" in the Korean War, and, most recently, following the Vietnam War, "posttraumatic stress disorder" (PTSD), a designation that has continued to be in use through the Gulf War, the conflict in Somalia, and combat in Afghanistan and Iraq.[1]

Like all wars, the Second World War brought immense emotional hardship to the American men and women who fought, as well as to those family members who remained behind. Latinos went to war in unprecedented numbers in Europe and in the Pacific theater, as well as in some of the lesser-known theaters, and many distinguished themselves by their contributions. Following the war, many Latino veterans returned home to new opportunities, and some were empowered by their wartime experiences to struggle for full rights as American citizens. Other contributors in this volume address the implications of these important developments for Latino identity, political organization, and language, among a variety of other issues. Less well known, however, since these struggles have been underreported and underacknowledged, is that the war took a heavy emotional toll on the lives of many of the veterans and their families.[2] Specifically, Latinos showed greater lifetime generalized anxiety, alcohol use and drug dependence, readjustment difficulties, and marriage problems than did other veterans.[3]

Posttraumatic Stress Disorder: The Syndrome

PTSD has become recognized in unprecedented ways as a psychological disorder affecting 10 to 15 percent of those who experience combat.[4] The experience of Vietnam veterans, in particular, played a key role in helping mental health professionals and others, including Veterans Administration personnel and especially veterans' families, understand the psychological cost often paid by soldiers who are exposed to combat and the horrors of war.

PTSD is the development of characteristic and persistent symptoms, along with difficulty in functioning, after exposure to a life-threatening experience.[5] The American Psychiatric Association classified this syndrome as a disorder for the first time in 1980 and published criteria for it that year in the *Diagnostic and Statistical Manual of Mental Disorders*, third edition (DSM-III). Since this original classification, the criteria for PTSD have evolved as informed by research and clinical work with patients afflicted with the disorder. The evolution of a common language for PTSD also reflects changes in how it has been understood and how treatment has evolved as a result.[6] The classification criteria for PTSD allowed patients and health providers to use common conventions when speaking about the phenomenon. Patients present the symptoms most commonly after incidents such as military combat, sexual assault, motor vehicle accidents, or any event witnessed or experienced that threatens the life of an individual.[7]

The symptoms that result in PTSD are varied, but they can have a pervasive impact on a veteran's life following combat experience. These symptoms include sleep disorders, hypervigilance and paranoid thinking, chronic flashbacks, and intrusive thoughts.[8]

There is often a powerful need to blunt the emotional impact of the traumatic events, resulting in alcohol and drug abuse, for example, or in psychic numbing.[9] At the same time, veterans suffering from PTSD may become thrill seekers and otherwise sensation seekers following their exposure to combat, because ordinary life simply does not yield the kinds of intense sensory stimuli that were at times a part of combat. High levels of depression and suicidal feelings are not uncommon in these veterans. Veterans suffering from PTSD also frequently feel a great deal of guilt—for having survived, for what they've seen, for what they've participated in. Iraq War veterans, for instance, frequently witnessed devastating events such as the destruction of homes and cities, the injury or death of fellow Americans or allies in combat, and found themselves among people who were homeless and begging for assistance. These soldiers suffering from PTSD find it difficult to negotiate the intense feelings associated with such horrifying situations.[10]

The symptoms of PTSD often have direct implications for how veterans interact with others. They may be prone to isolation and withdrawal, for example, because being around other people is extremely taxing. More generally, the symptoms lead victims of PTSD to feel extremely alienated from others and to be cynical in their views of the world around them. Not surprisingly, such symptoms also lead veterans to have tremendous difficulties in getting close to others, including members of their own families, and as a consequence, forming and maintaining intimate relationships become very problematic for them. Indeed intimate relationships are often casualties of this syndrome.

The sources of such psychological conflicts and symptoms are obvious. Combat involves experiences that are profound and that evoke horror of such proportions as to defy the ability to put words to them or otherwise use language to help organize them in a way that provides understanding of and meaning to this experience. See, for example, Rea Ann Trotter's description, in chapter 7 of this volume, of the invocation of religious thought and experience by combat soldiers when facing the overwhelming reality of war. When catastrophic events overwhelm individuals, the resulting experiences are all but impossible to integrate into ordinary emotional life.[11]

Such experiences cannot be understood, and all too often they are hard to share with others, precisely because words are inadequate to the task, but also because complex defenses interfere with such efforts. An individual may feel too anxious or too guilty, for example. Such soldiers may have frequently had their lives endangered and may have been wounded. In addition, their friends and fellow soldiers may have been wounded or killed. They may also have witnessed massive destruction of cities, towns, and villages, for example, perhaps taking part in such actions directly, involvement that sometimes may have included the killing of other combatants or even innocent individuals. Finally, factors such as exhaustion, chronic fear and uncertainty, and the sense of ever-present danger generate chronic stress and anxiety that simply overpower the senses in the context of having little or no control over the events that surround one. As Trotter points out, such conditions also mobilize profound moral dilemmas.

Any of these experiences, singly or in combination, may create significant symptoms in veterans, making them "psychiatric casualties" of war.[12] For some veterans, especially those who are unable to assimilate such war memories into their psychic structure, these concerns constantly intrude into their thoughts and feelings long after they have returned home, leading to psychological and somatic symptoms that hobble them, sometimes for the remainder of their lives. Just as important, however, is that such symptoms often have a long-term impact upon veterans' families as well.

As noted earlier, current research suggests that PTSD affects approximately 10 to 15 percent of combat veterans.[13] Although there are not statistics regarding the Latino men and women who served during World War II, it is evident that a great number of Latino veterans returning from this war may have suffered from PTSD-related symptoms. As we noted above, no such accounting is presently available, given that neither medical nor military authorities had a clear understanding of the psychological impact and thus the symptoms were poorly documented or monitored. In addition, studies focusing on Latino veterans of the Vietnam War found that they were at higher risk for war-related PTSD than their White and African American counterparts.[14]

Kulka et al. reported that most ethnic minority veterans groups have a higher rate of PTSD than White veterans. They theorized that this may be due to psychological conflicts related to identification with the "enemy" and due to higher exposure to war zone stressors. This trend suggests that belonging to an ethnic minority may cause one to be at higher risk for PTSD. These authors also found differences among Hispanic, African American, and White Vietnam veterans in terms of readjustment after military service. Hispanic veterans had higher rates of PTSD and more distressing symptoms in various diagnostic domains than other ethnic minorities and Whites.[15] Hispanics also had more problems with substance abuse and drug dependence and showed higher rates of generalized anxiety disorder than other veterans.[16]

Given that the percentage of veterans suffering from PTSD has been relatively stable across different combat experiences, we can only assume that a high number of Latino World War II veterans came home suffering from PTSD, although no reliable statistics are available for estimating the number of Latinos who fought in World War II, because such data were not systematically recorded at the time.

What seems certain is that, with the exception of the most flagrant symptoms, after World War II the emotional problems created by combat were largely ignored and not recognized as an enduring product of combat experiences. Historically, it was assumed that returning war veterans would find a way of reintegrating themselves into society.[17]

Families were expected to simply figure out what to do with their loved ones with minimal assistance from military and nonmilitary medical professionals who, in any event, had but a limited understanding of veterans' struggles. In many respects, this disjuncture between the veterans' war experiences and how family, friends, the military, and medical professionals made sense of them served only to accentuate the symptoms and the postwar adjustment difficulties. Veterans tended to feel alone and misunderstood by those around them.

The harsh realities that soldiers endured and the unparalleled destruction that they often witnessed during the war deeply affected many of them and changed them psychologically, affecting the way they responded to everyday events in which civilians engaged without thought or reflection. Obviously, operating from a combat-related paradigm did not translate well when returning to civilian life, and many of these veterans found it difficult to shift gears when it came time for normalcy.[18] Their symptoms made efforts to adapt to life outside the war zone quite challenging and compromised their efforts to reestablish prewar relationships within their families and their communities.

Impact on la Familia

The horrors of war do not stop with the individual. When a soldier with PTSD returns home, the signs and symptoms of the disorder infiltrate the family and those closest to the veteran. The veteran is a changed person, and in the time the soldier was away, the family learned to exist independently. The reunion of the soldier and family exerts stresses that are felt by both sides. Both parties must learn to live together again. This can become a strenuous situation under the best of circumstances but proves even more difficult for a family faced with managing PTSD symptoms.

Returning soldiers may find it difficult to enter into close contact with loved ones. They may feel that no one can be trusted, and therefore they may be unable to engage intimately with members of their family. Veterans may become hypervigilant in protecting themselves and their families. They may also become anhedonic—that is, unable to enjoy things they once did. This new and complex outlook on life is unusual to family members, and confusion and chaos result from the stressful new reality within the family. Considered together, family members may feel scared, withdrawn, and resentful toward the veteran and toward a situation they must now manage.

Individuals within the family have difficulty when accommodating a loved one who is enacting behaviors consistent with PTSD symptomatology. Matsakis identified several responses that families commonly exhibit when living with a returned veteran who has been exposed to traumatic events. While family members often feel sympathy and sorrow for the soldier who endured combat, they may also become depressed when recognizing how the war changed their loved ones and feeling the war's impact on their family relationships, finances, and quality of life.[19] Fear and worry are felt by many family members, who may frequently be reminded of the harsh realities of the world from the accounts of the returning vet. The family may also be concerned about its future and about the implications of the veteran's symptoms and behavior for the family as a whole. Family members may also be afraid of the vet when symptoms of anger or substance abuse appear. When vets return, avoidance, guilt, and shame are common within families, and in many cases there is little or no discussion of these stressors. Guilt and shame may surface when family members cannot "fix" the situation or help their loved one stop recurrent memories of traumatic events. Anger may be directed at anything associated with the source of the conflict—from specific incidents to the war in general, "the system," God, or the veteran for having these problems and not being able to overcome them. Like the struggling veteran, family members too may use alcohol and drugs as ways of dealing with these uncomfortable feelings and situations. Together these stresses may take a toll on both the emotional and the physical health of family members and thereby affect family relationships more generally.

It is imperative to consider the family in the identification and treatment of individuals with PTSD. A 2006 cohort study conducted by Stimpson, Masel, Rudkin, and Peek found that within the Mexican American population, health behaviors were associated within families.[20] Especially in the context of families dealing with PTSD, given the intense symptoms that are often produced, one can see the reciprocal importance of the affected individual on the family and the family on the individual. According to this criterion, simply by virtue of being members of the same family and living within the same context, families are at risk for sharing and developing the PTSD-related symptoms of the affected individual.

Before mental health services were available for veterans with PTSD, spouses and other caregivers simply did not know how to manage their loved ones who were suffering from this condition. Thus, considerable confusion and stress were added to the caregivers' management of their own complex feelings about tending to veterans who were trying to readapt to civilian life after the Second World War.

Illustrations from Latino World War II Oral History Interviews

Upon returning from service during World War II, Raul Chávez still had nightmares and felt guilt associated with being a survivor of the war:

> I have a lot of nightmares, bad nightmares. I have suicidal thoughts. I cry, I cry . . . and a lot of bad thoughts keep coming back to me. I keep remembering my buddies. What would they look like today if they were alive? Why did they get killed and why did I survive? You know, instead of them getting killed, they should have just gotten wounded and that's it. You know, stuff like that, it bothers me a lot.[21]

Chávez' statement illustrates a common experience of veterans suffering from PTSD, regardless of the specific war they fought in. This Latino World War II veteran had chronic nightmares that were exceedingly disturbing and were accompanied by suicidal thoughts, all suggestive of strong guilt feelings regarding his status as a survivor. He also described a number of other symptoms associated with PTSD such as sleep disturbances, flashbacks, and intrusive thoughts. The presence of such symptoms kept this vet chronically poised and on alert, lest those feelings enter his life, but such efforts were typically not successful in shielding him from them. The soldier was no longer able to trust his environment. On the contrary, he was constantly on guard and anxious, feeling that every situation held the potential for danger.

Sallie Castillo Castro, the wife of another World War II veteran, explained a related dilemma:

Raul Chávez. Courtesy of the U.S. Latino & Latina World War II Oral History Project.

There were times when he would wake up in the middle of the night and scream or yell at somebody like he was yelling at somebody to look out or something. I never could understand it completely. One time he was out on Sixth Street. He was selling insurance, and he went into this, I think it was a shop or something. They knew him real well because it was near his house. Some car went by and backfired. The man said that he [Castro's husband]— he just dove under a car. So it was still with him, his reactions. But he couldn't—and for a long time he couldn't talk about what happened.[22]

Clearly, for this veteran ordinary events in civilian life, such as walking down a street when a car backfired, triggered reactions that were no doubt suitable to a life-threatening combat situation but appeared odd in a postwar civilian context. In this family, the vignette became emblematic of the veteran's difficulties in adjusting to civilian life. However, the story was framed as describing an eccentricity of the man rather than as a symptom of a broader set of concerns about how the war had affected him.

Another vignette similarly illustrates the profound impact the war had on another veteran. Guadalupe Conde, of the Rio Grande Valley of Texas, was assigned first to North Africa and later to Italy, serving as a cook. But besides feeding men, he also had to help out collecting dog tags from men whose bodies were still warm when he got to them. In Naples, Conde hurt both legs when he jumped from a truck, but he didn't report his injury until he couldn't bend his knees to sit. After being taken to a hospital, he suffered severe anxiety attacks and was sent stateside. He remained in a state of terror following the war. Sleeping alone or even being alone in his house were intolerable for him. Thus, as a grown man, Conde was frightened of being alone, and at night his symptoms were so intense that he had to sleep with a family member, a situation that must have been embarrassing to him and stressful for his family: "I couldn't sleep. I was afraid to stay at home. . . . My daddy said, 'I am going to take you to a doctor.' So he took me to the doctor, and he started telling him what was wrong with me and everything. I couldn't stay in my house. My daddy had to sleep with me. I had to sleep with my daddy, with my papa."[23] Conde said that the doctor recommended that he find a good woman to marry to help him stabilize himself. In January 1945, Conde married María Gallegos and, in an interview conducted by his son, credited his wife with restoring his peace of mind.

After the Second World War, when soldiers were returning to their families, the Veterans Administration had not yet set up psychological services

Sallie Castillo Castro. Courtesy of the U.S. Latino & Latina World War II Oral History Project.

Guadalupe Condé. Courtesy of the U.S. Latino & Latina World War II Oral History Project.

tailored to treat PTSD. Veterans returning home with serious mental illness were sometimes hospitalized in psychiatric units. But once they were discharged from those settings, the burden of caring for these veterans, many of whom continued to suffer from severe symptoms, fell to their families, with little or no support from government sources. It was the families of these individuals who became the primary caregivers. One such example is that of Willie García, who married Elizabeth Ruiz after knowing her for only three months before he was shipped to North Africa and Italy. Six months later, García was discharged for "shell shock." In an interview, Elizabeth García said that the profound changes in her husband after his return from the European theater of war affected her life:

> Well, my life after the war . . . I was so taken up with my husband coming back from overseas, very sick, and he had what you call posttraumatic stress. He came back very sick. He couldn't eat; he didn't know himself. What he went through there [in the war], he couldn't take it. I went to Waco [where a VA hospital was located] every weekend to see him, and it was bad. They kept him there and they started giving him electric shock, and they did that

until they discharged him to me and that was in [19]45. So then I was with a
big responsibility . . . something to get adjusted [to]. [When] we finally took
him out of the hospital, I was advised by the doctors that I couldn't go live by
myself with him because they were afraid. So I had to live with my parents
for five years before I could move out.[24]

As we can see from this account, the families of soldiers with PTSD often
did not know how to care for them. One consequence of circumstances such
as those just described is that PTSD in returning war veterans could generate significant emotional strains within their families. The emotional toll of
overwhelming war traumas in a sense became generalized in veterans, affecting those around them once they returned home. Often family members
developed secondary psychological disorders in response to these stressors,
displaying a variety of symptoms such as depression, guilt, and fear, and, like
many of the returning veterans suffering from PTSD, these family members
also turned to avoidance, substance abuse, or other psychological mecha-
nisms to help them manage the emotional conflicts at home.

World War II veteran Raul Chávez described the impact of his emotional
conflicts on his wife:

I wake up at night kicking the walls and hitting the walls. In fact I am going
to tell you one thing—my wife will not even sleep with me . . . and I don't
blame her. I used to push her and push her, and one time I got her and I
started hitting her. I had never ever done that before to my wife. I've never
put a finger on her. We'd argue just like regular people, but we never hit
each other.[25]

Symptoms such as flashbacks, intrusive thoughts, hyperalertness, and hypervigilance in soldiers with PTSD often lead to depression, suicidal thoughts,
isolation, and withdrawal. Many times these symptoms baffle the family
members who are left to rehabilitate their loved one. The strained communication between the veteran and his family initiates many problems, one
being a decrease of intimacy in their relationships. The sleep disturbances of
Chávez were related to feelings of guilt and flashbacks about old trauma that
he experienced. He describes the nightmares he was having: "But that day I
was having a [war-related] nightmare . . . because I do get a lot of nightmares,
bad ones too. Nightmares where I dream I see—you know things come back
after all these years. And I always wonder, I ask myself, 'Why me?'"[26]

Conclusion

For veterans suffering psychological symptoms following their service in World War II, there were few resources available to help them with the traumas that had overwhelmed their psychological equilibrium. Even though every war, dating back to the Civil War, has produced its own psychiatric terminology to capture the psychological toll on soldiers, understanding of the emotional consequences of war was quite limited in the past. In addition, for Latino veterans, the toll of war must have been exacerbated by the fact that their postwar lives back home often included a return to a societal context in which racism and other social barriers created additional obstacles and stresses.

With the growing numbers of Hispanics within the U.S. population, it is likely that an increasing number of Latino military men and women will return with symptoms of posttraumatic stress disorder when the United States sends men and women into war. Although the Veterans Administration developed unprecedented sophistication in understanding PTSD as a combat-related disorder after the Vietnam War, creating inpatient and outpatient clinics to treat these veterans and developing mental health programs in an attempt to reduce the emotional toll of war on them and their families, recent reports suggest that a significant number of veterans continue to suffer from PTSD.

9

MOTHER'S LEGACY

Cultivating Chicana Consciousness during the War Years

BRENDA SENDEJO

I told them, I told my girls . . . when they were growing up . . . to always defend themselves . . . because "nobody's better than you. . . . You can always defend yourself, and try to get educated . . . your education, nobody can take it away from you." —AURORA OROZCO, worker in Texas vegetable packing plant during World War II

Women such as Aurora Orozco who became mothers following the Second World War edged away from the prescribed gender roles of their earlier years and those of their mothers, to raise children who became professionals, political activists, artists, and educators. These Mexican women of the World War II generation extended the Mexican American occupational reach to unprecedented heights by influencing the subsequent generation to make use of socioeconomic opportunities during the 1960s and 1970s. The World War II generation of Tejanas were the beneficiaries of wartime opportunities and relaxed gender roles, and they represented a transition from the experiences of the Great Depression to life in the postwar period.[1] Whether they opted to return to prewar roles or not, they afforded their daughters and granddaughters a new form of feminist consciousness as they demonstrated new heights of self-sufficiency and independence. This shift in consciousness shaped the lives of future family generations and their communities.

Orozco's unwavering commitment to her daughters' educational advancement and personal growth resonates in other interviews found in the U.S. Latino & Latina World War II Oral History Project archives. Fathers, husbands, and other family members also influenced the lives of their children, but an examination of the mothers' roles reveals singular contributions. Aside from underscoring the importance of mothers in family decisions and the significant wartime gains that women like Orozco made, the interventions by these women on their daughters' behalf suggest that World War II–generation Tejanas exercised broadly defined roles as both caregivers and active participants in the social advancement of women across time. This observation challenges the idea of motherhood that is largely confined to the domestic and maternal spheres and posits that women, especially the Mexican women of the 1940s, also contributed to the important material and psychological changes experienced by their daughters, who in turn influenced subsequent generations.[2]

It is important to note that World War II–generation women in turn attribute many of their own attitudes to their mothers, women of the Depression era who also made lasting impressions on their daughters. The narratives addressed here speak to this. Mothers taught their daughters about politics, helped them to advance in school, and set examples of hard work and fortitude that their daughters respected greatly and strove to emulate. Elena De Peña describes her mother as such a woman:

> My mother was a visionary.... [W]e wanted to go into nurses training ...
> [and] my father said, "Oh no ... what, leave home? No." So my mother said,
> "No. If they want to go into training, they'll go into training." ... Thanks to
> my mother, who was ahead of her years at that time, ... my sister and I ...
> went into nurses training.[3]

So while the war was very likely a catalyst for the evolution of the feminist consciousness of World War II women, such thinking was already in motion among Mexican women of the Depression era. These women instilled upon their daughters ideals that can be read as early forms of feminism and precursors to Chicana feminist thought.

This chapter examines the lives of three groups of women. The first ones were born in the late nineteenth century and lived through the Great Depression. The second group consists of women who were born around the time of the Depression and secured wartime employment outside the home. The last group includes women born after World War II, the generation that contributed significant numbers to the first wave of college graduates of the so-called Chicana era of the 1960s and 1970s.[4] The focus is on three women of the war years—Elena De Peña, Aurora Orozco, and Henrietta Rivas. Scholars studying American women of the 1940s have focused largely on Anglo women, with scant attention to Mexican women.[5] However, their work provides useful contextual information.

A close examination of women's individual stories illuminates how social change and shifts in race and gender consciousness occur, and it uncovers the nuances and intricacies of women's personal and distinct experiences. Such narratives also uncover how changes in women's attitudes and beliefs about themselves, as well as societal understandings of gender roles, occur over time. Sherna Berger Gluck speaks to this in reference to her oral histories of World War II women defense workers:

> I now appreciate the subtle and incremental nature of change and understand that change and changes in consciousness are not *necessarily* or *immediately* reflected in dramatic alterations in the public world. They may be very quietly played out in the private world of women, yet expressed in a fashion that can both affect future generations and eventually be expressed more openly when the social climate is right.[6]

Furthermore, as Jan Vansina states, narratives such as those explored here serve as valuable sources of information that transmit and generate messages. Examining these stories illuminates questions that need to be further pursued, such as how and why the construction and transmission of attitudes and beliefs, in this case about Mexican women, have occurred and under what historical circumstances.[7]

Maureen Honey offers a point of departure with her review of disagreements among scholars who have studied the long-term impact of World War II on women's traditional occupational roles and the social forces that often moved women into nontraditional work environments. She concludes that the war provided unprecedented employment opportunities for women. The improvements in women's roles, however, did not keep pace with the gains made by men, and the advances that women attained dissipated after the war in part because government policies and media campaigns encouraged them to return to their previous jobs, often as homemakers or low-skilled workers.[8] Despite this setback into "normal" roles for women, did the high expectations generated by the Second World War continue? Did women remain unchanged after achieving mobility and enjoying the attendant sense of accomplishment and self-worth? And how did the experience

of mobility and high expectations differ when women were subjected to racial discrimination? Oral narratives provide some answers, especially when
they are informed by the history of Anglo women during the 1940s and by
Chicana feminist scholarship, which asserts that race, ethnicity, class, and
sexuality reveal a greater multiplicity of women's experiences.[9]

The previously noted oral histories suggest that wartime experiences
in the labor force, military service, and households generated feelings of
independence and self-reliance among women and that this new sense of
empowerment led them to challenge social injustices and inequalities later
in their lives.[10] Wartime experiences also encouraged women to raise their
daughters differently from how they themselves had been raised. The interviews also tell us that this change involved an emphasis on education, expressions of self-reliance, and the development of social consciousness. The
historical literature supports much of this, especially the importance of war-
related jobs in altering gender roles and in generating a more self-reliant and
independent outlook toward life.[11]

The Women of World War II

Women played important roles at both the war and home fronts. They served
as nurses, Teletype operators, typists, and cooks in the Women's Army
Corps and the Women Accepted for Volunteer Emergency Service. They
bought war bonds, rolled bandages for the American Red Cross, planted victory gardens, and provided support services to the troops. Women also contributed to the war effort as workers. Their numbers in the workforce grew
by more than 50 percent, from 11,970,000 in 1940 to 18,610,000 in 1945. By
war's end, women constituted 36.1 percent of the civilian labor force.[12] Although many of them assumed lower-skilled and lower-paying jobs in the
cotton fields, food processing plants, and the urban-based service industry, a
growing number of them secured employment in the manufacturing industry, including aircraft construction and repair plants, garment factories, and
military camps. Their greater labor force participation and the higher-skilled
and better-paying jobs that they obtained represented major employment
gains for women, especially for those who had never worked outside their
homes or the cotton fields. Women, like minority workers, however, were
never incorporated into the labor market on an equal basis. They were concentrated in the lower-skilled and lower-paying jobs, even in the industries
producing critical material for the war effort. Minority women also benefited from additional employment opportunities but fared worse than Anglo
women in obtaining the better jobs.[13]

The turn in women's fortunes resulted from expanded production and the growing demand for workers by a wartime economy. The conscription of increasing numbers of male workers also contributed to the mobilization of women workers. The government, often in collaboration with employers, led major mobilization campaigns that were symbolically identified with the popular government propaganda icon "Rosie the Riveter." Such images, appearing in government buildings and work sites throughout the country, recognized the importance of women in the war effort and promoted their greater utilization. The government also encouraged women to join the industrial workforce with uplifting declarations like "We Can Do It!" Women responded overwhelmingly to the patriotic call for women workers and took advantage of the increasing employment opportunities.

According to the oral narratives consulted for this study, Mexican women answered the call for workers and joined in to do their patriotic duty. They served in the military, got involved in community campaigns in support of the war effort, and participated in the home front cause for increased production. They joined the workforce in growing numbers and obtained jobs that had been previously out of reach. Mexican women performed almost every kind of job imaginable, including "men's work." In the Southwest and the Midwest, they labored as riveters, welders, airplane mechanics, farmworkers, vegetable packers, seamstresses, nurses, secretaries, shipbuilders, crane operators, and munitions workers. However, like their male counterparts, Mexican women faced much discrimination. They, along with African American women, most often assumed a distant position in a queuing system that gave hiring and upgrading preferences to males, especially Anglo males. On the other hand, the wartime opportunities allowed Mexican women to share in the development of a new consciousness among the greater numbers of women in the workforce.

Participation in the military and in the workforce made women feel that they were making significant contributions to the war effort as well as to the livelihood of their families. The government's public information campaigns were especially important in validating their roles as partners at a critical time in history. Women reinforced this view by carrying out important tasks in workplaces throughout the country and by assuming greater family responsibilities in their homes. Defense worker Victoria Morales provided a pithy description of the psychological changes that accompanied the new opportunities and responsibilities: "By the end of the war we had transformed into young mature women with new job skills, self-confidence, and a sense of worth as a result of our contributions to the war effort. Just as the war had changed boys into men, the same thing happened to us girls."[14] This chapter explores the impact of such changes on women and the possibility that expanded opportunities coalesced into an expanded consciousness that would come to affect future generations of Mexican American women.

Elena Tamez De Peña

Elena De Peña was born on 19 February 1916 in the South Texas town of San Benito. She married Hector De Peña in 1942 and had three children—two sons and a daughter. Her father was born in the northern Mexican state of Nuevo León, and her mother in Brownsville, Texas. De Peña noted that her mother was very intelligent and singly managed the family store. She recalled that her parents were supportive and caring, and though their schooling experience was limited, they believed that their children should be educated: "They set a fine example.... [M]other thought that we wanted further education, and she saw to it that we got it." De Peña benefited from this influence; she earned a bachelor's degree in public health from the Incarnate Word Academy in San Antonio and a master's degree in the same field from Sam Houston State University in Huntsville, Texas. She worked as a public health nurse for nearly twenty years. De Peña remembered that her mother was a wise counselor who encouraged her and her sister to search for opportunities beyond their immediate and limiting surroundings. She also recalled a strict father, suggesting that her mother had negotiated the girls' eventual departure against some serious odds. De Peña added that she had an open and friendly relationship with her father that the mother no doubt helped fashion to allow for fair and caring family decisions:

> I can appreciate her much more than I probably did growing up or as a younger person. Now that I am more or less in her age group, I can appreciate how smart she was. In fact my father would have preferred that we had stayed ... in San Benito. I used to kid him that probably we would marry the first fellow that smiled at us, you know.[15]

When the time came to make use of an opportunity rarely available to Mexicans in Texas—a nurses' training program—she recalled that the sisters "decided" to do it, but that their mother's decision to allow them, measured against their father's serious misgivings, had been decisive. De Peña understood, from her mother's admonitions, that the decision was based on an apparent understanding that De Peña's mother had with her father. The sisters learned that their mother had extended herself on their behalf and that they could not minimize the sacrifice or squander the opportunity: "We decided and found an opening and mother . . . said yes. I mean, we went in nurses' training, and I remember she would admonish us and say, 'Now, you behave, because if you do anything you shouldn't do, I'll never hear the end from your daddy because he would have preferred for you to have stayed here.'"[16]

The memory of a strict and somewhat constraining father and a support-ive and fairly independent mother, especially regarding decisions involving the daughters, runs through De Peña's narrative. It appeared early in her life, when she decided to leave home for a university education. The family's relatively comfortable financial standing, made possible by their small store, and the recovery from the Depression that began in the late 1930s no doubt contributed to the decision. Going away to college, however, was very rare for Mexicans, especially for young Mexican women. De Peña nevertheless attended the university and obtained her two degrees.

Soon after starting college and the nurses' training program, she married Hector De Peña, an ambitious young man from South Texas. He was fresh out of law school and interested in setting up his practice in his hometown in Duval County, a ranching area west of Corpus Christi. Political differ-ences between his father and a local political boss ended his law practice, and the family decided to move to Corpus Christi, where Hector became the legal counsel for the Mexican consulate. Meanwhile, De Peña continued her studies and eventually obtained a college degree. The couple also integrated themselves into the political life of Corpus Christi. Hector worked as a legal counsel with the Mexican consul, and he and Elena became active in the local council of the League of United Latin American Citizens (LULAC).

The couple's only daughter, Carla De Peña Cook, recalled a middle-class upbringing with social expectations that were decidedly higher than in her grandmother's household. Her parents stressed an education to the point that attending college became a natural decision for Carla Cook. She would later acknowledge this important influence in her life: "I tease mother I never even realized I even had a choice about whether or not to go to college. It was just . . . 'You are going.' And that's all there was to it."[17]

Carla received her bachelor's degree in psychology and was currently working as a licensed counselor for Nueces County. Although she acknowl-edged the influence of both her father and mother, she also expressed special admiration for her mother. Carla was especially impressed with her moth-er's accounts of her grandmother, speaking of her in exalted terms with the obvious intent of inculcating values that would serve De Peña well in life. Carla recalled recurring stories of her grandmother:

What an intelligent woman she was, and she was quite intelligent. She read a lot—all kinds of poetry and all kinds of literature . . . and she worked for a doctor for a period of time and ran a business . . . and did a really good job of raising her sons and daughters and was very adventurous. . . . She was, I think, probably an early feminist.[18]

Carla's interpretation of her grandmother as an "early feminist" communicated a model of behavior that De Peña Cook promulgated and emulated.

De Peña and her mother were independent and forward-looking, but they also lived in a world of financial difficulties, stricter racial hierarchies, and more traditional gender roles. These circumstances underscored the degree to which they departed from convention as well as the restrictions that defined their worlds. Their vantage point explains why they helped their daughters challenge norms at the same time that they encouraged marriage, for example. Carla acknowledged this seeming inconsistency, but with a good measure of understanding. She obviously understood that intergenerational change necessarily involved a transitional experience for women who reached into the future while living in their present. What was more important was that Carla described the "double message" of "you need to get an education and . . . of course you are going to get married" without expressing any regret or resentment against her mother. Although she may have shared her mother's views and overlooked any inconsistency in the advice, Carla appreciated her mother's love and guidance to the point of indulging their possible differences and making intergenerational change natural and understandable.[19]

Her parents' association with the Mexican social movement, especially LULAC, also prepared Carla for her experiences with discrimination. Carla, in other words, knew of discrimination and her right to protest and overcome it. It became an especially glaring experience sometime in the early 1970s when a co-worker apparently overlooked her Mexican heritage and complained that government policies were forcing their employer, the Lubbock telephone company, to promote equal employment opportunities. The co-worker, an Anglo woman, expressed resentment when she stated, "Well, you know, honey, we just have to work with everyone, Mexicans included."[20]

Incensed, Carla immediately informed the Anglo woman, "I am a Hispanic. I am a Mexicana." Carla was light-skinned, and her co-worker probably mistook her for a fellow Anglo and assumed that she shared her racial prejudice. Although Carla concluded that the co-worker and other like-minded individuals mostly spoke out of ignorance, she decided that "while

I was there, I was going to make some noise." Her resolute response to the affronts that she faced at work reflected a strong personality that her family had nurtured over time.[21]

Aurora Estrada Orozco

Aurora Estrada Orozco assumed the traditional role of wife and mother at the same time that she inculcated independent thinking among her daughters. She was born on 8 May 1918 in Cerralvo, a town near the northern industrial city of Monterrey, Nuevo León, Mexico. Unlike Elena De Peña, she lived a financially comfortable childhood in Mexico, but her family experienced a major financial downturn and the hard times of the Depression. Orozco, like De Peña, thusly became a transitional figure who represented the traditional outlook of her mother as well as a new independent orientation that she passed on to the next generation of women in her family. The war years offered her an opportunity to make this transition.

Orozco was six when her family moved to Texas in 1924. Her father, Lorenzo Estrada, was a Jamaican immigrant who had a good command of both English and Spanish. He used his bilingual skills to parlay a job as a foreman and bookkeeper for a U.S.-owned mining company that worked gold, silver, and coal in Cerralvo. The political instability of the Mexican Revolution, however, forced the company to establish its operations in the United States. Estrada followed and soon sent for his family. After his job with the mining company ended, he found work where he could, but adjusting to the new country was difficult. Estrada worked in various jobs, including keeping books for a button factory in South Texas and herding cattle on a ranch in Bishop, Texas. The devastation of the Depression worsened the family's socioeconomic situation and forced Aurora and her siblings to work. In 1949, Aurora met Primitivo Estrada Orozco Vega at a church fiesta. He too was an immigrant, from Guadalajara, who worked as a boot maker in Texas. After they married, the couple raised their six children in Cuero, approximately 150 miles southwest of Houston.[22]

Aurora Orozco had been raised in a conservative household. This conservativism was especially evident in the gender roles that the children were expected to observe. She and her sisters, for instance, were required to help with the cooking and cleaning around the house, while her brothers cut the grass and performed other duties that took them outside the home. The young women also had to abide by a stricter set of rules when venturing outside the home. They could not leave the house in the evenings unless they

Aurora Estrada Orozco. Courtesy of the U.S. Latino &
Latina World War II Oral History Project.

were accompanied by a chaperone. They were told that failure to abide by
these expectations would disgrace the family and invite serious reprimands.
The boys had more freedom and usually exercised it. Orozco continued to
observe gendered rules when she married. Once she had children, she stayed
at home with them and ran the household, as was common for women during the late 1940s and 1950s.[23]

Although the strict gender roles fostered a conservative cultural outlook
in Orozco's childhood and later life, her experiences varied enough to provide her and, later, her daughters with opportunities to pursue other forms of
personal development. Orozco had been raised in a household where young
ladies did not work outside of the home, but this core value was overridden
by financial necessity. Orozco and her sisters, for example, contributed to
the family income by working outside the home at an early age—her sisters
in the cotton fields and Orozco in a vegetable packing plant when she graduated from high school. This contributed positively to their sense of worth, as
they recognized their capabilities and took pride in the ability to contribute
to the family income.

Orozco's older sisters made an especially important contribution that Orozco and her parents recognized. Their combined labor added sufficiently to the family income to allow Orozco to stay in school longer. Her educational accomplishments also became a source of family gratification. She attended a private Mexican school and also enrolled in public schools until she graduated from the local high school in 1939. This was an especially important achievement because Mexicans, especially women, did not usually finish high school during the 1930s.[24]

The need for children's labor in a working-class household may have kept Orozco's sisters from drawing greater benefit from educational opportunities. However, their parents' emphasis on schooling as a basis for development and self-sufficiency was nevertheless evident in them and then later in their daughters.

Cynthia, one of Orozco's daughters, acknowledged this influence in her mother's educational success. Orozco's husband also gave great importance to education and was even "relentless" in urging his daughters to attend college. Parenting in the Orozco household—as in the De Peña home—was obviously a shared responsibility. Orozco, however, played a more active role in defending her daughters against discrimination in the schools and in urging them to stand up for their rights.[25]

The memory of discrimination in the schools left an early and indelible impression on Orozco and informs her sense of Mexican identity to the present day, an identity that she wore with great pride. Her recollection characterized her as a precocious child who spoke her native language and defiantly faced the wrath of one teacher: "I was one of those little girls that used to speak a lot in the class . . . Spanish in the class. So this teacher . . . she would hit my hand with a little rubber band that she had. . . . My hand would turn real red, but she never did break me at it."[26]

Discrimination against Mexicans continued during the 1940s and 1950s, when Orozco's children reached school age. Orozco recounted this experience in large part to underscore her continuing defiance, this time in defense of her children, but also to explain how her daughters first learned to stand up for their rights as Mexicans and as women. One such instructive confrontation involved a school principal who questioned her daughter's onetime use of a government-sponsored lunch program:

I always leave my kids money for their lunch. But . . . when my husband was sick . . . I just didn't have enough money. [My daughter] María Teresa . . . and another girl [were the only Mexican Americans] that were members of the gifted club . . . so they [the school officials] gave her some tickets . . . for lunch . . . but then she came one day, and she was upset. And I said, "What's the matter with you?" "Well," she said, "the principal, Mr. Smith, said that I would have to stay after school if I wanted to get those tickets, I would have to stay after school and help the janitor clean." . . . And I said, "Well, that's all right, María Teresa. I'm gonna send him a little note in the morning with you." So I sent him a little note. And I said, "Mr. Smith, María Teresa told me so-and-so. . . . How would you like for your fourteen-year-old daughter . . . to stay after school and work cleaning with the janitor that you don't know who he is and what he might do? How would you like that?" And I said, "In the first place, Mr. Smith, I didn't ask you to give her tickets. And in the second place, Mr. Smith, the tickets are not yours. They belong to the government. And the government is the one giving out to the children." And I said, "So from now on, Mr. Smith, I don't know where I'm gonna get my little change. But I have change so María Teresa will never have to have another ticket from you." Oh boy. So she took it to the office. And then at noon, somebody was knocking at my door . . . it was his secretary. And she said, "Are you Mrs. Orozco?" And I said, "Yes." And she said, "Well, Mrs. Orozco, Mr. Smith got this note this morning. He was very upset, and so was I." And I said, "Mr. Smith has no business telling my daughter to stay after school to clean with the janitor." I said, "Because like I told him, those tickets were not his. They are from the government."[27]

Orozco often urged her daughters to stand up for their rights, as the quote at the opening of this chapter illustrates. Like De Peña, Orozco underscored the strategy of an education as a way for young women to achieve a measure of independence, noting the common refrain that working-class parents used to suggest the enduring value of schooling: "You can always defend yourself, and try to get educated. . . . Your education, nobody can take it away from you."[28]

Orozco did not confine her attention to the schools or the educational needs of her daughters. She also became active in other community affairs and, according to Cynthia, further modeled the idea that women should be involved in activities outside the home. Cynthia recalled that her mother made sure that her daughters knew of her activities and political issues that were current at the time. The conversations were frequent and rich. "We always talked about civics and political stuff at the dinner table," she noted.[29]

As a young mother in Cuero, Orozco was a key participant in the local Catholic Church. She served on the church council from 1972 to 1981 and was an active member of Las Guadalupanas, a Catholic women's service group, for most of her adult life. She also took part in organizing a LULAC council in Cuero and served as secretary of the local organization between 1972 and 1979. Beginning in the late 1960s, Orozco joined her daughters in various activities throughout Texas that were associated with the Mexican social movement. As La Raza Unida Party's chief representative in her hometown between 1974 and 1978, she played an especially important role in the organization's third-party challenge against the Republican and Democratic parties. In addition, Orozco has shared her experiences and views regarding women's rights and the Mexican social movement in public venues like scholarly conferences and in her writings, primarily in the form of poetry and personal remembrances.[30]

Orozco was primarily motivated by the influence of her parents and her concern that discrimination would undermine her daughters' educational opportunities. The more egalitarian sociocultural setting of the Second World War, however, also informed the more independent outlook that she and her sisters adopted and transmitted to the next generation of women in the family. To illustrate the change, Orozco underscored the new roles that women assumed as workers and soldiers:

> In the [Rio Grande] Valley there were these packing sheds where they packed tomatoes and lettuce. . . . There were not enough men to work so they started hiring women. Everyone was shocked because women had never worked there. But then they [the women] liked it because they'd make money, so pretty soon it was the women who were running things. So see, that is when it started to change a little more in women's lives. They were calling from the government for women to go and work in the factories. . . . Then they started calling women into the army. And first it was, like, "Oh my goodness, *Dios mío*! How can these women go over there by themselves?" Everybody was shocked because we were not used to seeing women leave the house. You didn't leave the house until you were married. With señoritas [unmarried women] everything was so strict, and then came this change . . . and I think that was wonderful because it opened a new world for women. It showed that women can be independent. This was a real break for women.[31]

Orozco added that her parents allowed her to work in the packing shed because they wanted the family to contribute to the war effort. The national emergency, in other words, opened up unprecedented opportunities for women as workers. Although most Mexican women, much like African

American women, had been wage earners at one time in their lives, the dire need for women's wartime work opened up new possibilities for earning higher wages and often in jobs typically reserved for males.[32] The family's sense of patriotic duty also contributed to the decision by Orozco, her sister Gertrudis, and another Mexican woman from Mercedes, Texas, to move to Dickinson, a town near Galveston, in response to the call for war workers on the Gulf Coast. The women went to Dickinson for approximately three months during the packing season to process figs.[33]

Orozco stated that she, her sister, and the other women felt "liberated" by the experience of working outside the home and contributing to the income of their families. She also credited her views on equal rights for Mexicans and women to her life-changing experience as a worker during World War II. This does not mean that Orozco discarded or even repudiated the world of her youth, but it suggests that this historical moment in the early 1940s was pivotal in her personal development into a woman who bridged tradition with her present as a mother. The experience undoubtedly also informed her sense of gender and ethnic identity as well as a feminist consciousness. The melding of her two generally defined realities explained the seeming inconsistencies involved in the parenting of her daughters. Cynthia recalled, for instance, that her mother expected her daughters but not her son to help with the cleaning and cooking. Aurora Orozco, in other words, promoted separate gender roles. Cynthia noted, "She trained all the girls to do everything that women were expected to do. My brothers were only obligated to cut the yard and take out the trash, so those roles were pretty set actually."[34]

Cynthia also recalled, however, that Orozco taught her daughters that they could be anything they wanted. Orozco obviously lived in the gendered world of her own upbringing but nevertheless provided her daughters the means to question the inequalities associated with the different roles assigned to men and women. More importantly, her daughters grew to understand their mother's cultural dilemma and to appreciate how the experience of discrimination moved her to nurture a different life for them. This understanding, previously seen in the way Carla comprehended her mother's relationship with her father, was as important as the constructive parental influence itself.

Orozco's influence on her daughters can be best measured in two ways. First, they acknowledge the special role that their mother played in encouraging them to make use of educational opportunities and to develop a Mexicanist and feminist identity. Second, the daughters have accomplished much in the area of education. The four daughters have obtained bachelor's degrees, secured professional positions in academia, the arts, education, and business, and continued their mother's civic activism. Cynthia, one of the major sources of information for this study, has earned a doctorate in history and promotes the understanding of Mexican and women's history, including her mother's experiences, in her publications, the classroom, and public talks.[35]

Henrietta López Rivas

Henrietta López Rivas was born in San Antonio on 14 February 1924.[36] Her father, Pablo López, died in 1925, when she was only one year old, leaving his wife, Concepción Garza López, with two small children. The young widow supported her family by sewing and taking in laundry before marrying Juan Luna and having four more children with him.

Concepción Garza López taught her children at home. Before they entered school on the south side of San Antonio in the 1920s, Rivas and her older brother could read and recite the multiplication tables—in Spanish. This, however, was not enough to help her succeed. According to Rivas, her teachers did not value her knowledge of Spanish and mathematics, nor did they encourage her sufficiently. She failed first grade.[37]

During the Depression, Juan Luna lost his job with the railroad company, and the family had no other recourse but to join the migrant workforce, requiring them to leave San Antonio in the spring, before the school term ended, and return after the next school term had begun. The spotty attendance in school hampered Rivas' learning and eventually discouraged her from continuing her studies. By the eighth grade, she had dropped out of school. After that, she worked cleaning houses, until the war years ushered in new employment options. Rivas worked in Civil Defense as a Spanish-language interpreter and subsequently as an airplane instrument repair technician at Duncan Field in San Antonio. Rivas also secured work repairing airplane altimeters at Kelly Field, a military base in San Antonio. Her pay, which had been as low as $1.50 per week as a domestic worker, now increased to $90 per month. On 20 February 1945 she married Ramón Rivas, and together they raised seven children, first in San Antonio and, after 1956, in Devine, a small town south of San Antonio. One of her most memorable accomplishments was gaining a general equivalency diploma at fifty-five years of age.[38]

Like Elena De Peña and Aurora Orozco, Rivas became a confident young woman as a result of her employment outside the home. She was especially gratified by her translation skills and her ability to do well in the examinations required to secure wartime employment:

Henrietta López Rivas. Courtesy of the U.S. Latino &
Latina World War II Oral History Project.

I think it made me feel like I was equal or even more intelligent. Because
what I did, very few Anglos could do. Because we were given a lot of tests to
get our jobs. And that didn't make me feel as dumb as I thought I was. And
this is the way it was—you're not as dumb as you think you are. Someone
has made you feel like you're dumb, but you're not.[39]

Her references to feeling "dumb" are consistent with the degrading racial
stereotypes that rationalized discrimination and the unequal social relations
in the United States between a generally privileged Anglo population and
a submerged Mexican community. Mexicans, in other words, often internalized the stereotypical views of Mexicans as ignorant.[40] Contributing to
the prejudiced views of Mexicans was the social distance that discrimination
and inequality reinforced. The only Anglos that Rivas knew prior to the war,
for instance, were the ones whose homes she had cleaned. She met more
Anglos in wartime industries, but the discrimination, unequal relations,
and racial slurs continued. Improved employment opportunities, in other

words, did not necessarily abate the tensions associated with the racialized social relations between Mexicans and Anglos. Relations, in fact, became more strained as segregationists sought to resume their racial practices in war industries while Mexicans like Rivas exercised their newfound sense of equal worth.[41]

Rivas remembered an instance when an Anglo supervisor at Kelly tried to intimidate her with the accusation that she had broken a very expensive piece of equipment. He almost drove her to tears, but she later learned that the situation was not as bad as the supervisor had claimed. He had told her that the broken equipment would cost $5,000 to replace, but it was really only worth $5. Other Mexican women, according to Rivas, endured the same kind of unfair pressure so that they could keep their better-paying jobs. Although male workers of all ethnic backgrounds also had disagreements with their supervisors, Rivas believed that Mexicans, especially women, faced an inordinate amount of conflict that resulted from racial and gender discrimination.

Rivas was especially concerned that Anglo men regularly spoke of Mexican women in demeaning terms, as easy sexual prey. According to her daughter Maggie Rivas-Rodríguez, Rivas was deeply affected by this view and made sure that her daughters understood the challenge of being a Mexican woman in a racialized world:

> She once heard an Anglo soldier tell one of his buddies that he ought to go out with one of these Mexican girls, that they are "easy meat." I think that that made a big impression on her, and she was still angry about it several years later and wanted to make sure that her daughters knew that that was the reputation and, "So you be careful. Don't think they are thinking you are so smart and nice and pretty. They are really looking at you in this particular way." I think that they made a real big impression on her.[42]

Despite the dispiriting experience of racism and sexism, Rivas shared her memories of discrimination and her newfound identity as a self-assured woman with her children. Maggie once again shared her mother's memory and lessons in life as if they were her own when she underscored the important change that Rivas underwent as a war worker:

> During the war she worked at Kelly Field and had a chance to do these jobs that required a lot of skill, and she realized she was as smart or smarter as the other girls. To this day she is really, really sharp. Her self-esteem went way up. I think that if nobody ever told her that, she had a chance to see it

for herself. And I think that's what self-esteem is all about. Everybody can tell you how great you are, but until you've had a chance to really internalize it . . . I think that is what happened to her.[43]

Maggie added a note of profound affection that resulted from her mother's abilities and special standing in her community during the postwar period:

She was really a beautiful woman and had a beautiful voice. She was really smart. She was the woman in the neighborhood that people would get to interpret papers they would get from the city office. She would read it and translate it into Spanish. "Doña Enriqueta" is how she was known, which was a big title in Devine, Texas.[44]

Rivas, however, did not transform herself completely; like De Peña and Orozco, she retained values from her past that were evident in her parenting practices. She loved her wartime work and recognized its importance in becoming a self-assured and somewhat independent young woman, but she insisted that "raising my children was more important than my job."[45] Rivas recognized that she reared her children in a traditional way, but that she did it with a renewed sense of her capabilities and self-esteem.

The new person that Rivas had become was evident to Maggie as she also recalled her mother's active involvement in school affairs, especially one instance when a public school administrator demonstrated his almost blind adherence to the idea of tracking children in school:

When I was going to first grade, in Devine, Texas, I was going in to register. My mother went with me, and they had three or four first-grade classrooms in the public schools. They had one classroom for the mentally retarded kids and for the Spanish-speaking kids—all in one classroom.

And so I go in and the superintendent is filling out my paperwork and said he was going to assign me to that teacher, the one who teaches the mentally retarded kids and the Spanish-speaking kids, and my mother says, "Now"—my mother speaks flawless English, so there is no reason for him to assume that I wouldn't speak English. He says, "So she'll go into that classroom." And my mother says, "Why is that?" And he said, "Because she doesn't speak English—now, do you, Mary?" And I will always remember being a smart-ass and thinking, "Well, what do you think I speak? French?" But I didn't say that. I said, "Yes, sir." And so he said, "Well, okay, I'll put her in the other class." If my mother had not spoken up, I would have been in that classroom.[46]

Ramón Rivas even exceeded Henrietta Rivas' influence in the upbringing of their children, especially in the decision to attend college, demonstrating once again that Mexican women did not act alone in the practice of raising children, nor did they always lead in important practices. Maggie noted that her father always stressed that education was the one thing that could never be taken from you. Her mother, however, also encouraged her children and left memorable impressions of making a difference. Maggie recalled one occasion:

> Even though my mother didn't push me to go to college, she did support that. For instance, I wanted to go to UT [the University of Texas] and my counselor didn't think that was the path for me. So my mother went with me to talk to this man [who worked with SER—Jobs for Progress, a federally funded job and educational referral program in San Antonio]. He was really great; he helped me to get the paperwork done and send in my application and get a test waiver . . . it was actually a waiver on the fee to take an advanced placement test. . . . So my mother would always be with me but wouldn't push me. She would wait for me or whoever to do what we wanted, and she would support our decision.[47]

Maggie noted that her mother continued to be active in her life after high school graduation:

> When I was in college, she helped me get my first job. She went down to Monterrey, Mexico, so I could get this [newspaper] internship. . . . She did all the talking for me. That's my mom—she was one of those people who may not initiate something but she was always there, making sure that her kids did well.[48]

In recent years Rivas has used her Spanish and English readings skills to serve as a copy editor for the Latino & Latina World War II Oral History Project at the University of Texas at Austin. In this way, she continues to assist Maggie, who as of this writing is an associate professor in the University of Texas School of Journalism, and to promote the view that Mexicans made important contributions to the war effort at the same time that the experience transformed the lives of the Mexican women of the war years in ways that are also evident in the successful lives of their daughters.

Conclusion

The study of Mexican women on the U.S. home front during the 1940s is still in its infancy, despite the recent and deserved attention that historians and anthropologists have given other minorities and women in general. The experiences of Elena De Peña, Aurora Orozco, and Henrietta Rivas and the influence these women had on their daughters provides an initial examination of the transformation of Mexican women's lives during the war years and the generational reach of these changes into the 1960s and beyond. More work is required to determine the extent to which their lives reflect trends in the larger and varied population of Mexican women. Their transformed lives, however, conform with findings in the historical literature on Anglo women and suggest significance beyond the cases that this study has addressed.

World War II was a turning point for Mexican women as much as it was for other women in the United States.[49] Their greater labor participation, their service in the military, and the public discourse that acknowledged their importance to the war effort improved their self-esteem and broadened their life possibilities. As contradictory as it was to be simultaneously valued and devalued—as when men mostly returned to their prewar jobs after 1945 and women lost their wartime jobs—they had acquired a new sense of their worth and potential as women that enriched their lives.

Mexican women benefiting from wartime work represented a shift in a pattern of low-paying wage labor in sectors such as farmwork, canning, pecan shelling, and orchard harvesting during the early to mid-twentieth century, work that contributed to the racialization of women, that is, the social construction and oppression of the working-class Mexican female.[50] While wartime work was liberating for women, they still faced gender and racial discrimination, as illustrated by the case of Henrietta Rivas and in Joanne Rao Sanchez' chapter in this volume.

The cases of De Peña, Orozco, and Rivas demonstrate that the significance of their new outlook and positive identity can be measured generationally as the women married, had children, and influenced them in ways that could not have been possible without the experience of the war years. As transitional figures, the women of the war years reached into their past to transmit important traditional values along with an egalitarian outlook that allowed their daughters to achieve even more than them. This connection between women's pasts, their sense of self as cultivated during the war years, and the ways in which women influenced their children cannot be easily examined in isolation from one another. For as Vicki Ruiz states, the "feminist edifice of separate spheres" is not applicable, as family and work are intimately linked for women of color and immigrant women in the United States. "Integration, rather than separation," Ruiz observes, "provides a more illuminating construct in exploring the dynamics of Mexicana/Chicana work and family roles."[51]

The experience of World War II allowed women to challenge social norms and broaden opportunities for the next generation. They, for instance, challenged discrimination as a practice in conflict with their new understanding that Mexicans, including women, had made important contributions to the war effort and could, as a consequence, expect to be treated as valued members of society. Often working in unison with their equally attentive husbands, they also urged their daughters to make use of educational opportunities. Moreover, the women fostered assertiveness in their daughters, even to the point of encouraging them to challenge discrimination as individuals and as members of the larger communities of Mexicans and women. Orozco, in particular, did so openly and consistently, while De Peña chose to occasionally offer private counsel and model the preferred behavior in the public arena. Rivas did not so much encourage assertiveness verbally as she did by setting a strong example for her children.

While some scholars contend that women went back to prewar jobs and domestic roles after the war with little change, the narratives presented here and in Joanne Rao Sanchez' chapter in this volume suggest a different experience for women of color. For Mexican women, the material realities of social inequality played a pivotal role in their access to opportunity. A historical consciousness of racial, class, *and* gender discrimination played into their identity formation and understanding of their roles as Mexican women in the United States.[52] The double standards experienced by the Chicana and World War II–generation Mexican women discussed here reflect the melding of social realities from different periods and the resulting shifts in consciousnesses. They demonstrate the fluid nature of cultural attitudes and beliefs and how Mexican women have navigated them in order to cultivate and sustain meaningful lives for themselves and their families.

Both the women of the war years and their daughters acknowledged their mothers as critical sources of influence in their lives. In one way or another, De Peña, Orozco, and Rivas credited their mothers with helping them make the most of the opportunities that the war offered them. Their daughters singled out their mothers to an even greater extent, suggesting that the generational leap into their own world as politically conscious Chicana women could not have been possible without the equally significant experience of

their mothers. Their obvious sense of joined history and shifts in consciousness strengthens their relations and reinforces this view, demonstrating how
Mexican women in Texas have left a legacy as constant agents in the making
of history and culture.[53]

AUTHOR'S NOTE: I thank the women who agreed to be interviewed and who
appear in this study. I also wish to dedicate this article to my grandmother
María Balcazar Castañon Sendejo, who was a machinist at the Corpus
Christi Naval Air Station during World War II. Finally, my appreciation
goes to the Center for Women's and Gender Studies and the College of
Liberal Arts at the University of Texas at Austin, which provided support
for research conducted over the summer of 2005. This chapter is informed
by and includes interviews conducted for my master's report, entitled "Cultivating a Chicana Consciousness on the Texas-Mexico Border: Influences
of World War II Generation Women on the Chicana Generation" (Department of Anthropology, University of Texas at Austin, 2005).

NOTES

INTRODUCTION

1. The following studies address the story of wartime production: Richard Polenberg, *America at War: The Home Front, 1941–1945* (Englewood Cliffs, N.J.: Prentice-Hall, 1968); William O'Neill, *A Democracy at War: America's Fight at Home and Abroad in World War II* (New York: Free Press, 1993); Allan M. Winkler, *Home Front U.S.A.: America during World War II* (Wheeling, Ill.: Harlan Davidson, 2000); Avid Reynolds, *From World War to Cold War: Churchill, Roosevelt, and the International History of the 1940s* (New York: Oxford University Press, 2006).

2. Home front experiences, including the contradiction between the rhetoric of democracy and justice and the reality of discrimination and inequality involving workers, minorities, and women, are addressed in the following: John Morton Blum, *V Was for Victory: Politics and American Culture during World War II* (New York: Harcourt Brace Jovanovich, 1976); Ruth Milkman, *Gender at Work: The Dynamics of Job Segregation by Sex during World War II* (Champaign: University of Illinois Press, 1987); O'Neill, *Democracy at War*; Elizabeth Cohen, *Making a New Deal: Industrial Workers in Chicago, 1919–1939* (New York: Cambridge University Press, 1990); Ronald Takaki, *Double Victory: A Multicultural History of America in World War II* (Boston: Little, Brown, 2000); Emilio Zamora, *Claiming Rights and Righting Wrongs in Texas: Mexican Workers and Job Politics during World War II* (College Station: Texas A&M University Press, 2009).

3. Juan Gonzalez, *Harvest of Empire: A History of Latinos in America* (New York: Penguin Books, 2001); Suárez-Orozco and Páez, eds., *Latinos: Remaking America* (Berke-

ley: University of California Press, 2002); Flores, "From Bomba to Hip-Hop: Puerto Rican Culture and Latino Identity," in *Popular Cultures, Everyday Lives*, edited by Robin G. Kelley and Janice Radway (New York: Columbia University Press, 2000); Alamillo, "Bibliographic Essay on U.S. Latino/a History," National Park Service, 2008, http://www.nps.gov/history/history/resedu/latino.pdf.

4. See the following additional works that examine the history and contemporary experiences of distinct Latino/a groups with varying degrees of attention to comparability in the wider Latino/a population: Clara E. Rodríguez and Virginia Sánchez Korrol, eds., *Historical Perspectives on Puerto Rican Survival in the United States* (Princeton, N.J.: Markus Wiener, 1980); Juan Gómez-Quiñones, *Chicano Politics: Reality and Promise, 1940–1990* (Albuquerque: University of New Mexico Press, 1990); Ramona Hernández, *The Mobility of Workers under Advanced Capitalism: Dominican Migration to the United States* (New York: Columbia University Press, 2002); Felix Masud-Piloto, *With Open Arms: Cuban Migration to the United States* (New York: Rowman and Littlefield, 1988). Three of the most recent reference books are David Gutiérrez, ed., *The Columbia History of Latinos in the United States since 1960* (New York: Columbia University Press, 2004); Suzanne Oboler and Deena J. González, eds., *The Oxford Encyclopedia of Latinos and Latinas in the United States* (New York: Oxford University Press, 2005); Vicki L. Ruiz and Virginia Sánchez Korrol, eds., *Latinas in the United States: A Historical Encyclopedia*, 3 vols. (Bloomington: Indiana University Press, 2006).

5. Castañeda, "The Second Rate Citizen and Democracy," in Alonso Perales, comp., *Are We Good Neighbors?* (San Antonio: Artes Gráficas, 1948).

6. For an examination of the persistence of inequality in the face of improved wartime opportunities, see Zamora, *Claiming Rights and Righting Wrongs*.

7. M. T. García, *Mexican Americans: Leadership, Ideology, and Identity, 1930–1960* (New Haven, Conn.: Yale University Press, 1989); Montejano, *Anglos and Mexicans in the Making of Texas, 1836–1886* (Austin: University of Texas Press, 1987); Sánchez, *Becoming Mexican American: Ethnicity, Culture, and Identity in Chicano Los Angeles, 1900–1945* (New York: Oxford University Press, 1993); San Miguel, *"Let All of Them Take Heed": Mexican Americans and the Campaign for Educational Equality in Texas, 1910–1981* (Austin: University of Texas Press, 1987); Gómez-Quiñones, *Chicano Politics*.

8. Pauline Kibbe, *Latin Americans in Texas* (Albuquerque: University of New Mexico Press, 1946); Carey McWilliams, *North from Mexico: The Spanish-Speaking People of the United States* (New York: Greenwood Press, 1948); Perales, *Are We Good Neighbors?* Raul Morín, *Among the Valiant: Mexican-Americans in WW II and Korea* (Alhambra, Calif.: Borden Publishing Co., 1963).

9. The long-lasting view that military service and battlefield sacrifice encouraged Mexican soldiers to adopt a stronger sense of self-worth and civic confidence and that this realization morphed into an Americanized ethnic identity and renewed civil rights cause is examined in the following: M. T. García, *Mexican Americans*; Sánchez, *Becoming Mexican American*; Manuel G. Gonzales, *Mexicanos: A History of Mexicans in the United States* (Bloomington: Indiana University Press, 1999); Matt García, *A*

World of Its Own: Race, Labor, and Citrus in the Making of Greater Los Angeles, 1900–1970 (Chapel Hill: University of North Carolina Press, 2001).

10. Castañeda, a borderlands historian and librarian at the University of Texas at Austin, worked as a field examiner and the principal investigator of Mexican worker complaints with the Fair Employment Practice Committee, the wartime agency responsible for implementing President Franklin D. Roosevelt's executive orders that prohibited discrimination according to race, national origin, or religious creed in government employment, unions, and wartime industries. Lucey was the archbishop of the San Antonio Archdiocese and a prominent progressive leader on behalf of social equality, particularly for poor workers. Saenz was a cofounder of LULAC and the author of the World War I diary *Los méxico-americanos en la gran guerra y su contingente en pró de la democracia, la humanidad y la justicia* (San Antonio: Artes Gráficas, 1933). See also Félix D. Almaraz, *Knight without Armor: Carlos Eduardo Castañeda, 1896–1958* (College Station: Texas A&M University Press, 1999); Saul E. Bronder, *Social Justice and Church Authority: The Public Life of Archbishop Robert E. Lucey* (Philadelphia: Temple University Press, 1982); Stephen A. Privett, *The U.S. Catholic Church and Its Hispanic Members: The Pastoral Vision of Archbishop Robert E. Lucey* (San Antonio: Trinity University Press, 1988); Emilio Zamora, "Fighting on Two Fronts: José de la Luz Saenz and the Language of the Mexican American Civil Rights Movement," in *Recovering the U.S. Hispanic Literary Heritage*, vol. 4, edited by José F. Aranda Jr. and Silvio Torres-Saillant (Houston: Arte Público Press, 2002).

11. Morín, *Among the Valiant*, 10–11.

12. Bogardus, *The Mexican in the United States* (Los Angeles: University of Southern California Press, 1934); Tuck, *Not with a Fist; Mexican Americans in a Southwestern City* (New York: Harcourt, Brace and Co., 1946); Simmons, "Anglo Americans and Mexican Americans in South Texas: A Study in Dominant-Subordinate Group Relations," Ph.D. dissertation, Harvard University, 1952; Rubel, *Across the Tracks; Mexican Americans in a Texas City*, Hogg Foundation Research Series (Austin: University of Texas Press, 1961); Madsen, *The Mexican-Americans of South Texas* (New York: Holt, Rinehart and Winston, 1964); Burma, *Spanish-Speaking Groups in the United States* (Detroit: Blaine Ethridge Books, 1974).

13. Fogel, *Mexican Americans in Southwest Labor Markets*, Advance Report 10, Mexican-American Study Project (Los Angeles: UCLA Graduate School of Business Administration, 1967); López, *Chicano, Go Home! A Novel Based on the Life of Alfonso Rodríguez* (Hicksville, N.Y.: Exposition Press, 1976). See also the following works, which address the wartime experience: Mario Barrera, *Race and Class in the Southwest: A Theory of Racial Inequality* (Notre Dame: University of Notre Dame Press, 1979); Salvador Guerrero, *Memorias: A West Texas Life*, ed. Arnoldo de León (Lubbock: Texas Tech University Press, 1991); Ruth S. Lamb, *Mexican Americans: Sons of the Southwest* (Claremont, Calif.: Ocelot Press, 1970).

14. The Recovering the U.S. Hispanic Literary Heritage Project was established by Nicolás Kanellos in 1990 to accompany a highly successful publication program

known as Arte Público Press. The Latino & Latina Project, created in 1999 by Maggie Rivas-Rodríguez, is one of the leading oral history programs in the nation that focuses on Latinos and World War II. Debra D. Andrist, "An Interview with Nicolas Kanellos," *South Central Review* 19, no. 1 (2002): 15–25; University of Texas at Austin, "War Stories," http://www.utexas.edu/features/archive/2004/history.html.

15. The first scholarly publication that emerged out of the meetings sponsored by the Latino & Latina WWII Oral History Project is *Mexican Americans and World War II*, ed. Maggie Rivas-Rodríguez (Austin: University of Texas Press, 2005).

16. U.S. Latino & Latina World War II Oral History Project, *Themes from the U.S. Latino and Latina WWII Oral History Project*. Austin, Tex.: U.S. Latino & Latina World War II Oral History Project, 2004.

17. For a detailed discussion on the idea of shared authorship in oral history, see: Michael Frisch, *A Shared Authority: Essays on the Craft and Meaning of Oral and Public History* (Albany: State University of New York Press, 1990).

CHAPTER ONE

1. Mario T. García defined the Mexican American generation as the middle group in an acculturating continuum that began with the highly Mexicanized population of the 1890–1930 period and the highly Americanized community of "Chicanos" of the 1960s in *Mexican Americans: Leadership, Ideology, and Identity, 1930–1960* (New Haven, Conn.: Yale University Press, 1989); and "Americans All: The Mexican American Generation and the Politics of Wartime Los Angeles, 1941–45," *Social Science Quarterly* 65, no. 2 (1984): 279–289.

2. See the following historical works that address the midcentury: M. T. García, *Mexican Americans;* Juan Gómez-Quiñones, *Chicano Politics: Reality and Promise, 1940–1990* (Albuquerque: University of New Mexico Press, 1990); David G. Gutiérrez, *Walls and Mirrors: Mexican Americans, Mexican Immigrants, and the Politics of Ethnicity* (Berkeley: University of California Press, 1995); Gilbert G. González and Raúl A. Fernández, *A Century of Chicano History: Empire, Nations, and Migration* (New York: Routledge, 2003).

3. For an analysis of the process of "becoming" prior to World War II, see George J. Sánchez, *Becoming Mexican American: Ethnicity, Culture and Identity in Chicano Los Angeles, 1900–1945* (New York: Oxford University Press, 1993).

4. Betsy Glickman, "Antonio Campos," U.S. Latino & Latina World War II Oral History Project, *Narratives*, Spring 2002, 52.

5. Ibid.

6. Ibid.

7. Ibid., 48.

8. Deborah Bonn, "Moisés Flores," U.S. Latino & Latina World War II Oral History Project, *Narratives*, Spring 2003, 29.

9. Andrew Tamayo, interview by Ernest Eguía, videotape recording, Houston, 18 September 2002, U.S. Latino & Latina World War II Oral History Project, Nettie Lee

Benson Latin American Collection, General Libraries, University of Texas at Austin (hereafter cited as U.S. Latino & Latina WWII Oral History Project).

10. Luis Leyva, interview by Mary Alice Carnes, videotape recording, San Antonio, 23 November 2001, U.S. Latino & Latina WWII Oral History Project.

11. Ibid.

12. Raymond J. Flores, interview by Violeta Dominguez, videotape recording, Phoenix, Ariz., 4 January 2003, U.S. Latino & Latina WWII Oral History Project.

13. Ibid.

14. Ibid.

15. María Elisa Rodríguez, interview by Ryan Bauer, videotape recording, Austin, Tex., 10 May 1999, U.S. Latino & Latina WWII Oral History Project.

16. Ibid.

17. Ibid.

18. Ibid.

19. Andrew Aguirre, interview by René Zambrano, videotape recording, San Diego, Calif., 22 January 2001, U.S. Latino & Latina WWII Oral History Project.

20. Ibid.

21. Ibid.

22. Ibid.

23. Texas A&I University was renamed Texas A&M University–Kingsville in 1993, four years after it became part of the Texas A&M University System.

24. Hector De Peña Jr., interview by Karla E. Gonzalez, videotape recording, Corpus Christi, Tex., 18 August 2001, U.S. Latino & Latina WWII Oral History Project.

25. Ibid.

26. For more information about school segregation, see Guadalupe San Miguel Jr., *"Let All of Them Take Heed": Mexican Americans and the Campaign for Educational Equality in Texas, 1910–1981* (Austin: University of Texas Press, 1987).

CHAPTER TWO

1. Ramón Rivas, interview by Maggie Rivas-Rodríguez, videotape recording, San Antonio, 21 June 1999, U.S. Latino & Latina World War II Oral History Project, Nettie Lee Benson Latin American Collection, General Libraries, University of Texas at Austin Libraries (hereafter cited as Latino & Latina WWII Oral History Project).

2. Joe Bernal, telephone interview by Maggie Rivas-Rodríguez, tape recording, 7 August 2008, U.S. Latino & Latina WWII Oral History Project.

3. Ibid.

4. For more on the early years of radio and how it shaped the country, see Michele Hilmes' *Radio Voices: American Broadcasting, 1922–1952* (Minneapolis: University of Minnesota Press, 1997), 93–96. This section, "Blackness on Radio," details how African Americans were portrayed and later developed their own programming. Though not addressing Spanish-language radio, it considers how minority Americans addressed mainstream radio. For a discussion on how radio was affected by, and

affected, the nation's polity, see Robert J. Brown, *Manipulating the Ether: The Power of Broadcast Radio in Thirties America* (Jefferson, N.C.: McFarland and Co., 1998). See also Bruce Lenthall, *Radio's America: The Great Depression and the Rise of Modern Mass Culture* (Chicago: University of Chicago Press, 2007). Lenthall notes: "To most of the radio scholars in the 1930s, mass communication held out the elusive possibility of keeping the modern world's mass public democratically informed . . . a means of making essential communication possible in the twentieth century" (144).

5. There are several sources that point to this increase, including Lenthall, *Radio's America.*

6. Dennis J. Bixler-Márquez, "The Mass Media and the Retention of Spanish by Chicanos," *International Journal of the Sociology of Language* (1985): 21–29. Bixler-Márquez concludes that those who are most successful at maintaining Spanish-language fluency make use of Spanish-language periodicals and broadcasts. He says that the "phenomenal growth of Spanish mass media, particularly electronic media, can be a powerful ally of Spanish maintenance efforts by Chicanos in the United States." See also Diana I. Rios and Stanley O. Gaines Jr., "Latino Media Use for Cultural Maintenance," *Journalism and Mass Communication Quarterly* 75, no. 4 (1998): 746–761.

7. Rudolf Arnheim and Martha Collins Bayne, "Foreign Language Broadcasts over Local American Stations," in *Radio Research, 1941*, ed. Paul F. Lazarsfeld and Frank N. Stanton (New York: Duell, Sloan and Pearce, 1941).

8. José R. "Joe" Jasso, interview by Evelyn Jasso García, videotape recording, San Antonio, 18 June 2001, U.S. Latino & Latina WWII Oral History Project.

9. U.S. Federal Communications Commission, *Sixth Annual Report of the Federal Communications Commission* (Washington, D.C.: Federal Communications Commission, 1940), http://www.fcc.gov/ftp/Bureaus/Mass_Media/Databases/documents _collection/annual_reports/1940.pdf.

10. Joshua A. Fishman, *Language Loyalty in the United States: The Maintenance and Perpetuation of Non-English Mother Tongues by American Ethnic and Religious Groups* (The Hague: Mouton, 1966), 21–33. Fishman's first chapter, "The Historical and Social Contexts of an Inquiry into Language Maintenance Efforts," articulates the inherent contradictions between "Americanization" and cultural and language maintenance: "Part of the national consciousness of all Americans is the awareness that successive waves of immigrants have been 'digested' and have become integral parts of the body politic. . . . To question the wisdom or the necessity or the naturalness of the de-ethnization of immigrant populations strikes many as questioning the very legitimacy or the very possibility of America's national and cultural existence. Both the *fact* and the *expectation* of de-ethnization have affected language maintenance in the United States, and both have probably done so in a cumulative and accelerating fashion" (24).

11. German Americans, in fact, were frequently singled out, particularly after World War I. For more on German-language maintenance, see Heinz Kloss, "German-American Language Maintenance Efforts," in Fishman, *Language Loyalty.*

12. For an examination of this issue, see Krysko, "'Gibberish' on the Air." The 1940 FCC report may be found at http://www.fcc.gov/ftp/Bureaus/Mass_Media/Databases /documents_collection/annual_reports/1940.pdf; see esp. pp. 51–52.

13. For a detailed treatment of the history of the Mexicans in the Southwest, see Rodolfo F. Acuña, *Occupied America: A History of Chicanos*, 6th ed. (New York: Pearson Longman, 2007).

14. Interviews for the U.S. Latino & Latina WWII Oral History Project are replete with examples of the punishment meted out to the offenders. The punishments ranged from a verbal chastisement to slaps on the hands and "wallopings." The corporal punishment was the case for Andrew Aguirre, who grew up in San Diego, Ca. Aguirre, interview by René Zambrano, videotape recording, San Diego, Calif., 22 January 2001, U.S. Latino & Latina WWII Oral History Project.

15. Hank Cervantes, telephone interview by Maggie Rivas-Rodríguez, tape recording, 12 August 2008, U.S. Latino & Latina WWII Oral History Project.

16. Ibid.

17. Ibid. See also Curtis Marez, "Subaltern Soundtracks: Mexican Immigrants and the Making of Hollywood Cinema," *Aztlán* 29, no. 1 (2004): 66. Marez writes about Pedro J. González, who hosted daily live broadcasts on the Burbank, California, station KELW, beginning at 4 a.m., to appeal to the Mexican migrant farmworkers.

18. Ibid.

19. Morley, *"This Is the American Forces Network."*

20. David Culbert. "Erik Barnouw's War: An Interview Concerning the Armed Forces Radio Services' Education Unit, 1944–1945," *Historical Journal of Film, Radio and Television* 22, no. 4 (2002): 475–490. One of the most fascinating parts of this interview details how the early developers of the AFRS wished to build on the "multiethnic nature of the country." Barnouw helped produce a series titled *They Call Me Joe* to celebrate American diversity. Barnouw describes it: "Each one was family history and had a first person singular narration. It always began 'They call me Joe, Giuseppe, Joe for short.' One week it was Joe who was Giuseppe, an Italian; and another one was Joe who was Joseph, or José. In fact, in almost any language you could have a Joe. That was the point" (479).

21. Martin Hadlow, "The Mosquito Network: American Military Radio in the Solomon Islands during World War II," *Journal of Radio Studies* 11, no. 1 (2004): 73–86. See also John McDonough, "The Longest Night: Broadcasting's First Invasion," *American Scholar* 63, no. 2 (1994): 193–211. McDonough offers a step-by-step chronology of the coverage of D-day, 6 June 1944, the moment at which broadcast journalism came into its own.

22. Mark Bernstein, "Inventing Broadcast Journalism," *American History* 40, no. 2 (2005): 40–46. Bernstein writes about how the practice of relying on eyewitnesses, reporting live from remote locations, evolved from covering the warfront.

23. Jerome S. Berg, "DXers/Dxing: Tuning In Distant Stations," in *Museum of Broadcast Communications Encyclopedia of Radio* (Routledge, 2004), 514–516. In this article, Berg describes the term "DXing" as deriving from the telegraphers' abbrevia-

tion for distance. DXing began in the 1920s in the United States as DXers sought the challenge of accessing radio transmitters from great distances. The practice was so prevalent and popular that, Berg notes, magazines dedicated to DXing sprang up. See also Michael C. Keith, *Sounds in the Dark : All-Night Radio in American Life*, 1st ed. (Ames: Iowa State University Press, 2001), 56. Keith writes about the ability of AM radio signals to cover great distances at night: "In the evening, a few hours past sunset, the ionosphere forms and radio's secondary signals, those that travel skyward, bounce off this nearly impenetrable layer of atmosphere. Thus, despite relatively low power levels, an AM station's sky wave can travel hundreds, sometimes thousands, of miles late at night."

24. Gene Fowler and Bill Crawford, *Border Radio: Quacks, Yodelers, Pitchmen, Psychics, and Other Amazing Broadcasters of the American Airwaves* (Austin: University of Texas Press, 2002), 9.

25. Thomas W. Hoffer, "TNT Baker: Radio Quack," in Bluem, *American Broadcasting: A Source Book on the History of Radio and Television*, ed. Lawrence W. Lichty and Malachi C. Topping (New York: Hastings House, Publishers, 1975).

26. Ibid., 575.

27. Maurice E. Shelby Jr., "John. R. Brinkley: His Contributions to Broadcasting," in *American Broadcasting: A Source Book on the History of Radio and Television*, edited by Lawrence W. Lichty and Malachi C. Topping (New York: Hastings House, 1975).

28. Ibid.

29. Ibid., 567, 685.

30. Fowler and Crawford, *Border Radio*, 65. After the war, a different station, XERF, operated out of the same building that had housed XERA. XERF would become known as the home of Wolfman Jack.

31. Hoffer, "TNT Baker: Radio Quack."

32. Fowler and Crawford, *Border Radio*, 85.

33. Hoffer, "TNT Baker: Radio Quack," 578.

34. Fowler and Crawford, *Border Radio*, 100, 101.

35. Chris Strachwitz and James Nicolopulos, *Lydia Mendoza: A Family Autobiography* (Houston: Arte Público Press, 1993). There is some disagreement about the call letters of the station, but the Mendoza family identifies it as KABC.

36. Ibid., 131.

37. Ibid., 130–131.

38. Ibid., 87.

39. Hank Cervantes, telephone interview by Maggie Rivas-Rodríguez, tape recording, 8 August 2008, U.S. Latino & Latina WWII Oral History Project.

40. Armando Flores, interview by Bettina Luis, videotape recording, Corpus Christi, Tex., 24 March 2001, U.S. Latino & Latina WWII Oral History Project.

41. Nicanór Aguilar, interview by Maggie Rivas-Rodríguez, videotape recording, El Paso, Tex., 29 December 2001, U.S. Latino & Latina WWII Oral History Project.

42. Jorge Reina Schement and Ricardo Flores, "The Origins of Spanish-Language

Radio: The Case of San Antonio, Texas," *Journalism History* 4, no. 2 (1977): 56; Félix Gutiérrez and Jorge Schement, *Spanish-Language Radio in the Southwestern United States* (Austin: Center for Mexican American Studies, 1979), 6.

43. For more information on Raoul Cortez, see http://www.sintv.org/sintv/history .html. This website, constructed by his grandson Guillermo Nicolás, provides details about Cortez. His family came from Mexico and he became a street vendor, selling fresh eggs, to earn enough money to buy time on radio stations in Nuevo Laredo, Mexico. After coming to the United States, he bought Spanish-language airtime on KMAC in San Antonio. His shows on KMAC became so popular that he understood the potential for an all-Spanish station, and thus KCOR was born.

44. Schement and Flores, "Origins of Spanish-Language Radio," 47.

45. Vicente Ximenes, interview by Jim Morrison, videotape recording, Albuquerque, 10 October 2001. Ximenes' interview was conducted in a mixture of Spanish and English. The translations are the author's.

46. Robert Rivas, my brother, conducted a genealogy of our family several years ago, as part of his coursework at Our Lady of the Lake University in San Antonio.

47. Miguel Encinias, interview by Brian Lucero, videotape recording, Albuquerque, 3 December 2001, U.S. Latino & Latina WWII Oral History Project.

48. Guadalupe San Miguel Jr., *"Let All of Them Take Heed": Mexican Americans and the Campaign for Educational Equality in Texas, 1910–1981*, 1st ed. (Austin: University of Texas Press, 1987), 33.

49. Ibid., 192.

50. Ibid., 37.

51. Joe Bernal, interview by Valentino Mauricio, videotape recording, San Antonio, 12 February 2006.

52. Nicanór Aguilar, interview by Maggie Rivas-Rodríguez, videotape recording, El Paso, Tex., 29 December 2001.

53. KIFN later became KVAA, a Univision station that continues to broadcast completely in Spanish.

54. Pete Moraga, interview by Maggie Rivas-Rodríguez, videotape recording, 4 January 2003, U.S. Latino & Latina WWII Oral History Project.

55. Nicanór Aguilar interview, 29 December 2001.

CHAPTER THREE

Author's note: I use "Mexican" to refer to persons of Mexican origin. When it is necessary to note citizenship or nativity, I use terms such as "U.S.-born Mexicans" and "Mexican nationals."

The first epigraph is from *Survey of the Mexican Labor Problem in California* (California Development Association, 1928), 3, 9–10, in George P. Clements Papers, box 62, folder 1, Department of Special Collections, University of California at Los Angeles. The second epigraph is from an interview of William Croddy by Beverly

Croddy, tape recording, 29 June 1971, OH655, Center for Oral and Public History, California State University–Fullerton (hereafter cited as CSUF).

1. Hank Cervantes, interview by Maggie Rivas-Rodríguez, videotaped recording, Washington, D.C., 30 May 2004, U.S. Latino & Latina World War II Oral History Project, Nettie Lee Benson Latin American Collection, General Libraries, University of Texas Libraries, the University of Texas at Austin (hereafter cited as U.S. Latino & Latina WWII Oral History Project).

2. Walter J. Stein, "The 'Okie' as Farm Laborer," *Agricultural History* 49 (January 1975): 202–215.

3. Important literature on agricultural workers of Mexican origin during the 1930s and 1940s includes Carey McWilliams, *Ill Fares the Land: Migrants and Migratory Labor in the United States* (Boston: Little, Brown, 1942); Cletus E. Daniel, *Bitter Harvest: A History of California Farmworkers, 1870–1941* (Ithaca, N.Y.: Cornell University Press, 1981); Dennis Nodín Valdés, *Al Norte: Agricultural Workers in the Great Lakes Region, 1917–1970* (Austin: University of Texas Press, 1991); Devra Weber, *Dark Sweat, White Gold: California Farm Workers, Cotton and the New Deal* (Berkeley: University of California Press, 1994); Gilbert G. González, "Labor and Community: Mexican Citrus Worker Villages in a Southern California County, 1900–1950," *Western Historical Quarterly* 22, no. 3 (1991): 289–331; and Matt García, *A World of Its Own: Race, Labor and Citrus in the Making of Greater Los Angeles, 1900–1970* (Chapel Hill: University of North Carolina Press, 2001).

4. Reuben W. Hecht, *Farm Labor Requirements in the United States, 1939 and 1944*, Farm Manual 59 (Washington, D.C.: U.S. Department of Agriculture, 1947): 1–7.

5. For a meticulous account of Mexicans in cotton and all other major crops in specific locations throughout the country, see U.S. Extension Service, *Preliminary Survey of Major Areas Requiring Outside Agricultural Labor*, Circular 38 (Washington, D.C., 1947).

6. Texas Agricultural Extension Service, *Farm Labor Program in Texas, 1943–1947* (College Station: Texas A&M College Extension Service, 1947), 17.

7. George T. Edson, "Mexicans in Our Northcentral States," typescript (1927), Paul Taylor Papers, Bancroft Library, University of California, Berkeley (hereafter cited as Bancroft); Dennis Nodín Valdés, *Al Norte*, and "Settlers, Sojourners and Proletarians: Social Formation in the Great Plains Sugar Beet Industry," *Great Plains Quarterly* 10 (Spring 1990), 110–123; Frank P. Barajas, "Resistance, Radicalism, and Repression on the Oxnard Plain: The Social Context of the Betabelero Strike of 1933," *Western Historical Quarterly* 35 (Spring 2004): 29–52.

8. W. Ray Easton, interview by Vivian Allen, tape recording, 27 October 1974, OH1318, Center for Oral and Public History, CSUF.

9. U.S. Extension Service, *Preliminary Survey*, 85, 92, 95, 104, 143, 168, 171, 195.

10. Paul Schuster Taylor, *Mexican Labor in the United States: Imperial Valley* (Berkeley: University of California Press, 1928); Paul Schuster Taylor, *Mexican Labor in the*

United States: Dimmit County, Winter Garden District, South Texas (Berkeley: University of California Press, 1934).

11. U.S. Extension Service, *Preliminary Survey*, 107, 141, 159, 165, 174.

12. Jerry García, "The Racialization of Mexican and Japanese Labor in the Pacific Northwest, 1900–1945," in *Memory, Community, and Activism: Mexican Migration and Labor in the Pacific Northwest*, ed. Jerry García and Gilberto García (East Lansing: Julián Samora Research Institute and Michigan State University Press, 2005): 85–129.

13. Florida Citizens Advisory Committee on Migratory Labor, Minutes of Public Hearing, Homestead, Fla., 21 February 1956, 8, Special and Area Study Collection, P. K. Yonge Library of Florida History, University of Florida; Lucian Edward Fester, "Cultural and Economic Mediation among Spanish Speaking Migrant Farm Workers in Dade County, Florida" (master's thesis, University of Miami, 1970), 34.

14. Field notes on Patterson, Stuart Jamieson Collection, Bancroft.

15. Ruth Allen, *The Labor of Women in the Production of Cotton*, University of Texas Bulletin 3134 (Austin: University of Texas, 1931), 236.

16. Gonzalo Garza, interview by Juan Campos, videotape recording, Georgetown, Tex., 14 March 2001, U.S. Latino & Latina WWII Oral History Project.

17. Beatrice Escudero Dimas, interview by Maggie Rivas-Rodríguez, videotape recording, Phoenix, Ariz., 4 January 2003, U.S. Latino & Latina WWII Oral History Project.

18. Eliseo López, interview by Kimberly Tillis, videotape recording, Austin, Tex., 26 February 2001, U.S. Latino & Latina WWII Oral History Project.

19. Henry Falcón, interview by Paul R. Zepeda, videotape recording, Houston, 24 October 2003, U.S. Latino & Latina WWII Oral History Project.

20. Candelario Hernández, interview by Lucinda Guinn, videotape recording, Austin, Tex., 3 March 2002, U.S. Latino & Latina WWII Oral History Project.

21. Paul, Otis, and Narciso Gil, interview by Andrea Valdez, videotape recording, Austin, Texas, 20 October 1999, U.S. Latino & Latina WWII Oral History Project.

22. Augustine Lucio, interview by Denise Chavarri, videotape recording, San Marcos, Tex., 10 February 2003, U.S. Latino & Latina WWII Oral History Project.

23. Ester Arredondo Pérez, interview by Gail Fisher, videotape recording, San Antonio, 23 May 2002, U.S. Latino & Latina WWII Oral History Project.

24. Baltazar Villarreal, interview by Maggie Rivas-Rodríguez, videotape recording, Kansas City, Mo., 2 August 2003, U.S. Latino & Latina WWII Oral History Project.

25. Robert Zepeda, interview by Paul Zepeda, videotape recording, Bay City, Tex., 17 March 2000, U.S. Latino & Latina WWII Oral History Project.

26. Benito Morales, interview by William Luna, videotape recording, Cicero, Ill., 5 December 2002, U.S. Latino & Latina WWII Oral History Project.

27. Elvira Pardo, interview by Wilfredo Pardo López, videotape recording, Detroit, Mich., 20 June 2003, U.S. Latino & Latina WWII Oral History Project.

28. Ascención Ambros Cortez, interview by Desirée Mata, videotape recording, San Antonio, 25 October 2003, U.S. Latino & Latina WWII Oral History Project.

29. Herlinda Mendoza Buitrón Estrada, interview by Gloria Monita, videotape recording, Saginaw, Mich., 19 October 2002, U.S. Latino & Latina WWII Oral History Project.

30. Tomás Cantú, interview by Bettina Luis, videotape recording, Corpus Christi, Tex., 23 March 2001, U.S. Latino & Latina WWII Oral History Project.

31. Calixto Ramírez, interview by Karin Brulliard, videotape recording, Brownsville, Tex., 13 September 2003, U.S. Latino & Latina WWII Oral History Project. See also "$42,000 Added to E. P. Cotton Mill Payroll," *El Paso Herald-Post*, 10 July 1933.

32. Field notes on interview of Santos Vásquez, Stuart Jamieson Collection, Bancroft.

33. Victoria Partida Guerrero, interview by Gloria Monita, videotape recording, Saginaw, Mich., 19 October 2002, U.S. Latino & Latina WWII Oral History Project.

34. Joseph Alcoser, interview by René Zambrano, videotape recording, National City, Calif., 21 October 2000, U.S. Latino & Latina WWII Oral History Project.

35. Ibid.

36. Jesús Herrera, interview by Jane O'Brien, videotape recording, San Antonio, 25 October 2003, U.S. Latino & Latina WWII Oral History Project.

37. Pete Prado, interview by Gabriel Manzano, videotape recording, San Antonio, 14 March 2000, U.S. Latino & Latina WWII Oral History Project.

38. Armando Flores, interview by Bettina Luis, videotape recording, Corpus Christi, Texas, 24 March 2001, U.S. Latino & Latina WWII Oral History Project.

39. Herminia Cadena, interview by Erika Martínez, videotape recording, Austin, Tex., 24 June 2002, U.S. Latino & Latina WWII Oral History Project.

40. Henrietta López Rivas, interview by Verónica Flores, videotape recording, San Antonio, 6 June 1999, U.S. Latino & Latina WWII Oral History Project.

41. Herlinda Mendoza Buitrón Estrada, interview.

42. George Vásquez, interview by Angela Macías, videotape recording, Inver Grove Heights, Minn., 11 August 2002, U.S. Latino & Latina WWII Oral History Project.

43. The assertion that migratory labor in the northern sugar beet fields offered high wages and that the workers were an elite appeared in Selden C. Menefee, *Mexican Migratory Workers of South Texas* (Washington, D.C.: Government Printing Office, 1940), 29.

44. Henry M. Smith, "Farm Labor in the Lower Rio Grande Valley of Texas," M.A. thesis, Texas College of Arts and Industries, Kingsville, 1947, 16–17.

45. Eliseo Navarro, interview by Francisco Venegas, videotape recording, San Antonio, 13 October 2001, U.S. Latino & Latina WWII Oral History Project.

46. Victoria Partida Guerrero, interview.

47. George Graham, interview by Donna C. Barasch, tape recording, 27 March 1972, OH1128, Center for Oral and Public History, CSUF.

48. Sarah Deutsch, *No Separate Refuge: Culture, Class and Gender on an Anglo-Hispanic Frontier in the American Southwest, 1880–1940* (New York: Oxford University Press, 1987); Walter Quinn, "Conditions of Sugar Beet Workers in Colorado in 1937,"

in Records of the Work Projects Administration, Record Group 69, folder NBER/
NRP Beet Sugar, National Archives and Records Administration, Washington, D.C.

49. U.S. Extension Service, *Preliminary Survey*, 130, 136.

50. José M. "Joe" Venegas, interview by A. Dean Tatom, tape recording, 24 March
1971, OH515, Center for Oral and Public History, CSUF.

51. Ruben Casillas, interview by René Zambrano, videotape recording, Chula
Vista, Calif., 13 July 2001, U.S. Latino & Latina WWII Oral History Project.

52. Felícitas Noriega, interview by A. Dean Tatom, tape recording, 16 May 1971,
OH607, Center for Oral and Public History, CSUF.

53. Ibid.

54. Detailed studies of Mexican labor in Southern California citrus include Gil-
bert G. González, *Community and Labor: Mexican Citrus Worker Villages in a Southern
California County, 1900–1950* (Urbana: University of Illinois Press, 1994); and Matt
García, *A World of Its Own*.

55. C. Stanley Chapman, interview by Arlene R. Sayre, tape recording, 8 March
1968, OH52, Center for Oral and Public History, CSUF.

56. W. Ray Easton, interview.

57. Claude Ridgeway, interviews by Esther R. Cramer, tape recording, 13 February 1963 and 19 January 1965, OH125, Center for Oral and Public History, CSUF.

58. J. M. Thompson, *The Orange Industry: An Economic Study*, Bulletin 622 (Berkeley, Calif.: Agricultural Experiment Station, 1938): 5–12, 69.

59. Ensley J. Campbell, interview by Florence Smiley and Milan Pavlovich, tape
recording, 1 September 1970, OH85, Center for Oral and Public History, CSUF.

60. Benoit and Frank Oxandaboure, interview by Andrea Thies, tape recording, 18
November 1981, OH1710, Center for Oral and Public History, CSUF.

61. Chaoi Vásquez, interview by Ronald Banderas, tape recording, 17 May 1970,
OH609, Center for Oral and Public History, CSUF.

62. Dan Muñoz, interview by Maggie Rivas-Rodríguez, videotape recording, San
Diego, Calif., 25 October 2002, U.S. Latino & Latina WWII Oral History Project.

63. Lauro Vega, interview by René Zambrano, videotape recording, Chula Vista,
Calif., 8 October 2000, U.S. Latino & Latina WWII Oral History Project.

64. Garland W. Coltrane, interview by Milan Pavlovich, tape recording, 12 September 1970, OH1500, Center for Oral and Public History, CSUF.

65. Jane Deming, interviews by John Gallagher, tape recording, 5 April and 2, 9, 16,
and 23 May 1968, OH19, Center for Oral and Public History, CSUF.

66. Alfredo Esqueda, interview by Ronald Banderas, tape recording, 28 May 1970,
OH612, Center for Oral and Public History, CSUF.

67. Ensley J. Campbell, interview.

68. For an informed contemporary examination of the strike and the new migra-
tion, see Paul Schuster Taylor, *On the Ground in the Thirties* (Salt Lake City: Gibbs M.
Smith, 1983); and Rodolfo F. Acuña, *Corridors of Migration: The Odyssey of Mexican
Laborers, 1600–1933* (Tucson: University of Arizona Press, 2007).

69. Manuel Guilin, interview by A. Dean Tatom, tape recording, 16 May 1971, OH-606, Center for Oral and Public History, CSUF.

70. Gonzalo B. García, interview by Beverly Gallagher, 21 March 1971, OH604, Center for Oral and Public History, CSUF.

71. Ibid.

72. Andrew Aguirre, interview by René Zambrano, videotape recording, Chula Vista, California, 28 January 2001, U.S. Latino & Latina WWII Oral History Project.

73. Rudy Acosta, interview by Louis Sahagún, videotape recording, Upton, Calif., 12 November 2000, U.S. Latino & Latina WWII Oral History Project.

CHAPTER FOUR

1. Judy Barrett Litoff and David C. Smith, eds., *American Women in a World at War: Contemporary Accounts from World War II (Worlds of Women)* (Wilmington, Dela.: Scholarly Resources, 1997), xiii, 167; Susan B. Hartmann, *The Home Front and Beyond* (Boston: Twayne, 1982), 21. The number of Latinas who served in the U.S. military is unknown. They no doubt were included among the 250,000 to 500,000 Mexican Americans and more than 53,000 Puerto Ricans in the military. Manuel Gonzales, *Mexicanos: A History of Mexican Americans in the United States* (Bloomington: Indiana University Press, 1999), 161; U.S. Department of Defense, *Hispanics in Defense of America* (Washington, D.C.: Government Printing Office, 1990), 27.

2. Litoff and Smith, *American Women in a World at War*, 167.

3. Ibid., xiv. Also see Sherna Berger Gluck, *Rosie the Riveter Revisited: Women, the War, and Social Change* (New York: Penguin Books, 1988), 270; Emily Yellin, *Our Mothers' War: American Women at Home and at the Front during World War II* (New York: Free Press, 2004), xiv; and Sara Evans, *Born for Liberty: A History of Women in America* (New York: Free Press, 1997), 241. Evans notes, "The longer-term consequences of a generation of women shaped by their wartime experiences . . . can only be inferred, but its importance should not be underestimated. . . . This may well have shaped the mixed messages they gave their daughters who loudly proclaimed the rebirth of feminism two decades later" (241).

4. Hartmann, *Home Front and Beyond*, 77, 93. By 1950, approximately 29 percent of women were in the labor force, and they were 30 percent of all workers. Nearly one-fourth of all married women were in the labor force (up from 11 percent in 1940).

5. Throughout this essay, I use the term "Latina" to mean women of Latin American descent, including those who were foreign-born. The term "Mexican American" refers to persons of Mexican descent born in the United States. When it is not necessary to underscore nativity, I use the "Mexican" designation.

6. Christine Marín, "La Asociación Hispano-Americana de Madres y Esposas: Tuscon's Mexican American Women in World War II," in Renato Rosaldo Lecture Series, Monograph 1, ser. 1983–1984 (Tucson: Mexican American Studies and Research Center University of Arizona, 1985), 5.

7. Gluck, *Rosie the Riveter Revisited*, 264.

8. Richard Santillán, "Rosita the Riveter: Midwest Mexican American Women during World War II, 1941–1945," *Perspectives in Mexican American Studies* 2 (1989): 138, 140–141.

9. Vicki L. Ruiz, *Cannery Women, Cannery Lives: Mexican Women, Unionization, and the California Food Processing Industry* (Albuquerque: University of New Mexico Press, 1987).

10. Vicki L. Ruiz, *From Out of the Shadows: Mexican Women in Twentieth-Century America* (New York: Oxford University Press, 1998), 70, 82–84.

11. Teresa Palomo Acosta and Ruthe Winegarten, *Las Tejanas: 300 Years of History* (Austin: University of Texas Press, 2003), 180–182.

12. Cindy Weigand, *Texas Women in World War II* (Latham, Md.: Republic of Texas Press, 2003).

13. Yellin, *Our Mothers' War*, 199–224, 253–278.

14. Researchers associated with the U.S. Latino & Latina World War II Oral History Project at the University of Texas at Austin conducted the interviews.

15. Karen Anderson, *Changing Women: A History of Racial Ethnic Women in Modern America* (New York: Oxford University Press, 1996), 112.

16. See Ruiz, *From Out of the Shadows*, 64–65, for the changes that began for working Mexicanas in the 1920s and 1930s. I contend that these social changes were greatly accelerated by the war.

17. Gluck, *Rosie the Riveter Revisited*, 87.

18. Dennis Gilbert, *The American Class Structure in the Age of Growing Inequality*, 6th ed. (Belmont, Calif.: Wadsworth/Thomson Learning, 2003), 17, 270. I use Gilbert's class divisions throughout this essay. Since the income of the interviewees was not available, I determined their class standing by their stated professions. In one instance, I classified a woman's family as middle class because her father owned a meat market, although she said they were poor. In another case, an interviewee's father was a steelworker, but her mother was a public schoolteacher. I designated them as middle class according to her mother's profession. Gilbert defines the following classes: underclass, working poor, working, middle, upper middle, and capitalist. The underclass includes the unemployed and those in "part time menial jobs [or on] public assistance." The working poor category includes the "lowest paid manual, retail and service workers." The working class consists of "low-skill manual, clerical or retail sales" workers. The middle class includes "lower managers, semi-professionals, craftsmen, foremen, [and workers in] non-retail sales." The upper middle class consists of "upper managers, professionals, and medium sized business owners." Finally, the capitalist class is made up of "investors, heirs, and executives."

19. Catherine Fitch and Michael R. Haines, "Median Age at First Marriage by Sex and Race, 1850–1999," in *Historical Statistics of the United States*, ed. Susan B. Carter et al. (New York: Cambridge University Press, 2006), table Ae481–488, 1:685–686. Figures for 1941–1946 are unavailable.

20. Anderson, *Changing Women*, 111–112.

21. Maggie Rivas-Rodríguez, "World War II (1941–1945)," in *Latinas in the United States: A Historical Encyclopedia*, vol. 3, ed. Vicki L. Ruiz and Virginia Sánchez Korrol (Bloomington: Indiana University Press, 2006), 810–811.

22. Francisco E. Balderrama and Raymond Rodríguez, *Decade of Betrayal: Mexican Repatriation in the 1930's* (Albuquerque: University of New Mexico Press, 1995), 216.

23. Natalia Molina, *Fit to Be Citizens: Public Health and Race in Los Angeles, 1879–1939* (Berkeley: University of California Press, 2006), 136–137.

24. Balderrama and Rodríguez, *Decade of Betrayal*, 194, 222.

25. Robert R. McKay, "Mexican Americans and Repatriation," in *The Handbook of Texas Online*, http://www.tshaonline.org/handbook/online/articles/MM/pqmyk.html.

26. Henrietta López Rivas, interview by Verónica Flores, videotape recording, San Antonio, 6 June 1999, U.S. Latino & Latina World War II Oral History Project, Nettie Lee Benson Latin American Collection, General Libraries, University of Texas Libraries, the University of Texas at Austin (hereafter cited as U.S. Latino & Latina WWII Oral History Project); Henrietta López Rivas, telephone interview by Maggie Rivas-Rodríguez, 7 April 2007, U.S. Latino & Latina WWII Oral History Project.

27. Matt S. Meier and Feliciano Ribera, *Mexican Americans/American Mexicans: From Conquistadors to Chicanos* (New York: Hill and Wang, 1993), 151.

28. Henrietta López Rivas, interview by Verónica Flores.

29. Beatrice Escudero Dimas, interview by Maggie Rivas-Rodríguez, videotape recording, Phoenix, Ariz., 4 January 2003, U.S. Latino & Latina WWII Oral History Project. Dimas was proud that she later passed the General Education Development (GED) test and earned an associate's degree when she was sixty-two years old.

30. Plácida Peña Barrera, interview by Virgilio Roel, videotape recording, Laredo, Tex., 28 September 2002, U.S. Latino & Latina WWII Oral History Project.

31. Theresa Herrera Cásarez, interviews with author, videotape recording, Austin, Tex., 11 and 13 October 2000, U.S. Latino & Latina WWII Oral History Project.

32. Unlike the formal de jure segregation of African Americans, Mexican American school segregation was rarely written into formal school statutes. Some schools stipulated, however, that instruction would be in English, giving them an excuse to segregate Mexican American children. Restrictive real estate practices and covenants also had the effect of segregating Mexican American pupils. Vicki L. Ruiz, "South by Southwest: Mexican Americans and Segregated Schooling, 1900–1950," *Organization of American States Magazine of History* 15, no. 2 (2001): 23–27; Victoria-María MacDonald, *Latino Education in the United States: A Narrated History from 1513–2000* (New York: Palgrave Macmillan, 2004), 118–119.

33. María Isabel Solís Thomas, interview by Anna Zukowski, videotape recording, Brownsville, Tex., 13 September 2003, U.S. Latino & Latina WWII Oral History Project.

34. Herminia Guerrero Cadena, interview by Erika Martínez, videotape recording, Austin, Tex., 24 June 2002, U.S. Latino & Latina WWII Oral History Project.

35. Sally Castillo Castro, interview by Nicole Griffith, videotape recording, Austin, Tex., 1 March 2001, U.S. Latino & Latina WWII Oral History Project.

36. Ibid.

37. Henrietta López Rivas, interview by Verónica Flores.

38. Ibid.

39. Ibid.

40. Theresa Herrera Cásarez, interviews with author.

41. Ventura Terrones Campa, interview by Delia J. Luján, videotape recording, Newton, Kans., 1 August 2003, U.S. Latino & Latina WWII Oral History Project.

42. Martha Ortega Vidaurri, interview by Tammi Grais, videotape recording, Austin, Tex., 3 October 2001, U.S. Latino & Latina WWII Oral History Project.

43. Gloria Araguz Alaniz, interview by Yvonne Lim, videotape recording, Austin, Tex., 18 October 2003, U.S. Latino & Latina WWII Oral History Project.

44. Ruiz, *From Out of the Shadows*, 69.

45. Ibid., 52–62.

46. Delfina Luján Cuellar, interview by Erika L. Martínez, videotape recording, Albuquerque, 2 November 2002, U.S. Latino & Latina WWII Oral History Project.

47. Concepción Alvarado Escobedo, interview by Sandra Freyberg, videotape recording, Brownsville, Tex., 20 September 2003, U.S. Latino & Latina WWII Oral History Project.

48. Apolonia Muñoz Abarca, interview by Erika L. Martínez, videotape recording, Corpus Christi, Tex., 18 August 2001, U.S. Latino & Latina WWII Oral History Project.

49. Ibid.

50. Ventura Terrones Campa, interview.

51. Ruiz, *From Out of the Shadows*, 59.

52. Henrietta López Rivas, interview by Verónica Flores.

53. Martha Ortega Vidaurri, interview.

54. Apolonia Muñoz Abarca, interview by Erika L. Martínez.

55. Delfina Luján Cuellar, interview. V-mail, or Victory mail, was created in England to reduce the size and weight of correspondence to and from servicemen during the war. The message was written on specially designed thin sheets of paper that folded and sealed, forming both letter and envelope. When mailed, the letter was reduced in size on microfilm. A facsimile of the letter, which was one-fourth of its original size, was reproduced and delivered to the recipient. For more information, see the Smithsonian national Postal Museum website, http://www.postalmuseum.si.edu/exhibits/2d2a_vmail.html.

56. Ventura Terrones Campa, interview.

57. Theresa Herrera Cásarez, interviews with author.

58. U.S. Department of Labor, Children's Bureau, *If Your Baby Must Travel in Wartime*, Bureau Publication 307 (Washington, D.C., 1944), 5–24. The publication was reprinted in Litoff and Smith, *American Women in a World at War*, 138–147.

59. Beatrice Escudero Dimas, interview.

60. Ascención Ambros Cortez, interview by Desirée Mata, videotape recording, San Antonio, 25 October 2003, U.S. Latino & Latina WWII Oral History Project.

61. Theresa Herrera Cásarez, interviews with author.

62. Sally Castillo Castro, interview.

63. Hartmann, *Home Front and Beyond*, 22.

64. Sally Castillo Castro, interview.

65. Gloria Araguz Alaniz, interview.

66. Elena Tamez De Peña, interview by Erika L. Martínez, videotape recording, Corpus Christi, Tex., 18 August 2001, U.S. Latino & Latina WWII Oral History Project.

67. Apolonia Muñoz Abarca, interview by Erika L. Martínez.

68. Ibid.

69. Ibid.

70. The Women's Detention Hospital and Rapid Treatment Center opened in September 1943 and closed in 1946. *Corpus Christi Caller-Times*, 9 September 1943, 30.

71. Apolonia Muñoz Abarca, telephone interview with author, tape recording, 20 August 2008, audiotape in author's possession.

72. Hartmann, *Home Front and Beyond*, 79.

73. *Building Bridges: Report on Health and Welfare Planning; July 1947*, collection C4, box 1, folder 1.06, Special Collections, Corpus Christi Public Library, Corpus Christi, Tex. Also see *Annual Report of the Community House: 1940*, collection C4, box 1, folder 1.06, Special Collections, Corpus Christi Public Library. For an overview of the settlement house movement, see Ruiz, *From Out of the Shadows*, 34–50.

74. Apolonia Muñoz Abarca, telephone interview with author.

75. Apolonia Muñoz Abarca interview by Erika L. Martínez.

76. Elena Tamez De Peña, interview.

77. Carlos E. Castañeda, "Statement before the Senate Committee on Labor and Education, September 8, 1944," in *Are We Good Neighbors?* comp. Alonso S. Perales (San Antonio: Artes Gráficas, 1948), 95.

78. Eric Arnesen and Alex Lichtenstein, introduction to *Wartime Shipyard: A Study in Social Disunity*, by Katherine Archibald (1947; Chicago: University of Illinois Press, 2006), xxxvi.

79. As of this writing, in 2008, 95 women have been interviewed, according to project records. In addition to the three defense workers in this study, Delfina Cooremans Baladez balanced propellers at Kelly Field in San Antonio; her sister, Wilhemina Cooremans Vásquez, worked as an airplane mechanic at Kelly Field; Ester Arredondo Pérez worked as an airplane mechanic, first at Kelly Field, and then in Hawaii; and Alejandra Rojas Zúñiga assembled gliders at Gibson Company, a plant in Greenville, Michigan.

80. Henrietta López Rivas, interview by Verónica Flores.

81. Ibid.

82. Ibid.

83. Josephine Kelly Ledesma, interview by Monica Rivera, videotape recording, Austin, Tex., 17 February 2001, U.S. Latino & Latina WWII Oral History Project.

84. Ibid.

85. Arnesen and Lichtenstein, introduction to Archibald, *Wartime Shipyard*, xvi.

86. Hartmann, *Home Front and Beyond*, 59.

87. Yellin, *Our Mothers' War*, 58.

88. Arnesen and Lichtenstein, introduction to Archibald, *Wartime Shipyard*,, xxviii.

89. Ibid., xlii.

90. María Isabel Solís Thomas, interview.

91. Ibid.

92. Ibid.

93. Ibid.

94. Aurora González Castro, interview by Anna Zukovski, videotape recording, San Antonio, 25 October 2003, U.S. Latino & Latina WWII Oral History Project.

95. Ibid.

96. Ventura Terrones Campa, interview.

97. Herminia Guerrero Cadena, interview.

98. Plácida Peña Barrera, interview. Texas A&I University became Texas A&M University–Kingsville in 1993, after becoming part of the Texas A&M University System.

99. Theresa Herrera Cásarez, interviews with author.

100. Ascención Ambros Cortez, interview.

101. Beatrice Escudero Dimas, interview.

102. Litoff and Smith, *American Women in a World at War*, 147.

103. Martha Ortega Vidaurri, interview.

104. Rafaela Muñiz Esquivel, interview by author, videotape recording, San Antonio, 12 April 2001, U.S. Latino & Latina WWII Oral History Project.

105. Ibid.

106. Black women served in segregated units in the Women's Army Corps and the Army Nurse Corps, but near the end of the war, they were allowed in the Women Accepted for Volunteer Emergency Service (WAVES) or the Women's Reserve of the U.S. Coast Guard (SPARS); they were not allowed in the Women's Airforce Service Pilots (WASP); and they were admitted to the marines only after World War II. See Yellin, *Our Mothers' War*, 116. "SPAR" is short for the Coast Guard motto: *Semper paratus* (Always ready), as noted in ibid., 115.

107. Hartmann, *Home Front and Beyond*, 32.

108. Rafaela Muñiz Esquivel, interview.

109. Ibid.

110. Hartmann, *Home Front and Beyond*, 32. War nurses were commissioned as second lieutenants.

111. For discrepancies between male and female enlistees, see Yellin, *Our Mothers' War*, 116.

112. For more on the relations working with Anglos, see Richard Griswold del Castillo, "The Paradox of War," chap. 1 in this volume.

113. Cármen Contreras Bozak, interview by Vivian Torre, videotape recording, Miami, Fla., 14 September 2002, U.S. Latino & Latina WWII Oral History Project.

114. Ibid.

115. Concepción Alvarado Escobedo, interview.

116. Ibid. For a discussion of the motivation behind Anglo female enlistments, see June Allenz, "Invisible Veterans," *Educational Record* 75, no. 4 (1994): 46. For a discussion of the motivation behind male Mexican American enlistments, see Gonzales, *Mexicanos*, 162.

117. Concepción Alvarado Escobedo, interview.

118. Ibid.

119. Felícitas Cerda Flores, interview by Paul Zepeda, videotape recording, Houston, 2 February 2002, U.S. Latino & Latina WWII Oral History Project.

120. Ibid. In addition to the four women mentioned above, Emma Villareal Hernández of Pharr, Texas, also joined the military. She was sent to Rodd Field in Corpus Christi, where she logged the flight hours of servicemen. Emma Villareal Hernández, interview by Gary Villereal, videotape recording, McAllen, Tex., 1 July 2002, U.S. Latino & Latina WWII Oral History Project.

121. This is similar to what happened with other American women. Evans writes that many Anglo-American married women with children entered the workforce at this time: "In contradiction to privatized images of family life and the glorification of motherhood, white married women with children entered the labor force at an accelerating rate. From 1950 to 1960 their labor force participation rate grew from 17 to 30 percent" (*Born for Liberty*, 252). For an analysis of the effects three Mexican American women had on their daughters, see Brenda Sendejo, "Mother's Legacy: Cultivating Chicana Consciousness during the War Years," chap. 9 in this anthology.

122. Hartmann, *Home Front and Beyond*, 77.

123. Four were nurses, three were bookkeepers/accountants, one was a supervisor in a Civil Service position, another worked in Civil Service temporarily, one was a clerk in a courthouse, two were department store clerks, one was a doctor's receptionist, one was a maid supervisor, another worked as an interpreter for Immigration and Naturalization Service, one was a migrant farmer, and one worked in an egg packing plant.

124. Mario Barrera, *Race and Class in the Southwest: A Theory of Inequality* (Notre Dame, Ind.: University of Notre Dame Press, 1979), 131.

125. Hartmann, *Home Front and Beyond*, 101.

126. June A. Willenz, *Women Veterans: America's Forgotten Heroines* (New York: Continuum, 1983), 46.

127. The Women's Auxiliary Army Corps became the Women's Army Corps (WAC) in 1943.

CHAPTER FIVE

1. Luis G. Zorrilla, Blanca Torres, and Carmela Elvira Santoro provide excellent studies on Mexico-U.S. relations that focus on Mexican contributions during the Second World War. Frederick B. Pike offers an early examination of the United States' Good Neighbor Policy as a primary initiative that improved relations with Latin America. Josefina Zoraida Vázquez and Lorenzo Meyer, on the other hand, place wartime cooperation within a broader historical framework. María Emilia Paz, William S. Wood, and Stephen I. Schwab represent a contrary view, one that questions the importance of WWII in Mexico-U.S. relations and gives limited attention to Mexico's contributions to the war effort. Zorrilla, *Historia de las relaciones entre México y los Estados Unidos de América, 1800–1958*, vol. 2 (Mexico City: Editorial Porrúa, 1966); Torres, *Historia de la Revolución Mexicana, periodo 1940–52: México en la Segunda Guerra Mundial* (Mexico City: El Colegio de México, 1979); Santoro, "United States and Mexican Relations during World War II" (Ph.D. diss., Syracuse University, 1967); Vázquez and Meyer, *México frente a Estados Unidos (un ensayo histórico, 1776–1988)*, 2nd ed. (Mexico City: Fondo de Cultura Económica, 1992); Pike, *FDR's Good Neighbor Policy: Sixty Years of Gentle Chaos* (Austin: University of Texas Press, 1995); Paz, *Strategy, Security and Spies: Mexico and the U.S. as Allies in World War II* (University Park: Pennsylvania State University Press, 1997); Wood, "A Re-examination of Mexican Support for the United States during World War II" (Ph.D., diss., University of Missouri–Columbia, 1989); Schwab, "The Role of the Mexican Expeditionary Air Force in World War II: Late, Limited, but Symbolically Significant," *Journal of Military History*, 66, no. 4 (2002): 115–140.

2. The discussion on Mexican-U.S. relations during the Second World War is based on the previously noted works, but largely on Torres' *Historia de la Revolución Mexicana*. The following study corroborates Torres' observations on military relations: Stetson Conn and Byron Fairchild, "The United States and Mexico: Solidarity and Security," in *United States Army in World War II: The Western Hemisphere; The Framework of Hemisphere Defense* (Washington, D.C.: Center of Military History, 1989): 331–363.

3. The following work addresses Mexico's campaign against discrimination in the United States and the U.S. promise to address it, all of which elevated the issue to a level of hemispheric relations during World War II: Emilio Zamora, *Claiming Rights and Righting Wrongs in Texas: Mexican Workers and Job Politics during World War II* (College Station: Texas A&M University Press, 2009).

4. As a result of the war, Mexico lost more than half of its territory to the United States, including the rights over Texas, which it had asserted primarily on the grounds that the declaration of independence by the "Lone Star State" and its admission as a state were based on an unjust act of rebellion and fraudulent legal claims. The famed deportations as well as the accompanying self-repatriating movement sent an undetermined number of Mexicans back to Mexico. The massive movement included

between 500,000 and 600,000 Mexican nationals and U.S.-born Mexicans, and it occurred mostly between the late 1920s and the early 1930s. Richard Griswold del Castillo, *The Treaty of Guadalupe Hidalgo: A Legacy of Conflict* (Norman: University of Oklahoma, 1992); Francisco A. Rosales, ¡*Pobre Raza! Violence, Justice, and Mobilization among México Lindo Immigrants* (Austin: University of Texas Press, 1999); Juan Gómez-Quiñones, *Roots of Chicano Politics, 1600–1940* (Albuquerque: University of New Mexico Press, 1994).

5. Numerous reports on the popular support in Mexico for the war, including references to the long lines of young volunteers at the U.S. Embassy, appear in various diplomatic sources, including Archivo Histórico Genaro Estrada, Secretaría de Relaciones Exteriores, Mexico City (hereafter cited as Relaciones) and U.S. State Department, Confidential U.S. State Department Central Files, *Mexico, Internal Affairs, 1940–1944*, part 1, microfilmed ed. (Frederick, Md.: University Publications of America, 1987) (hereafter cited as U.S. State Department).

6. Diplomatic correspondence and numerous letters from Mexicans in the United States and northern Mexico that speak of draft evasions appear in the archives of Secretaría de Relaciones Exteriores. In some cases, the evasions reflected misunderstandings regarding draft responsibilities rather than conscious attempts to avoid the draft. Some Mexican nationals, for example, traveled to Mexico to visit family at the same time that their draft notices arrived at their U.S. addresses. For diplomatic correspondence on the subject, see Javier Osornio C., Mexican Consul, Laredo, Texas, to Secretaría de Relaciones Exteriores, 2 January 1946, Relaciones.

7. According to Santoro, the agreement guaranteed the inductees the same rights and privileges accorded to each country's nationals. "Border crossers" would be allowed to maintain their residence status in the country where they lived. Other "exemptions" included students and government officials. The signatories also agreed to exchange information on registrants and inductees and to release the other country's nationals who had been inducted but had not declared an interest in adopting a new citizenship. Santoro, "United States and Mexican Relations," 206.

8. The following sources provide information on numerous cases of discrimination as well as complaints by Mexican nationals against overzealous draft boards and other unfair local officials: Armando C. Amador to Vicente Sanchez Gavito, 15 June 1945; Javier Osornio to Secretaría de Relaciones Exteriores, 2 January 1946; Carlos A. Calderón to Secretaría de Relaciones Exteriores, 15 March 1945, in "Dificultades que tienen mexicanos en Texas, 1945"; "Mexicanos reclutados (en el) ejército norteamericano, 1939–45: Asuntos generales"; "Mexicanos enrolados en el ejército de los Estados Unidos," all in Relaciones. The latter extensive records, subtitled "Asuntos consulares," contain twenty-seven *legados*, or files of correspondence with Mexican nationals in the U.S. military, that the author reviewed.

9. The total number of "dead, injured, imprisoned, or disappeared" Mexican servicemen represented almost 10 percent of the total number (15,000). The comparable figure of combat deaths, nontheater deaths, and nonmortal injuries for all U.S. soldiers

in World War II was 6.6 percent. U.S. Department of Veterans Affairs, Public and Inter-governmental Affairs, "Fact Sheet: America's Wars, November 2006," http://www1 .va.gov/opa/fact/amwars.asp.

10. Torres, *Historia de la Revolución Mexicana*, 244, quoted correspondence from Cárdenas to General Handy, 23 September 1943.

11. For a discussion of the symbolic contribution by the Mexican air squadron, see Santoro, "United States and Mexican Relations," 211–217; and Schwab, "Role of the Mexican Expeditionary Air Force."

12. Santoro, "United States and Mexican Relations," 207. For an early devastating critique of the reciprocal agreement in the Mexican press and a report on the critique by the U.S. ambassador, see Nemesio García Naranjo, "Con, pero no debajo," *Hoy*, 7 November 1942; and George S. Messersmith to Cordell Hull, U.S. Secretary of State, 5 November 1942, U.S. State Department. According to García Naranjo, "No state, whether acting as friend or kin, can legislate over the lives of citizens who belong to another state. It is absurd to recruit under a foreign flag persons who were born under our flag."

13. Santoro, "United States and Mexican Relations," 207.

14. Richard Vara, an early recruit who was assigned to accompany young Mexicans from South Texas being transported by train to military installations, recalled that discrimination followed them into the military. Also, many of the young men were despondent because they had never left their small towns or isolated rural homes. Discrimination, according to Vara, complicated their already difficult experience. Richard Vara, interview with author, Houston, 16 May 1995, copy of transcript in author's possession. The author's translation and Vara's corresponding statement on discriminatory practices in the military are as follows: "They were so inconsiderate— they respected me because I could speak English. But they mistreated the other poor souls. Many of them still had the sense of pride of our grandparents. They slapped us if we spoke Spanish. They would tell us not to speak the language of dogs." [Eran infelices, a mí me respetaban porque sabía inglés. Pero a los otros pobres los maltra-taban. Muchos todavía teníamos el orgullo de nuestros abuelos. Nos cacheteaban si hablábamos español. Nos decían que no habláramos el idioma de perros.]

15. "Mexicanos reclutados (en el) ejército norteamericano," part 2, 1944–1945, Relaciones.

16. I borrow the concept of the "1.5 generation" from scholars who have studied Latino immigrant youth in U.S. schools. The following recent representative ex-ample refers to children born in Mexico but whose experiences were comparable to U.S.-born because of their length of residence in the United States: Angela Valenzu-ela, *Subtractive Schooling: U.S.-Mexican Youth and the Politics of Caring* (Albany: State University of New York Press, 1999).

17. A note on the comparability of the occupational data in table 2 is necessary in order to build confidence in the findings. The author coded the data reported by the respondents according to the 1940 index of occupations and industries published by

the U.S. Bureau of the Census. Although the 1940 census did not provide comparable data on Mexican-origin persons, its index offered the standard occupational and industrial definitions for the time period. U.S. Department of Commerce, Bureau of the Census, *Alphabetical Index of Occupations and Industries*, prepared by Alba M. Edwards (Washington, D.C.: Government Printing Office, 1940).

18. Ibid.; Robert Jenkens, "Processing and Tabulation," chap. 4 in *Procedural History of the 1940 Census of Population and Housing* (Madison: Center for Demography and Ecology, University of Wisconsin, 1983), 75–78. The author used the 1940 census index to train and supervise a graduate class at the University of Houston in 1994 to code the registration data. The students were Marquita E. Anderson, Matthew Burdette, Charles Burris, William Clark, George Cooper, Ann Quiroz, Jan Rosin, Elías Sanchez, Juan Sanchez, and David Urbano. Although the census report of 1940 was useful in coding the occupational data, it did not include comparable occupational data. The 1930 report provided a racial category of "Mexican" while the 1950 report offered numerous categories for the "Spanish-speaking" that allows one to make comparisons. The 1940 report, on the other hand, dropped the racial category "Mexican." The 1930 and 1950 reports have their own problems that undermine to some extent the comparability of the data. The 1930 report, for example, did not include U.S.-born in the Mexican category, and the 1950 report limited its enumeration to the five southwestern states. These data, however, offer the best basis for making comparisons, whereas the 1940 data are practically impossible to determine with any reliability. For a discussion of the data and their comparability, see Mark Reisler, *By the Sweat of Their Brow: Mexican Immigrant Labor in the United States, 1900–1940* (Westport, Conn.: Greenwood Press, 1976), 265–270; and Campbell Gibson and Kay Jung, "Historical Census Statistics on Population Totals by Race, 1790 to 1990, for Large Cities and Other Urban Places in the United States," Population Division Working Paper 76 (Washington, D.C.: U.S. Bureau of the Census, 2005).

19. Walter Fogel, Mario Barrera, David Montejano, and Emilio Zamora have examined the upward mobility experience of Mexicans with the use of census data from between 1930 and 1970. Fogel, Barrera, and Zamora have underscored an accompanying process of uneven mobility to explain the continued concentration of Mexicans in the lower-skilled occupations as well as in the lower segments of the higher-skilled and higher-status occupations. Fogel, *Mexican Americans in Southwest Labor Markets*, Advance Report 10, Mexican-American Study Project (Los Angeles: UCLA Graduate School of Business Administration, 1967); Barrera, *Race and Class in the Southwest: A Theory of Racial Inequality* (Notre Dame, Ind.: University of Notre Dame Press, 1979); Montejano, *Anglos and Mexicans in the Making of Texas, 1836–1986* (Austin: University of Texas Press, 1987); Zamora, *Claiming Rights and Righting Wrongs*.

20. My observation on the education levels of farmworkers is based on the following sources: Texas Farm Placement Service, *Origins and Problems of Texas Migratory Farm Labor* (Austin, 1940); Perry Morris Broom, "An Interpretative Analysis of the Economic and Educational Status of Latin-Americans in Texas, with Emphasis upon

the Basic Factors Underlying an Approach to an Improved Program of Occupational Guidance, Training, and Adjustment for Secondary Schools" (Ph.D. diss., University of Texas at Austin, 1942).

21. As previously noted, much of the correspondence from Mexican nationals in the U.S. military originates from the following source: "Mexicanos enrolados en el ejército de los Estados Unidos," Relaciones. The following videotaped interviews from the U.S. Latino & Latina World War II Oral History Project Collection, Nettie Lee Benson Latin American Collection, General Libraries, the University of Texas at Austin provide additional representative observations by Mexican soldiers and family members on discrimination in the military as well as at the home front, before and after the war: Rudy Acosta, interview by Louis Sahagún, Upton, Calif., 12 November 2000; Nicanór Aguilar, interview by Maggie Rivas-Rodríguez, El Paso, Tex., 29 December 2001; Elena Peña Gallego, interview by Maggie Rivas-Rodríguez, El Paso, Tex., 9 March 2002; Félix Treviño, interview by David Zavala, San Antonio, 13 October 2001.

22. "Mi deseo es ser ciudadano de los Estados Unidos si es que sea posible tan pronto como haya oportunidad."

23. "Aún no se pueden decidir si soy digno de ser ciudadano del país."

24. "Apesar de todo esto estos Pinches Gringos me metieron de soldado después de que yo les dije que mi anciana Madre estaba perdiendo su vista, que gente tan infame estos pinches hueros."

25. "Que abusan y pisotean la constitución . . . , que no quieren a los negros y a nosotros."

26. ". . . si a mí me toca la de perder defendiendo al continente en que bivimos a mi pueblo y a mi nación lo que le encargo es que se una."

27. Acosta was born in El Paso and raised in Los Angeles, where he worked as a machinist at the start of the war. Aguilar was born and raised in Falls City, Texas, and worked as an agricultural laborer in the early 1940s. Frank Trejo, "Rudy Acosta," and Claudia Farias, "Nicanór Aguilar, Sr.," U.S. Latino & Latina WWII Oral History Project, http://www.lib.utexas.edu/ww2latinos/browse-alpha.html.

28. David Zavala, "Felix Treviño"; Lindsay Peyton, "Elena Peña Gallego"; and Desirée Mata, "Aurora Estrada Orozco," all at U.S. Latino & Latina WWII Oral History Project, http://www.lib.utexas.edu/ww2latinos/browse-alpha.html.

29. Graduate students in search of a research topic may wish to conduct oral histories to explain the experiences of the Mexican soldiers, especially in relation to U.S.-born Mexicans, African Americans, and other U.S. soldiers. One of the most important tasks would be to determine how they reconciled their attachment to the homeland with their opportunity to incorporate themselves further into U.S. society, and how citizenship, in the cultural sense of the word, encouraged this process. It would also be useful to determine how military experience facilitated acculturation and social incorporation among themselves and their families.

CHAPTER SIX

1. Julio Enrique Monagas to Max Egloff, memorandum, n.d., Archivo General de Puerto Rico, Fondo Oficina del Gobernador, Serie Milicia 005, Tarea 96–20, Caja 1143 (hereafter AGPR); the translation is mine. Although Monagas' report is not dated, it was probably written in early October 1942. Monagas was an aide to Governor Rexford G. Tugwell.

2. Many of these letters are deposited in Fundación Archivo Luis Muñoz Marín, Sección IV LMM, Presidente del Senado 1941–1948, Serie 9 Asuntos Fuerzas Armadas (hereafter AFLMM).

3. Private Miguel Mateo to Luis Muñoz Marín, 11 December 1945, AFLMM.

4. Desmond King, *Black Americans and the US Federal Government* (Oxford: Clarendon Press, 1995).

5. Carl Allsup, *The American G.I. Forum: Origins and Evolution* (Austin: University of Texas Press, 1982), chap. 4.

6. Thurgood Marshall, "Summary Justice: The Negro GI in Korea," *Crisis*, May 1951, 297–355.

7. One of the classic works treating the subject of Jim Crowism is C. Van Woodward, *The Strange Career of Jim Crow* (New York: Oxford University Press, 1966).

8. *Plessy v. Ferguson*, 163 US 537 (1896). Some of the arguments in the majority opinion were as follows: "If one race be inferior to the other socially, the constitution of the United States cannot put them upon the same plane. . . . We consider the underlying fallacy of the plaintiff's argument to consist in the assumption that the enforced separation of the two races stamps the colored race with a badge of inferiority. If this be so, it is not by reason of anything found in the act, but solely because the colored race chooses to put that construction upon it. . . . A statute which implies merely a legal distinction between the white and colored races—a distinction which is founded in the color of the two races, and which must always exist so long as white men are distinguished from the other race by color—has no tendency to destroy the legal equality of the two races, or re-establish a state of involuntary servitude."

9. Jack D. Foner, *Blacks and the Military in American History: A New Perspective* (New York: Praeger, 1974).

10. For a brief but effective description of the relationship between racialist theories and science in the nineteenth century, see Stephen Jay Gould, *The Mismeasure of Man* (New York: W. W. Norton and Co., 1996).

11. For more on Charles White, see Marvin Harris, *The Rise of Anthropological Theory: A History of Theories of Culture* (New York: Crowell, 1968).

12. Foner, *Blacks and the Military*, 119–120.

13. Ibid, 13.

14. Tracy Creek notes: "During and after the First World War, Du Bois developed a critique of the war in Europe in which he argued that it was not, as many white Americans imagined, simply a fight among Europeans over European issues. Instead,

the war was a product of European imperialism and racial injustice. Du Bois also wrote extensively on the contributions of African Americans to the war effort and on the irony of seeing Black soldiers fight and die to restore democracy in Europe, while returning home to a land of intolerance and legal inequality. Returning black soldiers, he argued, should bring their struggle for equality back with them to their fatherland." Creek, annotation of selected W. E. B. Du Bois essays, http://www.library .umass.edu/spcoll/digital/writings.htm.

15. *Congressional Record*, 64th Cong., 2nd sess. (1917), 2250.

16. Jorge Rodríguez-Beruff, *Strategy as Politics: Puerto Rico on the Eve of the Second World War* (San Juan: Editorial de la Universidad de Puerto Rico, 2007): 31–32.

17. Ibid., 55.

18. "Objections to Negro Camp," *New York Times*, 21 August 1917, 13.

19. Governor [Arthur] Yager to Frank McIntyre, 19 November 1917, National Archives and Records Administration (NARA), Records of the Bureau of Insular Affairs, 1868–1945, Record Group 350, doc. 14-D.

20. Ibid.

21. For a short historical account of the regiment, see José Norat Martínez, *Historia del Regimiento 65 de Infantería, 1899–1960* (San Juan, Puerto Rico: Imprenta La Milagrosa, 1992).

22. NARA, Records of the War Department General and Special Staffs, Record Group 165, doc. 717.

23. William T. Bowers et al., *Black Soldier, White Army: The 24th Infantry Regiment in Korea* (Washington, D.C.: U.S. Army Center of Military History, 1996), 19.

24. Phillip McGuire, *He, Too, Spoke for Democracy: Judge Hastie, World War II, and the Black Soldier* (New York: Greenwood Press, 1988).

25. William H. Hastie, interview by Jerry N. Hess, tape recording, 5 January 1972, Harry S. Truman Library and Museum, Independence, Mo. Judge Hastie, who also served as governor of the U.S. Virgin Islands and a member of the Anglo-American Caribbean Commission in 1943, would later admit that his designation did not produce any dramatic changes. In this oral history interview, his opinion of Secretary of War Henry L. Stimson is illuminating:

> HESS: How receptive was Mr. Stimson?
>
> HASTIE: Well, Mr. Stimson was concerned, but he, in my judgment, had no feel for, no real perception of the problems of race in America, or their impact, or the relation of the military to them. He was a most honest and dedicated man, a patriot in the best and the highest sense of the word, but he was a man whose whole life in his practice of law, in his social contacts, his whole background, had isolated him from the areas, the problems, of which I was basically concerned.
>
> I can give one example of that: I was talking to him at one time about something that I'm sure had to do with the Air Force that troubled me from the beginning to the end of the period that I was there, because, as I say, I thought it was a place where it

was practical to make the most progress, and in fact, we were making the least progress. I'm sure that General [Henry H.] Arnold and others had talked to him about their point of view. In the course of the conversation, I will always remember one sentence, both what he said and the words he used, which to me reflected the problem of getting him to move in this area. He said, "Mr. Hastie, is it not true that your people are basically agriculturalists?"

HESS: Any other illustrations?

HASTIE: No, I think that one is both simple enough and dramatic enough to indicate that though Mr. Stimson was entirely well-meaning and I have no reason to believe that he was in any way a prejudiced person, I always felt that he was basically uncomprehending as to the realities of the problems of race in the army and in the American society generally.

26. Sergeant Major Nicolás Chiclana, interview with Silvia Alvarez Curbelo, tape recording, San Juan, Puerto Rico, 22 February 1990, in author's possession.

27. Foner, *Blacks and the Military*, 141.

28. Judge William H. Hastie to Governor Rexford G. Tugwell, 9 September 1942, AGPR.

29. Ibid.

30. Ibid.

31. Governor Rexford G. Tugwell to Judge William H. Hastie, 22 December 1942, AGPR.

32. Ibid.

33. I have analyzed this rhetoric in "Las lecciones de la guerra: Luis Muñoz Marín y la Segunda Guerra Mundial," in *Luis Muñoz Marín: Ensayos del Centenario*, ed. Fernando Picó (San Juan, Puerto Rico: Fundación Luis Muñoz Marín, 1999): 31–63.

34. The PDP leadership postponed the discussion of Puerto Rico's political destiny for the duration of the war. Penny M. Von Eschen, *Race against Empire: Black Americans and Anticolonialism, 1937–1957* (Ithaca, N.Y.: Cornell University Press, 1997).

35. Monagas to Egloff, memorandum.

36. Arjun Appadurai explains the role of the census in colonial contexts in his essay "El número en la imaginación colonial," in *La modernidad desbordada: Dimensiones culturales de la globalización* (Buenos Aires: Trilce, 2001), 125–144.

37. Tomás Blanco admits that there is "social" racism in Puerto Rico but argues that it is quite different from the "lynching" kind of racism practiced in the United States. Blanco, *El prejuicio racial en Puerto Rico* (San Juan: Ediciones Huracán, 1985).

38. Monagas to Egloff, memorandum.

39. Ibid.

40. I discuss the subject of nineteenth-century abolitionism as a modern discourse in my book *Un país del porvenir: El discurso de la modernidad en Puerto Rico (siglo XIX)* (San Juan, Puerto Rico: Ediciones Callejón, 2001).

41. Monagas to Egloff, memorandum.

42. Thomas R. Phillips, Chief of Staff [of Puerto Rico Military Department], to Max Egloff, 26 October 1942, AGPR.

43. Ibid.

44. Clarence Senior, for example, worked for the Social Sciences Research Center at the University of Puerto Rico. He is the author of *Preliminary Analysis of Puerto Rican Selective Service Rejections from May 18, 1937, to Jan. 5, 1946*, commissioned by the Division of Territories and Island Possessions, NARA, Record Group 126, doc. 6-A.

45. Harry Besosa, Director of the Selective Service Office in Puerto Rico, to Major General Lewis Hershey, Director of the Selective Service, 9 February 1943, NARA, Records of the Office of Territories, 1885–1976, Record Group 126, doc. 717-F.

46. Thomas Handy, Major General, Assistant Chief of Staff, Puerto Rico Military Department, memorandum, 12 January 1943, NARA, Record Group 126, doc. 717-P.

47. Ibid.

48. Col. Thomas R. Phillips to Lt. Col. Donald Wilson, 13 November 1942, NARA, Record Group 126, doc. 117-S.

49. Ibid.

50. Col. Thomas R. Phillips to Gov. Rexford Tugwell, 14 May 1943, AGPR.

51. *Establishment of a Policy in Regard to the Induction of Puerto Ricans in the Army,* 16 September 1945, NARA, Record Group 126, doc. 725-L.

52. Ibid.

53. Ibid.

54. Noemí Figueroa Soulet, a New York–based Puerto Rican, has collected the stories of individual Puerto Rican soldiers for a documentary titled *The Borinqueneers*. For more details, see http://www.prsoldier.com.

55. Sgt. James Bell to Luis Muñoz Marín, n.d., AFLMM.

56. For an account of the Portrex maneuvers, see *New York Times*, 5, 6, 8, 9, 10, 11, and 14 March 1950.

57. For a chronicle of these events, see *Historic Review on the 65th Infantry Regiment Court-Martial*, report provided by the U.S. Army's Center of Military History to the Puerto Rican–American Research Institute, Montgomery Village, Md. (n.d.).

CHAPTER SEVEN

1. León Leura to author, 27 June 1995. Additional videotaped interview by Frank O. Sotomayor, Los Angeles, 23 March 2002, is archived at the U.S. Latino & Latina World War II Oral History Project, Nettie Lee Benson Latin American Collection, General Libraries, University of Texas at Austin (hereafter cited as U.S. Latino & Latina WWII Oral History Project).

2. William D. Cleary, "The Chaplain," in *Religion of Soldier and Sailor*, ed. Willard L. Sperry (Cambridge, Mass.: Harvard University Press, 1945), 79.

3. Arlene Sánchez Walsh, "The Mexican American Religious Experience," in *Introduction to the U.S. Latina and Latino Religious Experience*, ed. Hector Avalos (Boston: Brill Academic, 2004), 12.

4. Orlando O. Espín, *The Faith of the People: Theological Reflections on Popular Catholicism* (Maryknoll, N.Y.: Orbis Books, 1997), 93–94.

5. Charles Chaput, e-mail message to author, 12 April 2005.

6. Elisha Atkins, "A Soldier's Second Thoughts," in *Religion of Soldier and Sailor*, ed. William L. Sperry (Cambridge, Mass.: Harvard University Press, 1945), 102.

7. Joe F. López, interviews by Rea Ann Trotter, tape recordings, Greeley, Colo., 12 October 1995, and Houston, 5 January 1996, U.S. Latino & Latina WWII Oral History Project.

8. Lt. Col. Dave Grossman, *On Killing: The Psychological Cost of Learning to Kill in War and Society*, 2nd ed. (New York: Back Bay Books, 1996), 93.

9. Charles Trujillo, interview by Rea Ann Trotter, tape recording, Avondale, Colo., 15 December 2000, U.S. Latino & Latina WWII Oral History Project.

10. Ceprian Armijo, interview by Rea Ann Trotter, tape recording, Avondale, Colo., 15 December 2000, U.S. Latino & Latina WWII Oral History Project.

11. Anonymous, interview by Rea Ann Trotter, tape recording, San Antonio, 21 June 1996, in author's possession.

12. Tony Olivas, interview by Rea Ann Trotter, tape recording, Avondale, Colo., 15 December 2000, U.S. Latino & Latina WWII Oral History Project.

13. Ernest Montoya, interviews by Rea Ann Trotter, tape recordings, Pueblo, Colo., 21 September 2000, and Avondale, Colo., 14 December 2000, U.S. Latino & Latina WWII Oral History Project.

14. Salvador Valadés, letter to author, 20 April 2005, in author's possession.

15. Salvador Valadés, "Mexican-American WW II Combat Experience" (unpublished manuscript, 1996), U.S. Latino & Latina WWII Oral History Project.

16. Gerald F. Linderman, *The World within War: America's Combat Experience in World War II* (New York: Free Press, 1997), 48, 54.

17. Karen Matthews, "A Salute to Friends," U.S. Latino & Latina World War II Oral History Project, *Narratives*, Spring 2004, 78.

18. Richard G. Candelaria, telephone interview by Rea Ann Trotter, tape recording, 19 February 2003, in author's possession. See also Candelaria interview by Mario Barrera, videotape recording, Las Vegas, Nev., 16 February 2003, U.S. Latino & Latina WWII Oral History Project.

19. Richard G. Candelaria, telephone interview by Rea Ann Trotter, tape recording, 11 April 2005, U.S. Latino & Latina WWII Oral History Project.

20. Ernest Montoya, interviews.

21. Charles Trujillo, interview.

22. Anonymous, interview.

23. Charles Trujillo, interview.

24. William P. Mahedy, *Out of the Night: The Spiritual Journey of Vietnam Vets* (New York: Ballantine Books, 1986), 11.

25. Ibid., 114.

26. M. Brewster Smith, "Ground Troop Combat Motivations," in *The American Soldier*, vol. 2, *Combat and Its Aftermath*, ed. Samuel A. Stouffer et al. (Princeton, N.J.: Princeton University Press, 1949; reprint, Manhattan, Kans.: Military Affairs, 1977), 174.

27. Joe F. López, interviews.

28. Smith, "Ground Troop Combat Motivations," 185.

29. Atkins, "Soldier's Second Thoughts," 106.

30. Joe F. López, interviews.

31. S. Valadés, "Mexican-American WW II Combat Experience."

32. Epifanio Salazar, interview by Rea Ann Trotter, tape recording, San Antonio, 20 June 1996, in author's possession. An additional interview of Mr. Salazar by Francisco Cortez in San Antonio, 13 March 2005, is archived at the U.S. Latino & Latina WWII Oral History Project.

33. Frank Arellano, interview by Rea Ann Trotter, tape recording, Alamosa, Colo., 10 September 2000, U.S. Latino & Latina WWII Oral History Project.

34. Ernest Montoya, interviews.

35. Atkins, "Soldier's Second Thoughts," 103, 105.

36. S. Valadés, letter to author.

37. José Martínez, interviews by Rea Ann Trotter, tape recordings, Fort Garland, Colo., 10 June and 30 September 2001, U.S. Latino & Latina WWII Oral History Project.

38. Joseph M. Autobee, interview by Rea Ann Trotter, tape recording, Pueblo, Colo., 15 December 2001, U.S. Latino & Latina WWII Oral History Project.

39. William Ornelas, interview by Rea Ann Trotter, tape recording, San Antonio, 20 June 1996, in author's possession. An additional interview of Mr. Ornelas by Maggie Rivas-Rodríguez in San Antonio, 25 August 1999, is archived at the U.S. Latino & Latina WWII Oral History Project.

40. S. Valadés, letter to author.

41. S. Valadés, "Mexican-American WW II Combat Experience."

42. Fred Vigil, interview by Rea Ann Trotter, tape recording, Longmont, Colo., 15 July 1998, in author's possession.

43. Joseph M. Autobee, interview.

44. Ruben Moreno, interview by Rea Ann Trotter, tape recording, Tucson, Ariz., 6 January 1999, in author's possession. A *manda* is a self-imposed obligation to fulfill a religious promise to God, Christ, or a specific saint.

45. Gilberto M. Hinojosa, "Mexican-American Faith Communities in Texas and the Southwest," in *Mexican Americans and the Catholic Church, 1900–1965*, ed. Jay P. Dolan and Gilberto M. Hinojosa (Notre Dame, Ind.: University of Notre Dame Press, 1994), 94.

46. Smith, "Ground Troop Combat Motivations," 185–186.

47. José Martínez, discussion with author, Greeley, Colo., 7 August 2004.

48. Leura, letter to author.

49. Elwood C. Nance, ed., *Faith of Our Fighters* (St. Louis: Bethany Press, 1944), 25, quoted in Daniel B. Jorgensen, *The Service of Chaplains to Army Air Units, 1917–1946* (Washington, D.C.: Office, Chief of Air Force Chaplains, 1961), 276.

50. Smith, "Ground Troop Combat Motivations," 186–187.

51. Leura, letter to author.

52. José Martínez, interviews.

53. S. Valadés, letter to author.

54. Barrage balloons were helium balloons that were tethered to the ground with metal cables and were used to defend against enemy bombers. Low-flying bombers risked running into the cables, which could shear off wings.

55. Richard G. Candelaria, interview by Rea Ann Trotter, tape recording, Las Vegas, Nev., 16 March 1998, in author's possession.

56. Ibid.

57. Smith, "Ground Troop Combat Motivations," 187.

58. Quoted in Jorgensen, *Service of Chaplains*, 196.

59. Larry Decker, "Including Spirituality," *Clinical Quarterly* 5, no. 1 (1995), 3, http://www.ncptsd.va.gov.

60. Charles Trujillo, interview.

61. Cleary, "The Chaplain," 77–78.

62. Joe F. López, interviews.

63. Jeffrey M. Burns, "The Mexican Catholic Community in California," in *Mexican Americans and the Catholic Church*, ed. Jay P. Dolan and Gilberto M. Hinojosa (Notre Dame, Ind.: University of Notre Dame Press, 1994), 178.

64. Atkins, "Soldier's Second Thoughts," 101.

65. Mahedy, *Out of the Night*, 19.

66. Luis Pineda, interview by Rea Ann Trotter, tape recording, San Antonio, 6 January 1996, in author's possession.

67. PTSD is addressed by Ricardo Ainslie and Daphny Domínguez in "Silent Wounds," chap. 8 in this volume.

68. William P. Mahedy, "Some Theological Perspectives on PTSD," *Clinical Quarterly* 5, no. 1 (1995): 7, http://www.ncptsd.va.gov/ncmain/nc_archives/clnc_qtly/V5N1.pdf.

69. Samuel J. Smith, interview by Rea Ann Trotter, Pigeon Forge, Tenn., 10 November 2000, in author's possession.

70. Angelita Garcia-Cabrera, "The Hispanic Veteran of the Armed Services and in the Veterans Administration" (Ph.D. diss., Brandeis University, 1978), 70; Hinojosa, "Mexican-American Faith Communities," 46, 122.

71. Gabriel Valadés to Rea Ann Trotter, 27 October 2000, U.S. Latino & Latina WWII Oral History Project.

72. Viktor Frankl, *Man's Search for Meaning*, trans. Ilse Lasch, 4th ed. (Boston: Beacon Press, 1992), 119.

73. Quoted in U.S. House Committee on Veterans' Affairs, Subcommittee on Health, *Hearing: Status of Department of Veterans Affairs Post-Traumatic Stress Disorder (PTSD) Programs, March 11, 2004* (Washington, D.C.: U.S. Government Printing Office, 2005), 39.

74. José Martínez, discussion.

75. José Martínez, interviews.

76. Richard G. Candelaria, telephone interview by Rea Ann Trotter, tape recording, 3 May 2005, U.S. Latino & Latina WWII Oral History Project.

77. Carlos Samarrón, interview by René Zambrano, tape recording, San Diego, Calif., 2 October 2000, U.S. Latino & Latina WWII Oral History Project.

78. S. Valadés, "Mexican-American WW II Combat Experience."

79. S. Valadés, letter to author.

80. Mahedy, "Some Theological Perspectives on PTSD," 6.

81. Chaput, e-mail message to author.

CHAPTER EIGHT

1. R. J. Bonwick and P. L. Morris, "Posttraumatic Stress Disorder in Elderly War Veterans," *International Journal of Geriatric Psychiatry* 11, no. 12 (1996): 1071–1076.

2. R. Rosenheck, "Impact of Posttraumatic Stress Disorder of World War II on the Next Generation," *Journal of Nervous and Mental Disease* 174, no. 6 (1986): 319–327.

3. A. M. Ruef, B. T. Litz, and W. E. Schlenger, "Hispanic Ethnicity and Risk for Combat-Related Posttraumatic Stress Disorder," *Cultural Diversity and Ethnic Minority Psychology*, no. 6 (2000): 245.

4. T. M. Keane, A. D. Marshall, and C. T. Taft, "Posttraumatic Stress Disorder: Etiology, Epidemiology, and Treatment Outcome," *Annual Review of Clinical Psychology* 2 (2006): 161–197.

5. L. M. Stevens, C. Lymn, and R. M. Glass, "Posttraumatic Stress Disorder," *Journal of the American Medical Association* 296, no. 5 (2006): 614.

6. Fessler, Geraldine A. (Dech), "The Historical Perspective," in *Posttraumatic Stress Disorder among Vietnam Veterans: The Inner War* (2000), http://www.vetsoutreach.org/ptsd-history.html.

7. From the American Psychiatric Association's *Diagnostic and Statistical Manual of Mental Disorders*, 4th ed. (Washington, D.C.: American Psychiatric Association, 2000).

8. Ibid.

9. Ibid.

10. P. O. Schnurr and A. Spiro, "Combat Exposure, Posttraumatic Stress Disorder Symptoms, and Health Behaviors as Predictors of Self-Reported Physical Health in Older Veterans," *Journal of Nervous and Mental Disease* 187, no. 6 (1999): 353–359.

11. J. J. Vasterling, S. P. Proctor, P. Amoroso, R. Kane, T. Heeren, and R. F. White, "Neuropsychological Outcomes of Army Personnel following Deployment to the Iraq War," *Journal of the American Medical Association* 296, no. 5 (2006): 519–529.

12. Judith L. Herman, *Trauma and Recovery*, rev. ed. (New York: Basic Books, 2006), 20.

13. Keane et al., "Posttraumatic Stress Disorder," 2006.

14. Richard Kulka, W. E. Schlenger, J. A. Fairbank, R. L. Hough, B. K. Jordan, C. R. Marmar, and D. S. Weiss, *Trauma and the Vietnam War Generation: Report of Findings from the National Vietnam Veterans Readjustment Study* (Philadelphia: Bruner/Mazel, 1990). See also Ruef et al., "Hispanic Ethnicity and Risk."

15. A. N. Ortega and R. Rosenheck, "Posttraumatic Stress Disorder among Hispanic Vietnam Veterans," *American Journal of Psychiatry* 157 (2000): 615–619.

16. Kulka et al., *Trauma and the Vietnam War Generation*.

17. B. I. Goderez, "The Survivor Syndrome: Massive Psychic Trauma and Posttraumatic Stress Disorder," *Bulletin of the Menninger Clinic* 51, no. 1 (1987): 96–113.

18. A. Matsakis, *Vietnam Wives: Facing the Challenges of Life with Veterans Suffering Posttraumatic Stress*, 2nd ed. (Baltimore: Sidran Press, 1996).

19. V. W. Savarese, M. K. Suvak, and L. A. King, "Relationships among Alcohol Use, Hyperarousal, and Marital Abuse and Violence in Vietnam Veterans," *Journal of Traumatic Stress* 14, no. 4 (2001): 717–732.

20. J. H. Stimpson, M. C. Masel, L. Rudkin, and M. K. Peek, "Shared Health Behaviors among Older Mexican American Spouses," *American Journal of Health Behavior* 30, no. 5 (2006): 495–502.

21. Raul Chávez, interview by Paul Zepeda, videotape recording, 28 August 2001, Houston, U.S. Latino & Latina World War II Oral History Project, Nettie Lee Benson Latin American Collection, General Libraries, University of Texas at Austin (hereafter cited as U.S. Latino & Latina WWII Oral History Project).

22. Sallie Castillo Castro, interview by Nicole Griffith, videotape recording, Austin, Tex., 1 March 2001, U.S. Latino & Latina WWII Oral History Project.

23. Guadalupe Conde, interview by Carlos Conde, videotape recording, 7 September 2002, San Benito, Tex., U.S. Latino & Latina WWII Oral History Project.

24. Elizabeth García, interview by Hannah McIntyre, videotape recording, 2 February 2000, Austin, Tex., U.S. Latino & Latina WWII Oral History Project.

25. Raul Chávez, interview.

26. Ibid.

CHAPTER NINE

Author's note: The epigraph is from an interview with Aurora Estrada Orozco by Desirée Mata, videotape recording, Austin, Tex., 17 October 2003, U.S. Latino & Latina World War II Oral History Project, Nettie Lee Benson Latin American Collection, General Libraries, University of Texas at Austin (hereafter cited as U.S. Latino & Latina WWII Oral History Project).

1. "Tejana" is the term used to refer to Texas women of Mexican descent. For an overview of Tejana history and culture, see Teresa Palomo Acosta and Ruthe Winegarten, *Las Tejanas: 300 Years of History* (Austin: University of Texas Press, 2003).

2. Vicki L. Ruiz and Sherna Berger Gluck explore the roles of women as mothers and active agents in the lives of their children and subsequent generations. Ruiz focuses on Mexican American women during the Depression years. Ruiz, *From Out of the Shadows: Mexican Women in Twentieth-Century America* (New York: Oxford University Press, 1998); Gluck, *Rosie the Riveter Revisited: Women, the War, and Social Change* (New York: Penguin Books, 1988). See also Naomi Quiñonez, "Rosita the Riveter: Welding Tradition and Wartime Transformation," in *Mexican Americans and WWII*, ed. Maggie Rivas-Rodríguez (Austin: University of Texas Press, 2005); and Emily Yellin, *Our Mothers' War: American Women at Home and at the Front during World War II* (New York: Free Press, 2004). Yellin's work is based on her mother's journal and emphasizes the different perspectives that women developed by virtue of their different experiences.

3. Elena Tamez De Peña, interview by Erika L. Martínez, tape recording, Corpus Christi, Tex., 18 August 2001, U.S. Latino & Latina WWII Oral History Project.

4. The ethnic identification "Chicana" is used in the title and throughout this chapter to reference a particular generation—the generation of children of the WWII generation—and for purposes of coherency in the chapter. While I use "Chicana" to refer to that younger generation, many of whom were active during the Mexican American civil rights movement, not all of the daughters interviewed here identify themselves as Chicana, nor do all women or men of that generation self-identify as Chicana or Chicano. Terms range widely among this generation and also include "Mexican American," "Latino," "Mexican," and "Hispanic," for instance.

5. See Joanne Rao Sánchez' contribution to this volume (chap. 4, "The Latinas of World War II: From Familial Shelter to Expanding Horizons"), which provides data to support Mexican women's varied contributions to the war effort in the areas of military service and home front work. Sánchez also provides a thorough assessment of the void in literature on Latinas in WWII, as does Richard Santillán in "Rosita the Riveter: Midwest Mexican American Women during World War II, 1941–1945," *Perspectives in Mexican American Studies* 2 (1989): 115–147.

6. Gluck, *Rosie the Riveter Revisited*, xii.

7. Jan Vansina, *Oral Tradition as History* (Madison: University of Wisconsin Press, 1985).

8. Maureen Honey, *Creating Rosie the Riveter: Class, Gender, and Propaganda during World War II* (Amherst: University of Massachusetts Press, 1984), 2–3.

9. Chicana feminist scholarship makes important theoretical and methodological contributions. This includes discussions around how the social locations of Chicanas, Latinas, and indigenous women, including migration, nativity, language, sexuality, and generation, situate women's experiences differently. This has provided rich terrain for the examination of multiple forms of feminisms, to which this chapter

seeks to contribute. See the following for readings on Chicana feminist history and theory: Irene I. Blea, *La Chicana and the Intersection of Race, Class, and Gender* (New York: Praeger, 1992). Chela Sandoval examines issues around power relations in "U.S. Third World Feminism: The Theory and Method of Oppositional Consciousness in the Postmodern World," *Genders*, Vol. 10 (Spring 1991): 1–23. Gloria Anzaldúa explores identity politics in *Borderland/La Frontera: The New Mestiza*, 2nd ed. (San Francisco: Aunt Lute Press, 1999). Patricia Zavella also provides insight into the dynamics of Chicana work and home life in her feminist ethnography: *Women's Work and Chicano Families: Cannery Workers of the Santa Clara Valley* (New York: Cornell University Press, 1987). See also Gabriela Arredondo, Aida Hurtado, Norma Klahn, Olga Nájera-Ramírez, and Patricia Zavella, eds., *Chicana Feminisms: A Critical Reader* (Durham, N.C.: Duke University Press, 2001); Martha Cotera, *Diosa y Hembra: History and Heritage of Chicanas in the U.S.* (Austin: Information Systems Development, 1976); and Martha Cotera, *The Chicana Feminist* (Austin: Information Systems Development, 1977).

10. Rao Sánchez explores the socioeconomic impact that war work had on women's lives in chapter 4 of this volume.

11. The following histories address the wartime experiences of women: Karen Anderson, *Wartime Women: Sex Roles, Family Relations, and the Status of Women during World War II* (New York: Berkeley Books, 2001); Honey, *Creating Rosie the Riveter;* Santillán, "Rosita the Riveter"; and Quiñonez, "Rosita the Riveter."

12. Susan M. Hartmann, *The Home Front and Beyond: American Women in the 1940s* (Boston: Twayne, 1982), 21.

13. See the following study of Texas workers for evidence that Mexican and Black women trailed behind their Anglo counterparts in the wartime labor market: Emilio Zamora, *Claiming Rights and Righting Wrongs: Mexican Workers and Job Politics during World War II* (College Station: Texas A&M University Press, 2009).

14. Quoted in Santillán, "Rosita the Riveter," 138. Santillán discusses the ways in which the war years "modified the social and political attitudes and behavior of many Mexican American defense workers regarding their roles in the home and in the community." He goes on to state that the midwestern women he interviewed, much like the Tejanas interviewed here, felt that the war was a pivotal moment in their lives, as it helped them gain self-worth, economic self-reliance, and independence.

15. Ibid.

16. Ibid.

17. Carla De Peña Cook and Elena Tamez De Peña, interview with author, videotape recording, Corpus Christi, Tex., 30 July 2005, U.S. Latino & Latina WWII Oral History Project.

18. Ibid.

19. Ibid.

20. Ibid.

21. Ibid.

22. Aurora Estrada Orozco, videotaped interview.

23. Ibid.

24. Ibid.

25. Ibid.

26. Aurora Estrada Orozco, telephone interview with author, tape recording, 31 July 2005, U.S. Latino & Latina WWII Oral History Project.

27. Ibid.

28. Ibid.

29. Cynthia Estrada Orozco, telephone interview with author, tape recording, 10 February 2007, U.S. Latino & Latina WWII Oral History Project.

30. Ibid.

31. Aurora Estrada Orozco, telephone interview.

32. Information about the status of Latina women workers may be found in several sources. Vicki L. Ruiz, in *Cannery Women, Cannery Lives: Mexican Women, Unionization, and the California Food Processing Industry, 1930–1950*, states that the majority of Spanish-speaking women, contrary to popular images of them tied solely to the domestic sphere, have been wage earners at some point in their lives. Additionally, according to *The Handbook of Texas Online* (s.v. "Mexican-American women," http://www.tshaonline.org/handbook/online/articles/MM/pwmly.html), at the turn of the century 15 percent of Mexican immigrant women in South Texas took work outside the home, as did 17 percent of El Paso Mexican women in 1920. Women earned wages through domestic work as well through sewing, doing laundry, and keeping boarders. They also worked in the textile industry in Houston, and both women and girls worked in the fields in South, Central, and West Texas. While working outside of the home occurred frequently, it was often looked down upon. In the years prior to World War II, store clerks constituted the middle class. Finally, in *Mexican Americans/American Mexicans: From Conquistadors to Chicanos* (New York: Hill and Wang, 1993), Matt S. Meier and Feliciano Ribera state that by the 1920s approximately one-third of the Mexican immigrant labor force was composed of women. They go on to say that, in California, women worked in canneries, packinghouses, and the garment industry and that in the 1930s three-fourths of the Texas pecan-shelling workers were Mexican women.

33. Gertrudis Estrada, telephone interview with author, 24 January 2008, notes in author's possession. Other Mexican women interviewed by the Latino & Latina World War II Oral History Project also credited the war effort for their being allowed to work outside their homes. Wilhelmina Cooremans Vasquez and her sister, Delfina Cooremans Baladez, from San Antonio, for instance, were able to move to Seattle to work at a Boeing manufacturing plant in response to the government's call for war workers. Cooremans Vasquez and Cooremans Baladez, interview with author, videotape recording, San Antonio, 28 July 2005, U.S. Latino & Latina WWII Oral History Project.

34. Cynthia Estrada Orozco, telephone interview.

35. At the time of this writing, Cynthia Orozco was the chair of and an instructor in the History and Humanities Department at Eastern New Mexico University, Ruidoso, and was a founding member of the Chicana caucus of the National Association for Chicano and Chicana Studies (NACCS). María Theresa had a bachelor's degree in psychology from Texas A&M University–Kingsville (previously Texas A&I University) and was the first Mexican American woman to earn a master's degree in public administration from the Lyndon B. Johnson School of Public Affairs at the University of Texas at Austin. Sylvia held a bachelor's degree in fine arts from the University of Texas at Austin and is the founder and executive director of Mexic-Arte Museum, a Mexican and Mexican American fine arts museum in Austin. Irma earned a bachelor's degree in journalism from the University of Texas at Austin and a master's degree in Spanish literature from the University of Texas at San Antonio. Orozco's oldest son, Edmundo, holds a bachelor's degree in business administration from the University of Texas at Austin. Robert earned a bachelor's degree in engineering from the University of Texas at San Antonio and works in the computer science field.

36. See her file at the U.S. Latino & Latina WWII Oral History Project.

37. Henrietta López Rivas, interview by Verónica Flores, videotape recording, San Antonio, 12 June 1999, U.S. Latino & Latina WWII Oral History Project.

38. Ibid.

39. Ibid.

40. See Laura M. Padilla's discussion on internalized racism among Latinos and the ways in which this is represented in U.S. laws. Padilla, "'But You're Not a Dirty Mexican': Internalized Oppression, Latinos and Law," *Texas Hispanic Journal of Law and Policy* (2001): 59–113.

41. Ibid.

42. Maggie Rivas-Rodríguez, interview with author, tape recording, Austin, Tex., 10 April 2005, U.S. Latino & Latina WWII Oral History Project. Maggie is one of López Rivas' seven children, six of whom are daughters. The oldest child, Robert, has a master's degree in clinical counseling from Our Lady of the Lake University in San Antonio and a bilingual endorsement from the University of Texas at San Antonio, as well as a bachelor's in history and government from Sul Ross University in Alpine, Texas; the fourth child, Carmen Aida Danna, earned a bachelor's degree in education from Texas A&I University (now Texas A&M University–Kingsville) and a master's from Incarnate Word University in San Antonio; Maggie earned a bachelor's degree in journalism from the University of Texas at Austin, a master's from the Columbia University Graduate School of Journalism, and a doctorate in mass communications from the University of North Carolina at Chapel Hill; Concepción Rivas Brown earned a bachelor's degree in government from the University of Texas at Austin. For information on the process of racialization among Mexicans in the American Southwest, see two of Martha Menchaca's books: *Recovering History, Constructing Race: The Indian, Black, and White Roots of Mexican Americans* (Austin: University of Texas Press, 2001) and *The Mexican Outsiders: A Community History of Marginaliza-*

tion and Discrimination in California (Austin: University of Texas Press, 1995). Also see *The Mexican Outsiders* for Menchaca's method of reconstructing the past of historically marginalized groups through the use of historical and anthropological research methods, including oral histories.

43. Maggie Rivas-Rodríguez, interview.

44. Ibid.

45. Henrietta López Rivas, interview.

46. Maggie Rivas-Rodríguez, interview.

47. Ibid.

48. Ibid.

49. See the discussion of the ways in which the war served as a watershed for Latinas in Rao Sánchez, "Latinas of World War II," in this volume.

50. See the following for data on twentieth-century Latina women's work experiences: José Alamillo, *Making Lemonade Out of Lemons: Mexican American Labor and Leisure in a California Town, 1880–1960* (Urbana: University of Illinois Press, 2006); Ruiz, *From Out of the Shadows* and *Cannery Women, Cannery Lives*; Gluck, *Rosie the Riveter Revisited*; Karen Anderson, *Changing Women: A History of Racial Ethnic Women in Modern America* (New York: Oxford University Press, 1996); Yolanda Leyva, "'Faithful Hard-Working Mexican Hands': Mexicana Workers during the Great Depression," in *Mexican American Women: Changing Images*, Perspectives in Mexican American Studies, vol. 5 (Tucson: Mexican American Studies and Research Center, University of Arizona, 1995), 63–78; and Acosta and Winegarten, *Las Tejanas*. See also the collection of oral histories of California WWII women defense workers housed in the Regional Oral History Office at the University of California, Berkeley.

51. Ruiz, *From Out of the Shadows*, xvi.

52. Maria Linda Apodaca, "The Chicana Woman: An Historic Materialist Perspective," *Latin American Perspectives 4, nos. 1–2* ("Women and Class Struggle," 1977): 70–89. See Apodaca's analysis on the historic material conditions of Chicanas in a capitalistic society. Apodaca also discusses the ways in which Mexican women have fought to improve labor conditions and increase wages.

53. In this piece I suggest that Orozco, Rivas, and De Peña experienced a shift in consciousness. Their wartime experiences afforded them a new way of conceiving of themselves and their abilities, a new form of consciousness that enabled them to create opportunities for their daughters later in life. In *Methodology of the Oppressed* (Minneapolis: University of Minnesota Press, 2000), Chela Sandoval examines the second wave of the U.S. feminist movement and puts forth a theory of consciousness that is useful here. Sandoval extends feminist theories of consciousness to create a new theory that addresses how marginalized groups use a differential consciousness to function "within yet beyond the demands of dominant ideology" (44). Sandoval aligns herself with U.S. Third World feminists, who consider the various locations from which marginalization occurs among groups, including the many classes, races, ethnicities, genders, and languages that make up such experiences. Such groups, ac-

cording to Sandoval, exhibit an oppositional way of thinking in conjunction with a historical consciousness. Together these provide a strategy for reaching a differential consciousness that originates from an instinct for survival and pushes the limits of social norms according to necessity. By applying Sandoval's concept to these WWII-generation women, we can see the possibility that in the postwar years women employed a historical consciousness of enduring racial and gender discrimination and a newfound sense of self-worth from their wartime experience to arrive at a different way of enacting their consciousness. Women arrived at new subject position where they were able to create change. They possessed the instinct for survival they had acquired as young girls and women in a gendered and raced society, and they employed various tactics in order to assure a better life for their daughters. Orozco and Rivas exhibited a differential consciousness by fighting institutional racism in their children's schools. They, along with De Peña and other women of this period confronted American gender and racial ideologies by instilling in their daughters a sense of entitlement to opportunity regardless of their gender, an oppositional move for Mexican women in the 1960s and 1970s. In these and other instances, women challenged the dominant social order while simultaneously working within it as an "effective means for transforming dominant power relations" (ibid.).

SELECTED BIBLIOGRAPHY

BOOKS, JOURNAL ARTICLES, AND REPORTS

Acosta, Teresa Palomo, and Ruthe Winegarten. *Las Tejanas: 300 Years of History*. Austin: University of Texas Press, 2003.

Acuña, Rodolfo F. *Corridors of Migration: The Odyssey of Mexican Laborers, 1600–1933*. Tucson: University of Arizona Press, 2007.

———. *Occupied America: A History of Chicanos*. 6th ed. New York: Pearson Longman, 2007.

Alamillo, José M. "Bibliographic Essay on U.S. Latino/a History." National Park Service, 2008. http://www.nps.gov/history/history/resedu/latino.pdf.

———. *Making Lemonade Out of Lemons: Mexican American Labor and Leisure in a California Town, 1880–1960*. Urbana: University of Illinois Press, 2006.

Allen, Ruth. *The Labor of Women in the Production of Cotton*. University of Texas Bulletin, 3134. Austin, 1931.

Allenz, June. "Invisible Veterans." *Educational Record* 75, no. 4 (1994): 46.

Allsup, Carl. *The American G.I. Forum: Origins and Evolution*. Austin: University of Texas Press, 1982.

Almaraz, Félix D. *Knight without Armor: Carlos Eduardo Castañeda, 1896–1958*. College Station: Texas A&M University Press, 1999.

Alvarez Curbelo, Silvia. "Las lecciones de la guerra: Luis Muñoz Marín y la Segunda Guerra Mundial." In *Luis Muñoz Marín: Ensayos del Centenario*, edited by Fernando Picó. San Juan, Puerto Rico: Ediciones Callejón, 1999.

————. *Un país del porvenir: El discurso de la modernidad en Puerto Rico (siglo XIX)*. San Juan, Puerto Rico: Ediciones Callejón, 2001.

American Psychiatric Association. *Diagnostic and Statistical Manual of Mental Disorders*. 3rd ed. Washington, D.C.: American Psychiatric Association, 1980.

————. *Diagnostic and Statistical Manual of Mental Disorders*. 4th ed. Washington, D.C.: American Psychiatric Association, 2000.

Anderson, Karen. *Changing Women: A History of Racial Ethnic Women in Modern America*. New York: Oxford University Press, 1996.

————. *Wartime Women: Sex Roles, Family Relations, and the Status of Women during World War II*. New York: Berkeley Books, 2001.

Andrist, Debra D. "An Interview with Nicolas Kanellos," *South Central Review* 19, no. 1 (2002): 15–25.

Anzaldúa, Gloria. *Borderlands/La Frontera: The New Mestiza*. 2nd ed. San Francisco: Aunt Lute Press, 1999.

Apodaca, Maria Linda. "The Chicana Woman: An Historic Materialist Perspective." *Latin American Perspectives 4, nos. 1–2* ("Women and Class Struggle," 1977): 70–89.

Appadurai, Arjun. "El número en la imaginación colonial." In *La modernidad desbordada: Dimensiones culturales de la globalización*. Buenos Aires: Trilce, 2001.

Archibald, Katherine. *Wartime Shipyard: A Study in Social Disunity*. Chicago: University of Illinois Press, 2006. First published in 1947.

Arnheim, Rudolf, and Martha Collins Bayne. "Foreign Language Broadcasts over Local American Stations." In *Radio Research, 1941*, ed. Paul F. Lazarsfeld and Frank N. Stanton. New York: Duell, Sloan and Pearce, 1941.

Arredondo, Gabriela, Aida Hurtado, Norma Klahn, Olga Nájera-Ramírez, and Patricia Zavella, eds. *Chicana Feminisms: A Critical Reader*. Durham, N.C.: Duke University Press, 2001.

Atkins, Elisha. "A Soldier's Second Thoughts." In *Religion of Soldier and Sailor*, edited by Willard L. Sperry. Cambridge, Mass.: Harvard University Press, 1945.

Balderrama, Francisco E., and Raymond Rodríguez. *Decade of Betrayal: Mexican Repatriation in the 1930's*. Albuquerque: University of New Mexico Press, 1995.

Barajas, Frank P. "Resistance, Radicalism, and Repression on the Oxnard Plain: The Social Context of the Betabelero Strike of 1933." *Western Historical Quarterly* 35 (Spring 2004): 29–52.

Barrera, Lisa Lizette. "Minorities and the University of Texas School of Law, 1950–1980." *Texas Hispanic Journal of Law and Policy* 4 (1998): 99–109.

Barrera, Mario. *Race and Class in the Southwest: A Theory of Racial Inequality*. Notre Dame, Ind.: University of Notre Dame Press, 1979.

Berg, Jerome S. "DXers/Dxing: Tuning In Distant Stations." In *Museum of Broadcast Communications Encyclopedia of Radio*. New York: Routledge, 2004.

Bernstein, Mark. "Inventing Broadcast Journalism." *American History* 40, no. 2 (2005): 40–46.

Bixler-Márquez, Dennis J. "The Mass Media and the Retention of Spanish by Chicanos." *International Journal of the Sociology of Language* (1985): 21–29.

Blanco, Tomás. *El prejuicio racial en Puerto Rico*. San Juan, Puerto Rico: Ediciones Huracán, 1985.

Blauner, Robert. *Colonized and Immigrant Minorities*. New York: Harper and Row, 1972.

Blea, Irene I. *La Chicana and the Intersection of Race, Class, and Gender*. New York: Praeger, 1992.

Blum, John Morton. *V Was for Victory: Politics and American Culture during World War II*. New York: Harcourt Brace Jovanovich, 1976.

Bogardus, Emory S. *The Mexican in the United States*. Los Angeles: University of Southern California Press, 1934.

Bonwick, R. J., and P. L. Morris. "Post-traumatic Stress Disorder in Elderly War Veterans." *International Journal of Geriatric Psychiatry* 11, no. 12 (1996): 1071–1076.

Bowers, William T., et al. *Black Soldier, White Army: The 24th Infantry Regiment in Korea*. Washington, D.C.: U.S. Army Center of Military History, 1996.

Bronder, Saul E. *Social Justice and Church Authority: The Public Life of Archbishop Robert E. Lucey*. Philadelphia: Temple University Press, 1982.

Broom, Perry Morris. "An Interpretative Analysis of the Economic and Educational Status of Latin-Americans in Texas, with Emphasis upon the Basic Factors Underlying an Approach to an Improved Program of Occupational Guidance, Training, and Adjustment for Secondary Schools." Ph.D. diss., University of Texas at Austin, 1942.

Brown, Robert J. *Manipulating the Ether: The Power of Broadcast Radio in Thirties America*. Jefferson, N.C.: McFarland and Co., 1998.

Burma, John H. *Spanish-Speaking Groups in the United States*. Detroit: Blaine Ethridge Books, 1974.

Burns, Jeffrey M. "The Mexican Catholic Community in California." In *Mexican Americans and the Catholic Church*, edited by Jay P. Dolan and Gilberto M. Hinojosa. Notre Dame, Ind.: University of Notre Dame Press, 1994.

Campbell, Randolph B. *Gone to Texas: A History of the Lone Star State*. New York: Oxford University Press, 2003.

Castañeda, Carlos E. "The Second Rate Citizen and Democracy." In Perales, *Are We Good Neighbors?*

———. "Statement before the Senate Committee on Labor and Education, September 8, 1944." In Perales, *Are We Good Neighbors?*

Cleary, William D. "The Chaplain." In *Religion of Soldier and Sailor,* edited by Willard L. Sperry. Cambridge, Mass.: Harvard University Press, 1945.

Cohen, Elizabeth. *Making a New Deal: Industrial Workers in Chicago, 1919–1939*. New York: Cambridge University Press, 1990.

Conn, Stetson, and Byron Fairchild. *United States Army in World War II: The Western Hemisphere; The Framework of Hemisphere Defense*. Washington, D.C.: Center of Military History, 1989.

Cotera, Martha P. *The Chicana Feminist*. Austin: Information Systems Development, 1977.

―――. *Diosa y Hembra: History and Heritage of Chicanas in the U.S.* Austin: Information Systems Development, 1976.

Cottrol, Robert J., Raymond T. Diamond, and Leland B. Ware. *Brown v. Board of Education: Caste, Culture, and the Constitution.* Lawrence: University of Kansas Press, 2003.

Craig, Douglas B. *Fireside Politics: Radio and Political Culture in the United States, 1920–1940.* Baltimore: Johns Hopkins University Press, 2000.

Culbert, David. "Erik Barnouw's War: An Interview Concerning the Armed Forces Radio Services' Education Unit, 1944–1945." *Historical Journal of Film, Radio and Television* 22, no. 4 (2002): 475–490.

Daniel, Cletus E. *Bitter Harvest: A History of California Farmworkers, 1870–1941.* Ithaca, N.Y.: Cornell University Press, 1981.

―――. *Chicano Workers and the Politics of Fairness: The FEPC in the Southwest, 1941–1945.* Austin: University of Texas Press, 1991.

Decker, Larry. "Including Spirituality." *Clinical Quarterly* 5, no. 1 (1995): 3. http://www.ncptsd.va.gov.

De León, Arnoldo. *They Called Them "Greasers": Anglo Attitudes toward Mexicans in Texas, 1821–1900.* Austin: University of Texas Press, 1983.

Deutsch, Sarah. *No Separate Refuge: Culture, Class and Gender on an Anglo-Hispanic Frontier in the American Southwest, 1880–1940.* New York: Oxford University Press, 1987.

Du Bois, W. E. B. *The Souls of Black Folk.* Chicago: McClurg and Co., 1903.

Eriksen, Thomas Hylland. "Linguistic Hegemony and Minority Resistance." *Journal of Peace Research* 29, no. 3 (1992): 313–332.

Espín, Orlando O. *The Faith of the People: Theological Reflections on Popular Catholicism.* Maryknoll, N.Y.: Orbis Books, 1997.

Evans, Sara. *Born for Liberty: A History of Women in America.* New York: Free Press, 1997.

Fessler, Geraldine A. (Dech). "The Historical Perspective." In *Post-Traumatic Stress Disorder among Vietnam Veterans: The Inner War.* 2000. http://www.vetsoutreach.org/ptsd-history.html.

Fester, Lucian Edward. "Cultural and Economic Mediation among Spanish Speaking Migrant Farm Workers in Dade County, Florida." Master's thesis, University of Miami, 1970.

Fishman, Joshua A. *Language Loyalty in the United States: The Maintenance and Perpetuation of Non-English Mother Tongues by American Ethnic and Religious Groups.* The Hague: Mouton, 1966.

Fitch, Catherine, and Michael R. Haines. "Median Age at First Marriage by Sex and Race, 1850–1999." In *Historical Statistics of the United States*, 5 vols., edited by Susan B. Carter et al. New York: Cambridge University Press, 2006.

Flores, Juan. "From Bomba to Hip-Hop: Puerto Rican Culture and Latino Identity." In *Popular Cultures, Everyday Lives*, edited by Robin G. Kelley and Janice Radway. New York: Columbia University Press, 2000.

Fogel, Walter. *Mexican Americans in Southwest Labor Markets.* Advance Report 10, Mexican-American Study Project. Los Angeles: UCLA Graduate School of Business Administration, 1967.

Foley, Neil. "Straddling the Color Line: The Legal Construction of Hispanic Identity in Texas." In *Not Just Black and White: Contemporary Perspectives on Immigration, Race, and Ethnicity in the United States,* edited by Nancy Foner and George M. Frederickson. New York: Russell Sage Foundation, 2004.

Foner, Jack D. *Blacks and the Military in American History: A New Perspective.* New York: Praeger, 1974.

Fowler, Gene, and Bill Crawford. *Border Radio: Quacks, Yodelers, Pitchmen, Psychics, and Other Amazing Broadcasters of the American Airwaves.* Austin: University of Texas Press, 2002.

Frankl, Viktor. *Man's Search for Meaning.* Trans. Ilse Lasch. 4th ed. Boston: Beacon Press, 1992.

Frederickson, Kari. *The Dixiecrat Revolt and the End of the Solid South, 1932–1968.* Chapel Hill: University of North Carolina Press, 2001.

Frisch, Michael. *A Shared Authority: Essays on the Craft and Meaning of Oral and Public History.* Albany: State University of New York Press, 1990.

Galarza, Ernesto. *Merchants of Labor: The Mexican Bracero Story.* Santa Barbara, Calif.: McNally and Loftin, 1964.

García, Jerry. "The Racialization of Mexican and Japanese Labor in the Pacific Northwest, 1900–1945." In *Memory, Community, and Activism: Mexican Migration and Labor in the Pacific Northwest,* edited by Jerry García and Gilberto García. East Lansing: Julián Samora Research Institute and Michigan State University Press, 2005.

García, Maria-Cristina. "Macario García." The Handbook of Texas Online, http://www.tshaonline.org/handbook/online/articles/GG/fga76.html.

García, Mario T. "Americans All: The Mexican American Generation and the Politics of Wartime Los Angeles, 1941–45." *Social Science Quarterly* 65, no. 2 (1984): 278–289.

———. *Mexican Americans: Leadership, Ideology, and Identity, 1930–1960.* New Haven, Conn.: Yale University Press, 1989.

García, Matt. *A World of Its Own: Race, Labor and Citrus in the Making of Greater Los Angeles, 1900–1970.* Chapel Hill: University of North Carolina Press, 2001.

Garcia-Cabrera, Angelita. "The Hispanic Veteran of the Armed Services and in the Veterans Administration." Ph.D. diss., Brandeis University, 1978.

Geertz, Clifford. *The Interpretation of Cultures.* New York: Basic Books, 2000.

Gibson, Campbell, and Kay Jung. "Historical Census Statistics on Population Totals by Race, 1790 to 1990, for Large Cities and Other Urban Places in the United States." Population Division Working Paper 76. Washington, D.C.: U.S. Bureau of the Census, 2005.

Gilbert, Dennis. *The American Class Structure in the Age of Growing Inequality.* 6th ed. Belmont, Calif.: Wadsworth/Thomson Learning, 2003.

Gluck, Sherna Berger. *Rosie the Riveter Revisited: Women, the War, and Social Change.* New York: Penguin Books, 1988.

Goderez, B. I. "The Survivor Syndrome: Massive Psychic Trauma and Posttraumatic Stress Disorder." *Bulletin of the Menninger Clinic* 51, no. 1 (1987): 96–113.

Gómez-Quiñones, Juan. *Chicano Politics: Reality and Promise, 1940–1990.* Albuquerque: University of New Mexico Press, 1990.

———. *Roots of Chicano Politics, 1600–1940.* Albuquerque: University of New Mexico Press, 1994.

Gonzales, Manuel. *Mexicanos: A History of Mexicans in the United States.* Bloomington: Indiana University Press, 1999.

González, Gilbert G. *Community and Labor: Mexican Citrus Worker Villages in a Southern California County, 1900–1950.* Urbana: University of Illinois Press, 1994.

———. "Labor and Community: Mexican Citrus Worker Villages in a Southern California County, 1900–1950." *Western Historical Quarterly* 22, no. 3 (1991): 289–331.

González, Gilbert G., and Raul A. Fernández. *A Century of Chicano History: Empire, Nations, and Migration.* New York: Routledge, 2003.

Gonzalez, Juan. *Harvest of Empire: A History of Latinos in America.* New York: Penguin Books, 2001.

Gould, Stephen Jay. *The Mismeasure of Man.* New York: W. W. Norton and Co., 1996.

Green, George N. "The Good Neighbor Commission and Texas Mexicans." In *Ethnic Minorities in Gulf Coast Society*, edited by Jerrell H. Shofner and Linda V. Ellsworth. Pensacola, Fla.: Gulf Coast History and Humanities Conference, 1979.

Griswold del Castillo, Richard. *The Treaty of Guadalupe Hidalgo: A Legacy of Conflict.* Norman: University of Oklahoma, 1992.

Grossman, Lt. Col. Dave. *On Killing: The Psychological Cost of Learning to Kill in War and Society.* 2nd ed. New York: Back Bay Books, 1996.

Guerrero, Salvador. *Memorias: A West Texas Life*, edited by Arnoldo de León. Lubbock: Texas Tech University Press, 1991.

Gutiérrez, David, ed. *The Columbia History of Latinos in the United States since 1960.* New York: Columbia University Press, 2004.

Gutiérrez, David G. *Walls and Mirrors: Mexican Americans, Mexican Immigrants, and the Politics of Ethnicity.* Berkeley: University of California Press, 1995.

Gutiérrez, Félix, and Jorge Schement. *Spanish-Language Radio in the Southwestern United States.* Austin: Center for Mexican American Studies, 1979.

Gutiérrez, Félix Frank. "Spanish-Language Radio and Chicano Internal Colonialism." Ph.D. diss., Stanford University, 1976.

Hadlow, Martin. "The Mosquito Network: American Military Radio in the Solomon Islands during World War II." *Journal of Radio Studies* 11, no. 1 (2004): 73–86.

Haney López, Ian. "Race and Colorblindness after *Hernandez and Brown*." *Chicano-Latino Law Review* 25 (Spring 2005): 61–76.

Harris, Marvin. *The Rise of Anthropological Theory: A History of Theories of Culture.* New York: Crowell, 1968.

Harris, William W. *Puerto Rico's Fighting 65th US Infantry: From San Juan to Chorwan.* San Rafael, Calif.: Presidio Press, 1980.

Hartmann, Susan M. *The Home Front and Beyond: American Women in the 1940s.* Boston: Twayne, 1982.

Hecht, Reuben W. *Farm Labor Requirements in the United States, 1939 and 1944.* Farm Manual 59. Washington, D.C.: U.S. Department of Agriculture, 1947.

Herman, J. L. *Trauma and Recovery.* Rev. ed. New York: Basic Books, 2006.

Hernández, Marie Theresa. *Cemeteries of Ambivalent Desire.* College Station: Texas A&M University Press, 2008.

————. "Reconditioning History: Adapting Knowledge from the Past into the Realities of the Present: A Mexican-American Graveyard." *Rethinking History* 3 (Autumn 1999): 289–308.

Hernández, Ramona. *The Mobility of Workers under Advanced Capitalism: Dominican Migration to the United States.* New York: Columbia University Press, 2002.

Hilmes, Michele. *Radio Voices: American Broadcasting, 1922–1952.* Minneapolis: University of Minnesota Press, 1997.

Hinojosa, Gilberto M. "Mexican-American Faith Communities in Texas and the Southwest." In *Mexican Americans and the Catholic Church, 1900–1965,* ed. Jay P. Dolan and Gilberto M. Hinojosa. Notre Dame, Ind.: University of Notre Dame Press, 1994.

Historic Review on the 65th Infantry Regiment Court-Martial. Report provided by the U.S. Army's Center of Military History to the Puerto Rican–American Research Institute, Montgomery Village, Md. N.d.

Hoffer, Thomas W. "TNT Baker: Radio Quack." In *American Broadcasting: A Source Book on the History of Radio and Television,* edited by Lawrence W. Lichty and Malachi C. Topping. New York: Hastings House, 1975.

Honey, Maureen. *Creating Rosie the Riveter: Class, Gender, and Propaganda during World War II.* Amherst: University of Massachusetts Press, 1984.

Hooks, Janet. *Women's Occupations through Seven Decades.* U.S. Department of Labor, Women's Bureau, Bulletin 218. Washington, D.C.: Government Printing Office, 1947.

Hyman, Harold M. *Oleander Odyssey: The Kempners of Galveston, Texas, 1854–1980s.* College Station: Texas A&M University Press, 1990.

Jeffries, John W. *Wartime America: The World War II Home Front.* Chicago: Ivan R. Dee, 1996.

Jenkens, Robert. "Processing and Tabulation." Chap. 4 in *Procedural History of the 1940 Census of Population and Housing.* Madison: Center for Demography and Ecology, University of Wisconsin, 1983.

Jorgensen, Daniel B. *The Service of Chaplains to Army Air Units 1917–1946.* Vol. 1 of *Air Force Chaplains.* Washington, D.C.: Office, Chief of Air Force Chaplains, 1961.

Keane, T. M., A. D. Marshall, and C. T. Taft. "Posttraumatic Stress Disorder: Etiology, Epidemiology, and Treatment Outcome." *Annual Review of Clinical Psychology* 2 (2006): 161–197.

Keith, Michael C. *Sounds in the Dark: All-Night Radio in American Life*. 1st ed. Ames: Iowa State University Press, 2001.

Kibbe, Pauline. *Latin Americans in Texas*. Albuquerque: University of New Mexico Press, 1946.

King, Desmond. *Black Americans and the U.S. Federal Government*. Oxford: Clarendon Press, 1995.

Krysko, Michael A. "'Gibberish' on the Air: Foreign Language Radio and American Broadcasting, 1920–1940." *Historical Journal of Film, Radio and Television* 27, no. 3 (2007).

Kulka, R. A., W. E. Schlenger, J. A. Fairbank, R. L. Hough, B. K. Jordan, C. R. Marmar, and D. S. Weiss. *Trauma and the Vietnam War Generation: Report of Findings from the National Vietnam Veterans Readjustment Study*. Philadelphia: Bruner/Mazel, 1990.

Lamb, Ruth S. *Mexican Americans: Sons of the Southwest*. Claremont, Calif.: Ocelot Press, 1970.

Latina Feminist Group. *Telling to Live: Latina Feminist Testimonios*. Durham, N.C.: Duke University Press, 2001.

Lazarsfeld, Paul Felix. *Radio and the Printed Page: An Introduction to the Study of Radio and Its Role in the Communication of Ideas*. New York: Duell, Sloan, and Pearce, 1940.

Lazarsfeld, Paul Felix, and Frank N. Stanton, eds. *Radio Research, 1941*. New York: Duell, Sloan, and Pearce, 1941.

Lenthall, Bruce. *Radio's America: The Great Depression and the Rise of Modern Mass Culture*. Chicago: University of Chicago Press, 2007.

Leyva, Yolanda. "'Faithful Hard-Working Mexican Hands': Mexicana Workers during the Great Depression." In *Mexican American Women: Changing Images*, Perspectives in Mexican American Studies, vol. 5. Tucson: Mexican American Studies and Research Center, University of Arizona, 1995.

Linderman, Gerald F. *The World within War: America's Combat Experience in World War II*. New York: Free Press, 1997.

Litoff, Judy Barrett, and David C. Smith, eds. *American Women in a World at War: Contemporary Accounts from World War II (Worlds of Women)*. Wilmington, Dela.: Scholarly Resources, 1997.

López, Tomás. *Chicano, Go Home! A Novel Based on the Life of Alfonso Rodríguez*. Hicksville, N.Y.: Exposition Press, 1976.

MacDonald, Victoria-María. *Latino Education in the United States: A Narrated History from 1513–2000*. New York: Palgrave Macmillan, 2004.

Madsen, William. *The Mexican-Americans of South Texas*. New York: Holt, Rinehart and Winston, 1964.

Mahedy, William P. *Out of the Night: The Spiritual Journey of Vietnam Vets*. New York: Ballantine Books, 1986.

———. "Some Theological Perspectives on PTSD." *Clinical Quarterly* 5, no. 1 (1995). http://www.ncptsd.va.gov/ncmain/nc_archives/clnc_qtly/V5N1.pdf.

Marez, Curtis. "Subaltern Soundtracks: Mexican Immigrants and the Making of Hollywood Cinema." *Aztlán* 29, no. 1 (2004): 57–82.

Marín, Christine. "La Asociación Hispano-Americana Madres y Esposas: Tuscon's Mexican American Women in World War II." In Renato Rosaldo Lecture Series, Monograph 1, ser. 1983–1984. Tucson: Mexican American Studies and Research Center University of Arizona, 1985.

Marquez, Benjamín. LULAC: *The Evolution of a Mexican American Political Organization*. Austin: University of Texas Press, 1993.

Marshall, Thurgood. "Summary Justice: The Negro GI in Korea." *Crisis*, May 1951, 297–355.

Martínez, Elizabeth. *500 Años del Pueblo Chicano/500 Years of Chicano History in Pictures*. Albuquerque: Southwest Organizing Project, 1991.

Martínez, George A. "Legal Indeterminacy, Judicial Discretion and the Mexican-American Litigation Experience: 1930–1980." *University of California-Davis Law Review* 27 (Spring 1994): 555–618.

Martínez, José Norat. *Historia del Regimiento 65 de Infantería, 1899–1960*. San Juan, Puerto Rico: Imprenta La Milagrosa, 1992.

Masud-Piloto, Felix. *With Open Arms: Cuban Migration to the United States*. New York: Rowman and Littlefield, 1988.

Matsakis, A. *Vietnam Wives: Facing the Challenges of Life with Veterans Suffering Post-Traumatic Stress*. 2nd ed. Baltimore: Sidran Press, 1996.

McDonough, John. "The Longest Night: Broadcasting's First Invasion." *American Scholar* 63, no. 2 (1994): 193–211.

McGuire, Phillip. *He, Too, Spoke for Democracy: Judge Hastie, World War II, and the Black Soldier*. New York: Greenwood Press, 1988.

McKay, Robert R. "Mexican Americans and Repatriation." In *The Handbook of Texas Online*, http://www.tshaonline.org/handbook/online/articles/MM/pqmyk.html.

McWilliams, Carey. *Ill Fares the Land: Migrants and Migratory Labor in the United States*. Boston: Little, Brown, 1942.

———. *North from Mexico: The Spanish-Speaking People of the United States*. New York: Greenwood Press, 1948.

Meier, Matt S., and Feliciano Ribera. *Mexican Americans/American Mexicans: From Conquistadors to Chicanos*. New York: Hill and Wang, 1993.

Menchaca, Martha. "History and Anthropology: Conducting Chicano Research." Occasional Paper 11, Latino Studies Series. East Lansing, Mich.: Julian Zamora Research Institute, Michigan State University, 1997.

———. *The Mexican Outsiders: A Community History of Marginalization and Discrimination in California*. Austin: University of Texas Press, 1995.

———. *Recovering History, Constructing Race: The Indian, Black, and White Roots of Mexican Americans*. Austin: University of Texas Press, 2001.

Menefee, Selden C. *Mexican Migratory Workers of South Texas*. Washington, D.C.: Government Printing Office, 1940.

Milkman, Ruth. *Gender at Work: The Dynamics of Job Segregation by Sex during World War II.* Champaign: University of Illinois Press, 1987.

Molina, Natalia. *Fit to Be Citizens: Public Health and Race in Los Angeles, 1879–1939.* Berkeley: University of California Press, 2006.

Montejano, David. *Anglos and Mexicans in the Making of Texas, 1836–1986.* Austin: University of Texas Press, 1987.

Morín, Raul. *Among the Valiant: Mexican Americans in WW II and Korea.* Alhambra, Calif.: Borden Publishing Co., 1963.

Morley, Patrick. "This Is the American Forces Network": The Anglo-American Battle of the Air Waves in World War II. Westport, Conn.: Praeger, 2001.

Nance, Elwood C., ed. *Faith of Our Fighters.* St. Louis: Bethany Press, 1944. Quoted in Daniel B. Jorgensen, *The Service of Chaplains to Army Air Units, 1917–1946.* Washington, D.C.: Office, Chief of Air Force Chaplains, 1961.

Nash, Gerald D. *The American West Transformed: The Impact of the Second World War.* Bloomington: Indiana University Press, 1985.

Oboler, Suzanne, and Deena J. González, eds. *The Oxford Encyclopedia of Latinos and Latinas in the United States.* New York: Oxford University Press, 2005.

Olivas, Michael A., ed. *"Colored Men" and "Hombres Aquí": Hernandez v. Texas and the Emergence of Mexican-American Lawyering.* Houston: Arte Público Press, 2006.

Omi, Michael, and Howard Winant. *Racial Formation in the United States.* Philadelphia: Temple University Press, 1994.

O'Neill, William. *A Democracy at War: America's Fight at Home and Abroad in World War II.* New York: Free Press, 1993.

Ortega, A. N., and R. Rosenheck. "Posttraumatic Stress Disorder among Hispanic Vietnam Veterans." *American Journal of Psychiatry* 157 (2000): 615–619.

Padilla, Laura M. "'But You're Not a Dirty Mexican': Internalized Oppression, Latinos and Law." *Texas Hispanic Journal of Law and Policy* (2001): 59–113.

Paniagua, Reinaldo, Jr., ed. *Roll of Honor.* San Juan, Puerto Rico: Imprenta Cantero, Fernández and Co., 1918.

Paz, María Emilia. *Strategy, Security and Spies: Mexico and the U.S. as Allies in World War II.* University Park: Pennsylvania State University Press, 1997.

Perales, Alonso, comp. *Are We Good Neighbors?* San Antonio: Artes Gráficas, 1948.

Pike, Frederick B. *FDR's Good Neighbor Policy: Sixty Years of Gentle Chaos.* Austin: University of Texas Press, 1995.

Plasencia de La Parra, Enrique. "Las infanterías invisibles: Mexicanos en la segunda guerra mundial." *Historia mexicana* 52, 4 (2003): 1021—1071.

Polenberg, Richard. *America at War: The Home Front, 1941– 1945.* Englewood Cliffs, N.J.: Prentice-Hall, 1968.

Privett, Stephen A. *The U.S. Catholic Church and Its Hispanic Members: The Pastoral Vision of Archbishop Robert E. Lucey.* San Antonio: Trinity University Press, 1988.

Proctor, Ben, and Archie P. McDonald, eds. *The Texas Heritage.* Arlington Heights, Ill.: Harlan Davidson, 1992.

Quiñonez, Naomi. "Rosita the Riveter: Welding Tradition and Wartime Transformation." In *Mexican Americans and WWII*, edited by Maggie Rivas-Rodríguez. Austin: University of Texas Press, 2005.

Ramos, Henry. *The American G.I. Forum: In Pursuit of the Dream, 1948–1983*. Houston: Arte Público Press, 1998.

Reisler, Mark. *By the Sweat of Their Brow: Mexican Immigrant Labor in the United States, 1900–1940*. Westport, Conn.: Greenwood Press, 1976.

Reynolds, Avid. *From World War to Cold War: Churchill, Roosevelt, and the International History of the 1940s*. New York: Oxford University Press, 2006.

Rios, Diana I., and Stanley O. Gaines Jr. "Latino Media Use for Cultural Maintenance." *Journalism and Mass Communication Quarterly* 75, no. 4 (1998): 746–761.

Rodríguez, Clara E., and Virginia Sánchez Korrol, eds. *Historical Perspectives on Puerto Rican Survival in the United States*. Princeton, N.J.: Markus Wiener, 1980.

Rodríguez-Beruff, Jorge. *Strategy as Politics: Puerto Rico on the Eve of the Second World War*. San Juan: Editorial de la Universidad de Puerto Rico, 2007.

Rosales, Francisco A. *¡Pobre Raza! Violence, Justice, and Mobilization among México Lindo Immigrants*. Austin: University of Texas Press, 1999.

Rosenheck, R. "Impact of Posttraumatic Stress Disorder of World War II on the Next Generation." *Journal of Nervous and Mental Disease* 174, no. 6 (1986): 319–327.

Rubel, Arthur J. *Across the Tracks: Mexican Americans in Texas City*. Hogg Foundation Research Series. Austin: University of Texas Press, 1961.

Ruef, A. M., B. T. Litz, and W. E. Schlenger. "Hispanic Ethnicity and Risk for Combat-Related Posttraumatic Stress Disorder." *Cultural Diversity and Ethnic Minority Psychology*, no. 6 (2000): 235–251.

Ruiz, Vicki L. *Cannery Women, Cannery Lives: Mexican Women, Unionization, and the California Food Processing Industry, 1930–1950*. Albuquerque: University of New Mexico Press, 1987.

———. *From Out of the Shadows: Mexican Women in Twentieth-Century America*. New York: Oxford University Press, 1998.

———. "South by Southwest: Mexican Americans and Segregated Schooling, 1900–1950." *Organization of American States Magazine of History* 15, no. 2 (2001): 23– 27.

Ruiz, Vicki L., and Virginia Sánchez Korrol, eds. *Latinas in the United States: A Historical Encyclopedia*. 3 vols. Bloomington: Indiana University Press, 2006.

Saenz, José de la Luz. *Los méxico-americanos en la gran guerra y su contingente en pró de la democracia, la humanidad y la justicia*. San Antonio: Artes Gráficas, 1933.

Salinas, Lupe S. "Gus Garcia and Thurgood Marshall: Two Legal Giants Fighting for Justice." *Thurgood Marshall Law Review* 28 (Spring 2003): 145–175.

Sánchez, George J. *Becoming Mexican American: Ethnicity, Culture and Identity in Chicano Los Angeles, 1900–1945*. New York: Oxford University Press, 1993.

Sandoval, Chela. *Methodology of the Oppressed*. Minneapolis: University of Minnesota Press, 2000.

———. "U.S. Third World Feminism: The Theory and Method of Oppositional Consciousness in the Postmodern World." *Genders* 10 (Spring 1991): 1–23.

San Miguel, Guadalupe, Jr. *"Let All of Them Take Heed": Mexican Americans and the Campaign for Educational Equality in Texas, 1910–1981.* Austin: University of Texas Press, 1987.

Santillán, Richard. "Rosita the Riveter: Midwest Mexican American Women during World War II, 1941–1945." *Perspectives in Mexican American Studies* 2 (1989): 115–147.

Santoro, Carmela Elvira. "United States and Mexican Relations during World War II." Ph.D. diss., Syracuse University, 1967.

Savarese, V. W., M. K. Suvak, and L. A. King. "Relationships among Alcohol Use, Hyperarousal, and Marital Abuse and Violence in Vietnam Veterans." *Journal of Traumatic Stress* 14, no. 4 (2001): 717–732.

Schement, Jorge Reina, and Ricardo Flores. "The Origins of Spanish-Language Radio: The Case of San Antonio, Texas." *Journalism History* 4, no. 2 (1977): 56.

Schnurr, P. P., and A. Spiro. "Combat Exposure, Posttraumatic Stress Disorder Symptoms, and Health Behaviors as Predictors of Self-Reported Physical Health in Older Veterans." *Journal of Nervous and Mental Disease* 187, no. 6 (1999): 353–359.

Schwab, Stephen I. "The Role of the Mexican Expeditionary Air Force in World War II: Late, Limited, but Symbolically Significant." *Journal of Military History* 66, no. 4 (2002): 115–140.

Sendejo, Brenda. "Cultivating a Chicana Consciousness on the Texas-Mexico Border: Influences of World War II Generation Women on the Chicana Generation." Master's report, Department of Anthropology, University of Texas at Austin, 2005.

Shelby, Maurice E., Jr. "John. R. Brinkley: His Contributions to Broadcasting." In *American Broadcasting: A Source Book on the History of Radio and Television*, edited by Lawrence W. Lichty and Malachi C. Topping. New York: Hastings House, 1975.

Simmons, Ozzie G. "Anglo Americans and Mexican Americans in South Texas: A Study in Dominant-Subordinate Group Relations." Ph.D. diss., Harvard University, 1952.

Smith, Henry M. "Farm Labor in the Lower Rio Grande Valley of Texas." M.A. thesis, Texas College of Arts and Industries, Kingsville, 1947.

Smith, M. Brewster. "Ground Troop Combat Motivations." In *The American Soldier*, vol. 2, *Combat and Its Aftermath*, edited by Samuel A. Stouffer et al. Princeton, N.J.: Princeton University Press, 1949; reprint, Manhattan, Kans.: Military Affairs, 1977.

Smith, Peter. *Talons of the Eagle: Dynamics of U.S.-Latin American Relations.* New York: Oxford University Press, 1996.

Stein, Walter J. "The 'Okie' as Farm Laborer." *Agricultural History* 49 (January 1975): 202–215.

Stevens, L. M., C. Lymn, and R. M. Glass. "Posttraumatic Stress Disorder." *Journal of the American Medical Association* 296, no. 5. (2006): 614.

Stimpson, J. P., M. C. Masel, L. Rudkin, and M. K. Peek. "Shared Health Behaviors among Older Mexican American Spouses." *American Journal of Health Behaviors* 30, no. 5 (2006): 495–502.

Strachwitz, Chris, and James Nicolopulos. *Lydia Mendoza: A Family Autobiography.* Houston: Arte Público Press, 1993.

Suárez-Orozco, Marcelo, and Mariela Páez. *Latinos: Remaking America.* Berkeley: University of California Press, 2002.

Takaki, Ronald. *Double Victory: A Multicultural History of America in World War II.* Boston: Little, Brown, 2000.

Taylor, Paul Schuster. *Mexican Labor in the United States: Dimmit County, Winter Garden District, South Texas.* Berkeley: University of California Press, 1934.

———. *Mexican Labor in the United States: Imperial Valley.* Berkeley: University of California Press, 1928.

———. *On the Ground in the Thirties.* Salt Lake City: Gibbs M. Smith, 1983.

Texas Agricultural Extension Service. *Farm Labor Program in Texas, 1943–1947.* College Station: Texas A&M College Extension Service, 1947.

Texas Farm Placement Service. *Origins and Problems of Texas Migratory Farm Labor.* Austin, 1940.

———. *Texas Labor Market Reports.* Austin, September 15–October 15, 1941.

———. *Texas Labor Market Reports.* Austin, July 15–August 15, 1943.

Thompson, J. M. *The Orange Industry: An Economic Study.* Bulletin 622. Berkeley, Calif.: Agricultural Experiment Station, 1938.

Thompson, Paul. *The Voice of the Past: Oral History.* New York: Oxford University Press, 1988.

Torres, Blanca. *Historia de la Revolución Mexicana, periodo 1940–52: México en la Segunda Guerra Mundial.* Mexico City: El Colegio de México, 1979.

Tuck, Ruth D. *Not with a Fist: Mexican Americans in a Southwestern City.* New York: Harcourt, Brace and Co., 1946.

U.S. Department of Commerce, Bureau of the Census. *Alphabetical Index of Occupations and Industries.* Prepared by Alba M. Edwards. Washington, D.C.: Government Printing Office, 1940.

U.S. Department of Defense. *Hispanics in Defense of America.* Washington, D.C.: Government Printing Office, 1990.

U.S. Department of Labor, Children's Bureau. *If Your Baby Must Travel in Wartime.* Bureau Publication 307. Washington, D.C., 1944. Reprinted in *American Women in a World at War: Contemporary Accounts from World War II, Worlds of Women,* edited by Judy Barret Litoff and David C. Smith. Wilmington, Del.: Scholarly Resources, 1997.

U.S. Department of Veterans Affairs, Public and Intergovernmental Affairs. *Fact Sheet: America's Wars, November 2006.* http://www1.va.gov/opa/fact/amwars.asp.

U.S. Extension Service. *Preliminary Survey of Major Areas Requiring Outside Agricultural Labor,* Circular 38. Washington, D.C., 1947.

U.S. Federal Communications Commission. *Sixth Annual Report of the Federal Communications Commission.* Washington, D.C.: Federal Communications Commission, 1940. http://www.fcc.gov/ftp/Bureaus/Mass_Media/Databases/documents_collection/annual_reports/1940.pdf.

U.S. Latino & Latina World War II Oral History Project. *Themes from the U.S. Latino and Latina WWII Oral History Project.* Austin, Tex.: U.S. Latino & Latina World War II Oral History Project, 2004.

U.S. State Department. Confidential U.S. State Department Central Files. *Mexico, Internal Affairs, 1940–1944,* part 1, microfilmed ed. Frederick, Md.: University Publications of America, 1987.

Valdés, Dennis Nodín. *Al Norte: Agricultural Workers in the Great Lakes Region, 1917–1970.* Austin: University of Texas Press, 1991.

———. "Settlers, Sojourners and Proletarians: Social Formation in the Great Plains Sugar Beet Industry." *Great Plains Quarterly* 10 (Spring 1990), 110–123.

Valdés, Dionicio. "The Mexican American Dream and World War II." In *Mexican Americans and World War II,* edited by Maggie Rivas-Rodríguez. Austin, University of Texas Press, 2005.

Valenzuela, Angela. *Subtractive Schooling: U.S.-Mexican Youth and the Politics of Caring.* Albany: State University of New York Press, 1999.

Vansina, Jan. *Oral Tradition as History.* Madison: University of Wisconsin Press, 1985.

Vasterling, J. J., S. P. Proctor, P. Amoroso, R. Kane, T. Heeren, and R. F. White. "Neuropsychological Outcomes of Army Personnel following Deployment to the Iraq War." *Journal of the American Medical Association* 296, no. 5 (2006): 519–529.

Vázquez, Josefina Zoraida, and Lorenzo Meyer. *México frente a Estados Unidos (un ensayo histórico, 1776–1988).* 2d ed. Mexico City: Fondo de Cultura Económica, 1992.

Von Eschen, Penny M. *Race against Empire: Black Americans and Anticolonialism, 1937–1957.* Ithaca, N.Y.: Cornell University Press, 1997.

Walsh, Arlene Sánchez. "The Mexican American Religious Experience." In *Introduction to the U.S. Latina and Latino Religious Experience,* edited by Hector Avalos. Boston: Brill Academic, 2004.

Weber, Devra. *Dark Sweat, White Gold: California Farm Workers, Cotton and the New Deal.* Berkeley: University of California Press, 1994.

Weigand, Cindy. *Texas Women in World War II.* Latham, Md.: Republic of Texas Press, 2003.

Wichersham, George W., II. *Marine Chaplain, 1943–1946.* Bennington, Vt.: Merriam Press, 1999.

Willenz, June A. *Women Veterans: America's Forgotten Heroines.* New York: Continuum, 1983.

Wilson, Steven H. "Brown over 'Other White': Mexican Americans' Legal Arguments and Litigation Strategy in School Desegregation Lawsuits." *Law and History Review* 21 (Spring 2003): 145–194.

Winkler, Allan M. *Home Front U.S.A.: America during World War II.* Wheeling, Ill.: Harlan Davidson, 2000.

Wood, Bryce. *The Dismantling of the Good Neighbor Policy.* Austin: University of Texas Press, 1985.

Wood, William S. "A Re-examination of Mexican Support for the United States during World War II." Ph.D. diss., University of Missouri-Columbia, 1989.

Woodward, C. Van. *The Strange Career of Jim Crow.* New York: Oxford University Press, 1966.

Yellin, Emily. *Our Mothers' War: American Women at Home and at the Front during World War II.* New York: Free Press, 2004.

Zamora, Emilio. *Claiming Rights and Righting Wrongs in Texas: Mexican Workers and Job Politics during World War II.* College Station: Texas A&M University Press, 2009.

———. "Fighting on Two Fronts: José de la Luz Saenz and the Language of the Mexican American Civil Rights Movement." In *Recovering the U.S. Hispanic Literary Heritage,* vol. 4, edited by José F. Aranda Jr. and Silvio Torres-Saillant. Houston: Arte Público Press, 2002.

———. "Mexico's Wartime Intervention on Behalf of Mexicans in the United States." In *Mexican Americans and World War II,* edited by Maggie Rivas-Rodríguez. Austin: University of Texas Press, 2005.

Zavella, Patricia. *Women's Work and Chicano Families: Cannery Workers of the Santa Clara Valley.* New York: Cornell University Press, 1987.

Zelden, Charles L. *Justice Lies in the District: The U.S. District Court, Southern District of Texas, 1902–1960.* College Station: Texas A&M University Press, 1993.

Zorrilla, Luis G. *Historia de las relaciones entre México y los Estados Unidos de América, 1800–1958.* Vol. 2. Mexico City: Editorial Porrúa, 1966.

ARCHIVAL MATERIAL

Archivo Fundación Luis Muñoz Marín (AFLMM). Sección IV Luis Muñoz Marín, Presidente del Senado 1941–1948. Serie 9 Asuntos Fuerzas Armadas.

Archivo General de Puerto Rico (AGPR). Fondo de la Oficina del Gobernador, Serie Milicia.

Bancroft Library, University of California, Berkeley.
Jamieson, Stuart, Collection. Field notes.
Taylor, Paul, Papers.

Center for Oral and Public History, California State University–Fullerton (CSUF). Tape-recorded interviews.
Campbell, Ensley J. Interview by Florence Smiley and Milan Pavlovich, OH85, 1 September 1970.
Chapman, C. Stanley. Interview by Arlene R. Sayre, OH52, 8 March 1968.
Coltrane, Garland W. Interview by Milan Pavlovich, OH1500, 12 September 1970.

Croddy, William. Interview by Beverly Croddy, OH655, 29 June 1971.

Deming, Jane. Interviews by John Gallagher, OH19, 5 April and 2, 9, 16, and 23 May 1968.

Easton, W. Ray. Interview by Vivian Allen, OH1318, 27 October 1974.

Esqueda, Alfredo. Interview by Ronald Banderas, OH612, 28 May 1971.

García, Gonzalo B. Interview by Beverly Gallagher, OH604, 21 March 1971.

Graham, George. Interview by Donna C. Barasch, OH1128, 27 March 1972.

Guilin, Manuel. Interview by A. Dean Tatom, OH606, 16 May 1971.

Noriega, Felícitas. Interview by A. Dean Tatom, OH607, 16 May 1971.

Oxandaboure, Benoit, and Frank Oxandaboure. Interview by Andrea Thies, OH1710, 18 November 1981.

Ridgeway, Claude. Interviews by Esther R. Cramer, OH125, 13 February 1963 and 19 January 1965.

Vásquez, Chaoi. Interview by Ronald Banderas, OH609, 17 May 1970.

Venegas, José M. Interview by A. Dean Tatom, OH515, 24 March 1971.

Harry S. Truman Library and Museum, Independence, Mo.

Hastie, William H. Interview by Jerry N. Hess. Tape recording, 5 January 1972.

Houston Public Library, Metropolitan Research Center.

Herrera, John J., Collection.

National Archives and Records Administration, Southwest Region, Fort Worth, Texas.

National Archives and Records Administration (NARA), Washington, D.C.

Records of the Fair Employment Practice Committee. Weekly Reports, 9 October and 6 November 1945.

Records of the Office of the Provost Marshal General. "Records of World War II Prisoners of War, 1942–1947." Record Group 389. Online: http://aad .archives.gov/aad/series-list.jsp?cat=WR26.

Records of the Office of Territories, 1885–1976. Record Group 126.

Records of the Work Projects Administration. Quinn, Walter, "Conditions of Sugar Beet Workers in Colorado in 1937." Record Group 69, folder NBER/ NRP Beet Sugar.

Regional Oral History Office, University of California, Berkeley. Rosie the Riveter WWII American Homefront Project.

Relaciones Exteriores, Archivos de la Secretaría de. Mexico City.

Calderón, Carlos A. Letter to Secretaría de Relaciones Exteriores, Mexico City, 15 March 1945.

"Mexicanos reclutados (en el) ejército norteamericano," part 2, 1944–1945.

Special and Area Study Collection, P. K. Yonge Library of Florida History, University of Florida.

Florida Citizens Advisory Committee on Migratory Labor. Minutes of Public Hearing, Homestead, Fla., 21 February 1956.

Special Collections, Corpus Christi Public Library, Corpus Christi, Tex.

Annual Report of the Community House: 1940. Collection C4, box 1, folder 1.06.

Building Bridges: Report on Health and Welfare Planning; July 1947, collection C4, box 1, folder 1.06, Special Collections, Corpus Christi Public Library, Corpus Christi, Tex.

U.S. Latino & Latina WWII Oral History Project Collection, Nettie Lee Benson Latin American Collection, General Libraries, University of Texas at Austin.

Abarca, Apolonia Muñoz. Interview by Erika L. Martínez. Videotape recording, Corpus Christi, Tex., 18 August 2001.

Acosta, Rudy. Interview by Louis Sahagún. Videotape recording. Upton, Calif., 12 November 2000.

Aguilar, Nicanór. Interview by Maggie Rivas-Rodríguez. Videotape recording, El Paso, Tex., 29 December 2001, and subsequent telephone interviews, 8 and 12 August 2008.

Aguirre, Andrew. Interview by René Zambrano. Videotape recording, San Diego, Calif., 22 January 2001.

———. Interview by René Zambrano. Videotape recording, Chula Vista, Calif., 28 January 2001.

Alaniz, Gloria Araguz. Interview by Yvonne Lim. Videotape recording, Austin, Tex., 18 October 2003.

Alcoser, Joseph. Interview by René Zambrano. Videotape recording, National City, Calif., 21 October 2000.

Armijo, Ceprian. Interview by Rea Ann Trotter. Tape recording, Avondale, Colo., 15 December 2000.

Arellano, Frank. Interview by Rea Ann Trotter. Tape recording, Alamosa, Colo., 10 September 2000.

Autobee, Joseph M. Interview by Rea Ann Trotter. Tape recording, Pueblo, Colo., 15 December 2001.

Baladez, Delfina Cooremans. Joint interview with Wilhelmina Cooremans Vásquez by Brenda Sendejo. Videotape recording, San Antonio, 28 July 2005.

Barrera, Plácida Peña. Interview by Virgilio Roel. Videotape recording, Laredo, Tex., 28 September 2002.

Bernal, Joe. Interview by Valentino Mauricio. Videotape recording, San Antonio, 12 February 2006.

———. Telephone interview by Maggie Rivas-Rodríguez. Tape recording, 7 August 2008.

Bozak, Cármen Contreras. Interview by Vivian Torre. Videotape recording, Miami, Fla., 14 September 2002.

Cadena, Herminia Guerrero. Interview by Erika L. Martínez. Videotape recording, Austin, Tex., 24 June 2002.

Campa, Ventura Terrones. Interview by Delia J. Luján. Videotape recording, Newton, Kans., 1 August 2003.

Candelaria, Richard G. Interview by Rea Ann Trotter. Tape recording, Las Vegas, Nev., 16 March 1998.

———. Telephone interviews by Rea Ann Trotter. Tape recording, 19 February 2003, 11 April 2005, and 3 May 2005.

———. Interview by Mario Barrera. Videotape recording, Las Vegas, Nev., 16 February 2003.

Cantú, Tomás. Interview by Bettina Luis. Videotape recording, Corpus Christi, Tex., 23 March 2001.

Cásarez, Theresa Herrera. Interviews by Joanne Rao Sánchez. Videotape recording, Austin, Tex., 11 and 13 October 2000.

Casillas, Ruben. Interview by René Zambrano. Videotape recording, Chula Vista, Calif., 13 July 2001.

Castro, Aurora González. Interview by Anna Zukovski. Videotape recording, San Antonio, 25 October 2003.

Castro, Sallie Castillo. Interview by Nicole Griffith. Videotape recording, Austin, Tex., 1 March 2001.

Cervantes, Hank. Interview by Maggie Rivas-Rodríguez. Videotape recording, Washington, D.C., 30 May 2004.

———. Telephone interview by Maggie Rivas-Rodríguez. Tape recording, 12 August 2008.

Chávez, Raul. Interview by Paul Zepeda. Videotape recording, 28 August 2001, Houston.

Conde, Guadalupe. Interview by Carlos Conde. Videotape recording, 7 September 2002, San Benito, Tex.

Cook, Carla De Peña. Joint interview with Elena Tamez De Peña by Brenda Sendejo. Videotape recording, Corpus Christi, Tex., 30 July 2005.

Cortez, Ascención Ambros. Interview by Desirée Mata. Videotape recording, San Antonio, 25 October 2003.

Cuellar, Delfina Luján. Interview by Erika L. Martínez. Videotape recording, Albuquerque, 2 November 2002.

De Peña, Elena Tamez. Interview by Erika L. Martínez. Videotape recording, Corpus Christi, Tex., 18 August 2001.

———. Joint interview with Carla De Peña Cook by Brenda Sendejo. Videotape recording, Corpus Christi, Tex., 30 July 2005.

De Peña, Hector, Jr. Interview by Karla E. Gonzalez. Videotape recording, Corpus Christi, Tex., 18 August 2001.

Dimas, Beatrice Escudero. Interview by Maggie Rivas-Rodríguez. Videotape recording, Phoenix, Ariz., 4 January 2003.

Eguía, León. Interview by Liliana Velázquez. Videotape recording. Houston, 2 March 2002.

Encinias, Miguel. Interview by Brian Lucero. Videotape recording, Albuquerque, 3 December 2001.

Escobedo, Concepción Alvarado. Interview by Sandra Freyberg. Videotape recording, Brownsville, Tex., 20 September 2003.

Esquivel, Rafaela Muñiz. Interview by Joanne Rao Sánchez. Videotape recording, San Antonio, 12 April 2001.

Estrada, Herlinda Mendoza Buitrón. Interview by Gloria Monita. Videotape recording, Saginaw, Mich., 19 October 2002.

Falcón, Henry. Interview by Paul R. Zepeda. Videotape recording, Houston, 24 October 2003.

Flores, Armando. Interview by Bettina Luis. Videotape recording, Corpus Christi, Tex., 24 March 2001.

Flores, Felícitas Cerda. Interview by Paul Zepeda. Videotape recording, Houston, 2 February 2002.

Gallego, Elena. Interview by Maggie Rivas-Rodríguez. Videotape recording, El Paso, Tex., 9 March 2002.

García, Elizabeth Ruiz. Interview by Hannah McIntyre. Videotape recording, 2 February 2000, Austin, Tex.

Garza, Gonzalo. Interview by Juan Campos. Videotape recording, Georgetown, Tex., 14 March 2001.

Gil, Paul, Otis Gil, and Narciso Gil. Interview by Andrea Valdez. Videotape recording, Austin, Tex., 20 October 1999.

Guerrero, Victoria Partida. Interview by Gloria Monita. Videotape recording, Saginaw, Mich., 19 October 2002.

Hernández, Candelario. Interview by Lucinda Guinn. Videotape recording. Austin, Tex., 3 March 2002.

Hernández, Emma Villareal. Interview by Gary Villareal, Videotape recording. McAllen, Tex., 1 July 2002.

Herrera, Jesús. Interview by Jane O'Brien. Videotape recording. San Antonio, 25 October 2003.

Jasso, José R. "Joe." Interview by Evelyn Jasso García. Videotape recording, San Antonio, 18 June 2001.

Ledesma, Josephine Kelly. Interview by Monica Rivera. Videotape recording, Austin, Tex., 17 February 2001.

Leura, León. Unpublished manuscript. 27 June 1995.

———. Interview by Frank O. Sotomayor. Videotape recording, Los Angeles, 23 March 2002.

Leyva, Luis. Interview by Mary Alice Carnes. Videotape recording, San Antonio, 23 November 2001.

López, Eliseo. Interview by Kimberly Tillis. Videotape recording, Austin, Tex., 26 February 2001.

López, Joe F. Interview by Rea Ann Trotter. Tape recording, Greeley, Colo., 12 October 1995.

———. Interview by Rea Ann Trotter. Tape recording, Houston, 5 January 1996.

López, José M. Interview by Manuel F. Medrano. Videotape recording, Brownsville, Tex., 6 October 2001.

Lucio, Augustine. Interview by Denise Chavarri. Videotape recording, San Marcos, Tex., 10 February 2003.

Martínez, José. Interviews by Rea Ann Trotter. Tape recording, Fort Garland, Colo., 10 June and 30 September 2001.

Montoya, Ernest. Interview by Rea Ann Trotter. Tape recording, Pueblo, Colo., 21 September 2000.

———. Interview by Rea Ann Trotter. Tape recording, Avondale, Colo., 14 December 2000.

Moraga, Pete. Interview by Maggie Rivas-Rodríguez. Videotape recording, Phoenix, Ariz., 4 January 2003.

Morales, Benito. Interview by William Luna. Videotape recording, Cicero, Ill., 5 December 2002.

Muñoz, Dan. Interview by Maggie Rivas-Rodríguez. Videotape recording, San Diego Calif., 25 October 2002.

Navarro, Eliseo. Interview by Francisco Venegas. Videotape recording, San Antonio, 13 October 2001.

Olivas, Tony. Interview by Rea Ann Trotter. Tape recording, Avondale, Colo., 15 December 2000.

Ornelas, William. Interview by Maggie Rivas-Rodríguez. Videotape recording, San Antonio, 25 August 1999.

———. Interview by Rea Ann Trotter, 20 June 1966.

Orozco, Aurora Estrada. Interview by Desirée Mata. Videotape recording, Austin, Tex., 17 October 2003.

———. Telephone interview by Brenda Sendejo, tape recording, 31 July 2005.

Orozco, Cynthia Estrada. Telephone interview by Brenda Sendejo. Tape recording, 10 February 2007.

Pardo, Elvira. Interview by Wilfredo Pardo López. Videotape recording, Detroit, Mich., 20 June 2003.

Pérez, Ester Arredondo. Interview by Gail Fisher. Videotape recording, San Antonio, 23 May 2002.

Prado, Pete. Interview by Gabriel Manzano. Videotape recording, San Antonio, 14 March 2000.

Ramírez, Calixto. Interview by Karin Brulliard. Videotape recording, Brownsville, Tex., 13 September 2003.

Rivas, Henrietta López. Interviews by Verónica Flores. Videotape recording, San Antonio, 6 and 12 June 1999.

Rivas, Ramón. Interview by Maggie Rivas-Rodríguez. Videotape recording, San Antonio, 6 June 1999.

Rivas-Rodríguez, Maggie. Interview with Brenda Sendejo. Tape recording, Austin, Tex., 10 April 2005.

Rodríguez, María Elisa Reyes. Interview by Ryan Bauer. Videotape recording, Austin, Tex., 10 May 1999.

Salazar, Epifanio. Interview by Francisco Cortez. Tape recording, San Antonio, 13 March 2005.

Samarrón, Carlos. Interview by René Zambrano. Videotape recording, San Diego, Calif., 2 October 2000.

Tamayo, Andrew. Interview by Ernest Eguía. Videotape recording, Houston, 18 September 2002.

Thomas, María Isabel Solís. Interview by Anna Zukowski. Videotape recording, Brownsville, Tex., 13 September 2003.

Treviño, Félix. Interview by David Zavala. Videotape recording, San Antonio, 13 October 2001.

Trujillo, Charles. Interview by Rea Ann Trotter. Tape recording, Avondale, Colo., 15 December 2000.

Valadés, Salvador. "Mexican-American WW II Combat Experience." Unpublished manuscript, 1996.

Vásquez, George. Interview by Angela Macías. Videotape recording, Inver Grove Heights, Minn., 11 August 2002.

Vásquez, Wilhelmina Cooremans. Joint interview with Delfina Cooremans Baladez by Brenda Sendejo. Videotape recording, San Antonio, 28 July 2005.

Vega, Lauro. Interview by René Zambrano. Videotape recording, Chula Vista, Calif., 8 October 2000.

Vidaurri, Martha Ortega. Interview by Tammi Grais. Videotape recording, Austin, Tex., 3 October 2001.

Vigil, Fred. Interview by Rea Ann Trotter. Tape recording, Longmont, Colo., 15 July 1998.

Villarreal, Baltazar. Interview by Maggie Rivas-Rodríguez. Videotape recording, Kansas City, Mo., 2 August 2003.

Ximenes, Vicente. Interview by Jim Morrison. Videotape recording, Albuquerque, 10 October 2001.

Zepeda, Robert. Interview by Paul Zepeda. Videotape recording, Bay City, Tex., 17 March 2000.

University of California at Los Angeles, Department of Special Collections.

Survey of the Mexican Labor Problem in California. California Development Association, 1928. In George P. Clements Papers, box 62, folder 1.

INDEX

Du Bois, W.E.B., 112, 204n14
Duncan Field, 51, 67, 170
Dutch Harbor, 21
DXing, 27, 185n23

Egloff, Max, 116, 117, 118
Eisenhower, Dwight D.: as general, 84;
  presidential library, 115
Encinias, Miguel, 32
Escobedo, Concepción (née Alvarado),
  72, 84
Espín, Orlando O., 126
Esquadrón 201 (201 Squadron), 96
Esqueda, Alfredo, 57, 58
Esquivel, Rafaela (née Muñiz), 81–83, 88
Estrada, Herlinda (née Mendoza Buitrón),
  47, 51
Evans, Sarah, 192n3

Falcón, Henry, 44
Federal Communication Commission,
  25, 28
Federal Radio Commission, 28
FEPC (Fair Employment Practice Com-
  mittee), 181n10
Figueroa Soulet, Noemí, 207n54
Fishman, Joshua, 184n10
Flores, Armando, 30, 31, 50
Flores, Felícitas (née Cerda), 85, 86
Flores, Moisés, 13
Flores, Raymond J., 15
Floresville, Texas, 30
Fogel, Walter, 5, 6
Fort Benning, 81
Fort Meade, 81
Fowler, Gene, 27

García, Elizabeth (née Ruiz), 153
García, Gonzalo, 59
García, Hector P., 19
García, Mario T., 182n1
García, Willie, 153
García Naranjo, Nemesio, 201n12
Garza, Gonzalo, 43–45

GI Bill (of Rights), 12, 15, 35, 86–89 pas-
  sim, 109
Gilbert, Dennis, 193n18
Gil family (Peter, Otis, Paul, and Narciso),
  44
Girl Scouts, 15
Gluck, Sherna Berger, 64, 158
Gonzalez, Juan, 2, 3
González, Pedro J., 26, 185n17
Good Neighbor Policy, 91, 92, 199
Gould, Stephen Jay, 204n10
Graham, George, 53
Grand Falls, Texas, 30, 33
Great Depression: citrus production dur-
  ing, 55; and deportations, 48; occupa-
  tions of Latinos before, 53
Great Depression, effects of: on agricul-
  tural industry, 40, 61; on Cervantes
  family, 40; on Escudero farming fam-
  ily, 44; on migration, 42; on sugar beet
  industry, 50; on WWII generation, 12,
  62, 156, 157
Grossman, Dave, 127
Guadalupanas, las, 168
Guerrero, Victoria, 48, 53
Guilin, Manuel, 58, 59
Gutiérrez, Félix, 30

Handbook of Texas Online, 215n32
Handy, Thomas, 119, 120
Hastie, William, 115, 116, 119, 205n25
Hernández, Candelario, 44, 45
Hernández, Emma (née Villareal), 87, 88,
  198n120
Hernández, Margarita, 58
Herrera, Jesús, 50
Hilmes, Michele, 183n4
Hinojosa, Gilberto, 134
Honey, Maureen, 158

Incorporated Mexican American Government Employees, 16

Jasso, José R., 23

Breinigsville, PA USA
21 March 2011
257992BV00002B/26/P

9 780292 725805